POISONED PROSPERITY

POISONED PROSPERITY

Development,
Modernization,
and the
Environment in
South Korea

Norman Eder

An East Gate Book

M.E. Sharpe
Armonk, New York
London, England

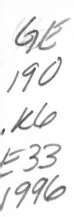

An East Gate book

Library of Congress Cataloging-in-Publication Data

Eder, Norman R.
Poisoned prosperity: development, modernization, and the
environment in South Korea / by Norman R. Eder.
p. cm.
"An East Gate book."
Includes bibliographical references and index.
ISBN 1-56324-686-4 (hardcover: alk. paper).
ISBN 1-56324-687-2 (pbk.: alk. paper)
1. Environmental policy—Korea (South)
2. Korea (South)—Environmental conditions. I. Title.
GE190.K6E33   1995
363.7′0095195—dc20
95-34229
CIP

Printed in the United States of America

BM (c)   10   9   8   7   6   5   4   3   2   1
BM (p)   10   9   8   7   6   5   4   3   2   1

Contents

Acknowledgments

My studies in Korea as a Senior Fulbright Scholar were made possible by the financial, intellectual, and emotional support provided by the Korean-American Educational Commission; the Army Environmental Policy Institute; my home institution, Oregon Graduate Institute of Science & Technology; and Hanyang University. Although the views expressed on these pages are my own, I owe a tremendous debt to the many people who shared their ideas and insights with me about a remarkable nation and its people.

Fred Carriere, former director of the Fulbright program in Seoul, Senator Mark O. Hatfield, and Col. James Thayer (ret.) each encouraged me to pursue my interests. Dr. Dwight Sangrey, former president of OGI, provided me with the opportunity to leave my administrative post to pursue my research in Korea. Dr. Shin Eung-Bae, director of Hanyang University's Environmental Research Center, was my constant intellectual mentor, confidant, and guide. His wife, Kim Kyung-Sook, made sure that we were never far from personal help and advice when we needed Korean life explained.

Dr. James Hartman and Ernest Eddy, of the U.S. Eighth Army, provided thoughtful and experienced counsel as well as hard questions. Dr. Hong Wuk-Hee, senior scientist at the KEPCO Environmental Research Centre, urged me to keep my sights high and to work to explain his country to mine. Robert Donaldson and Dr. Mel Gurtov were wonderfully insightful editors, and Dr. Adriano Gasperi, Tam Ormiston, and Dr. Ray Weisenborn all kept me going with their enthusiasm and understanding for the frustrations of a newly minted student of Korean affairs. The careful reading and editorial insight provided by Nancy Christie and Michelle De Lude immeasurably improved the manuscript long after my own patience had worn thin. And special thanks to Dr. George Hazelrigg of the National Science Foundation, whose curbside study, *100 Uses of Re-bar*, provided me with a unique touchstone for understanding Korean life and attitudes.

The views expressed in this book were indelibly shaped by many Koreans who openly shared their ideas with me in extensive interviews and numerous informal discussions. I give special thanks to Choi Joo-Sub, Dr. Kim Jung-Wk, Dr. Kwak Il-Chyun, Kwon Hyon-Youl, Lee Jina, Lee Sang-Duk, Dr. Lee Su-Hoon, Nam Sang-Min, Dr. Rho Yung-Hee, Shin Chang-Hyun, and Dr. Yoo Jae-Hyun. I also am most appreciative of the willingness of Dr. Chung Chin-Seung to trust me with his thoughtful unpublished manuscript. These and many others made every effort to graciously recommend a curious American, armed only with a laptop computer, to their friends and colleagues. In them all, I discovered the essential Korean spirit that assumes that all things are possible.

The author wishes to thank Korea Federation of Environmental Movements (KFEM), Center for Environmental Development, and Green Korea for their contribution of photographs for this book.

The production of this study was most of all a family event. Sherry, Benjamin, and David consented to taking a sabbatical from their lives in quiet Portland, Oregon. They tackled bustling Seoul with abandon and mostly good cheer: even in the face of my poor grocery shopping habits, a cold winter, and life without a car. Finally, this book would not have been written had it not been for our extended Korean family, Dr. Hwang Wan-Young and Professor Suh Cha-Young and their two sons. Their long-standing friendship, deep trust, and warm kindness made even the impossible possible.

Introduction

Over the past thirty years there has been a dramatic revolution in human thinking about nature and the earth's environment. The protection of the environment is no longer seen exclusively as a series of limited local, national, or regional problems. Today, it has emerged as an international question. The internationalization of the environment was first formally recognized in 1972, when the United Nations sponsored the Conference on the Human Environment in Stockholm to raise the issue of environmental decay to the international stage. Twenty years later the global importance of the environment was enshrined by Agenda 21 at the culmination of the 1992 United Nations Conference on Environment and Development (UNCED) in Rio de Janeiro. During this international conference on environment and development, world leaders and environmental activists laid a broad and principled foundation for global attention to the global environment.[1]

The Rio conference and subsequent worldwide activities have provided evidence that concern about environmental quality does not stand alone. It is intimately connected to questions of war and peace, development and social justice, democratization and the expansion of liberty, personal health, and public safety. The Rio conference also demonstrated that concern for the natural environment cannot be treated as a passing fad imposed on the underdeveloped world by the industrialized West. Instead, environmentalism is becoming one of the most powerful and far-reaching issues in global affairs.[2]

At the intersection of many of the world's most critical environmental questions lies the Republic of Korea (South Korea), a nation of enormous energy and drive coupled with an intense national pride, a cultural evolution that stretches back five thousand years, and political traditions that began nearly two millennia ago. Korea is also a country whose unyielding commitment to industrialization has left a tragic legacy of environmental damage to the air, water, and soils of a beautiful mountainous landscape. Today, every element of Korean society has come to accept the necessity of addressing Korea's environmental problems. However, acting upon this will take a Herculean effort: one that holds the potential for challenging many of the nation's core political and social conventions as well as the economic policies that have fostered development at the expense of all else.

It would be easy to paint the Korean contemporary environmental reality in dark terms. Unrestrained urban sprawl, massive traffic jams, toxic air and water laced with untreated municipal and industrial wastes, and bureaucratic gridlock are the environmental hallmarks of daily Korean life.[3] Still, to chronicle only these and to assume that the factors governing these near-crisis conditions are static would be a mistake. Moreover, such a conclusion would be a disservice to the many Koreans who are working with skill and intelligence to address their country's environmental problems. The difficulties facing them are enormous, and stabilizing—let alone repairing—environmental decay will be a stiff challenge. Yet, despite many limitations, the forces at work in Korea are dynamic and powerful and provide some room for cautious optimism. Already these forces have created a broad consensus in Korean society, business, and politics that environmental degradation must be stopped and some indication that improvement might be possible.

Although far from fully formed, there are unmistakable signs of the emergence of a new environmentalism within modern Korean society and government. It is too early to predict the success or failure of Korea's new environmentalism, but the outcome will have worldwide importance. No newly developed country has yet made the transition from growth at all costs to industrialization balanced by concern and protection for the environment. Developing economies that want to replicate Korean economic success may find lessons for avoiding environmental tragedy.[4] In turn, industrialized nations will see a vast, non-Western social and political experiment at work in Korea's struggle to come to terms with environmental degradation, an experiment that might reveal whether environmental destruction is the inevitable and perhaps irreversible result of rapid industrialization.[5]

Finally, a word of caution. Any study of contemporary Korea is bound to be a snapshot and have a limited shelf life. Korea is an incredibly dynamic society. It experiments daily with a robust mixture of ancient traditions, tribalism, and modern industrialism and globalization. This dynamism is no less present in environmental law, administration, policy, and politics. In capturing the state of Korean environmental affairs and their larger meaning, readers must be aware that over time the details of administration and management will change, as will the people involved. However, this book argues that in 1995, many of the pieces of improved environmental management are now evident and relatively constant; only the details will change. As a result, informed readers will find inaccuracies. I apologize for those but beg readers' forgiveness and understanding that that is the price for contemporary studies.

Notes

1. Report of the United Nations Conference on Environment and Development, June 3–14, 1992. For a summation of post-Rio activities, see Thorbjørn Bernsten, *Chairman's Summary*, Oslo Roundtable, Oslo, Norway, January 10, 1995. Also see Peter M. Haas, Marc A. Levy, and Edward A. Parson, "Appraising the Earth Summit: How Should We Judge UNCED's Success," *Environment*, vol. 34, no. 8, October 1992. Gilbert F. White et al., "Taking Stock of UNCED," *Environment*, vol. 34, no. 8, October 1992.

2. "All That Remains: A Survey of Waste and the Environment," *The Economist*, May 29, 1993.

3. This monograph is based on numerous official documents, the popular press, and many printed articles. Although those form the backbone of descriptions of programs and developments in Korean environmental law, regulation, and management, most of that material is neutral in its approach. During the course of research for this monograph, the author conducted numerous interviews with Koreans from all walks of life and of all political opinions. It is these that lie at the core of the judgments made. Many of the people interviewed spoke frankly and on the condition that they would not be directly cited. Because of this, no direct attribution will be made to specific individuals, and the evaluations of the themes discussed are those of the author.

4. Asia Development Bank, *Economic Policies for Sustainable Development: Ministerial Brief.* Manila, Philippines, 1991.

5. An excellent survey of environmental conditions in Asia appeared in "Southeast Asia: Facing Development Challenges," *Environmental Science and Technology*, special issue, vol. 27, no. 12, 1993. This touches on all the major issues affecting the region.

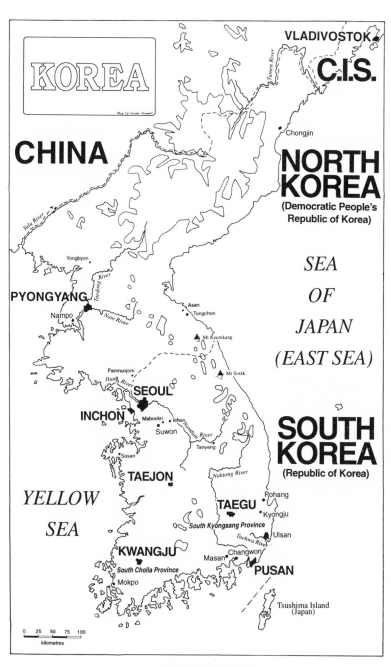

Map of Korea

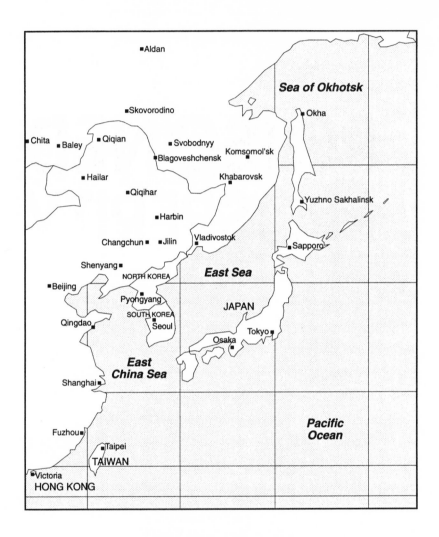

Map of Southeast Asia

POISONED PROSPERITY

1

The Human and Environmental Costs of Industrialization

Korea is one of the most homogeneous societies in the world; its culture and institutions all reflect a nearly complete lack of ethnic and racial diversity. Moreover, with the exception of a small Chinese minority and the international districts of Seoul, most Koreans have rarely come in contact with foreigners until very recently. To be sure, Koreans are increasingly bombarded by the international media and incessant twentieth-century consumerism, but the effect of this on the Korean way of thinking seems to have been far less than in other, more open societies. As a result, in Korea today, the modern and the traditional live uneasily, side by side, rarely reconciled and sometimes at odds with each other's demands.

The patterns of modern Korean daily life have been shaped by a mix of old and new. This frustrates and infuriates foreigners who live and work in Korean society and who try to study, influence, and interact with it from afar. Although traditional class consciousness has been reduced, it has been replaced by an equally strong class status system that still defies Western principles of pluralism and democracy. This uniquely Korean system is based on education, money, personal connections, and political position. Place and status at birth are no longer the exclusive determining factors of success and failure, yet they and the family connections they bring remain the critical elements in Korean life. Egalitarianism has grown in recent years, but personal relations remain hierarchical and paramount in all aspects of personal life, business, and government. Personal connection, whether based on friendship, family kinship, or business loyalty, will usually take precedence over principle and public policy. These precepts have been readily accepted by Koreans, who, with only a few exceptions, have for centuries conformed to them as the natural order of life. The result has been remarkable stability and order through hunger, conquest, and now industrialization. Today, though, the very elements that have long given stability and strength to Korean society make social and political change—indeed, any change—extremely difficult.[1]

Korean life has long been dominated by geographic position. Attached to the Asian continental land mass on one side and surrounded by ocean on three others, Korea and her history have been shaped by her larger and more powerful neighbors, China and Japan. The Chinese historically have been known as the "big brother" and cultural mentor. The Japanese have been a mortal enemy for a millennium. For both, though, Korea has been a battleground. Chinese Han and Tang emperors launched repeated invasions from the time of Christ, and in the thirteenth century the Mongols invaded and occupied the peninsula. Two brutal Japanese invasions swept over Korea in the late sixteenth century, followed by destructive Manchu invasions in the early seventeenth century. Each invasion destroyed native governments and robbed Korea of cultural and historic relics, leaving a sense of isolation and shameful defeat and a fierce national pride in those things that are uniquely Korean. The country's history also imbued Koreans with a clannishness, a deep sense of mistrust, and a suspicion of everything and anyone that might threaten the status quo and stability.[2]

The first glimmer of modernization in Korea came about as a result of conquest and tragedy. In 1910, imperial Japan brought an end to the native Yi dynasty and began its rule of Korea, which would last until the Japanese defeat in 1945. During the Japanese occupation, Koreans were classified as Japanese citizens (second-class, of course); the once-free nation was incorporated into Japan's domestic systems of government and treated as a province, as opposed to a conquered nation. Koreans were forced to give up their distinct language and culture and to adopt Japanese forms in all aspects of public and private life. The Japanese, in seeking to exploit the human and natural resources of their new conquest, reduced the native Korean ruling elite to subservience, eliminated feudalism, and recast everything from public education to civil administration to conform to the contemporary Japanese model. The Japanese rulers also began the transformation of Korea's preindustrial economic infrastructure. They constructed the first modern factories and brought modern communications and transportation systems to the peninsula. Japan also established the foundations of Korea's pattern of monopolistic capitalism, although this remained securely in the hands of Japanese bureaucrats, military officers, and expatriate business owners.

After the defeat of Japan, Korea was divided between the communist North and the capitalist South. The Second World War had left both north and south devastated, economically and socially, because although there were no major campaigns fought on the peninsula, the Japanese used Korean labor and resources to fuel their war machine. By 1945 the nation was destitute. The Korean War only added to the devastation. From 1950 to 1953, armies raced from one end of Korea to the other, leaving little except destruction and hungry refugees in their paths. At the signing of the armistice, the Korean people could rightfully claim that they lived in one of the most impoverished and brutalized nations on the face of the earth.

Throughout the second half of the 1950s, the Republic of Korea existed as a dependent state under the protection of the United States. Ruled by an authoritarian government and military, South Korea survived in nearly total poverty. In contrast, communist North Korea was the beneficiary of Soviet and Chinese political competition. This led to the creation of heavy industry and rising production rates that were viewed as a security threat by the rulers of South Korea and the United States government. In the face of this, Koreans and American supporters alike recognized that the South's security could not be maintained without economic growth and modernization at all levels of life. This realization formed the critical political foundation for the launching of economic development in the South, which in the early 1960s concentrated its national energies and talents on centrally managing the growth of heavy industry, from steel to chemicals to textiles, to create a modern industrial economy.[3]

This development was not accompanied by social or political modernization, however. Until very recently, Korean government was authoritarian, repressive of human rights, and abusive of individual liberties and political diversity. Unfettered industrial development has been the sole ambition of Korean national domestic policy over the past thirty years, and anything that stood in its way, from political dissent and labor organization to environmental concerns, was seen as demanding aggressive elimination by whatever means necessary.

The story of this "Korean economic miracle" is well known and often looked to as the standard for third world economic development. Following a policy of export-led growth and the creation of a heavy industrial manufacturing base, the Korean economy set world records for expansion.[4] From 1986 to 1989 real GNP growth averaged 11.3 percent. Per capita GNP nearly doubled, from $2,194 in 1984 to $4,127 in 1988. By the close of 1993, per capita GNP had risen to $7,007.[5] Although growth rates have slowed in recent years (3.8 percent in 1993, but above the 8 percent range for 1994), the Korean economy continues to expand. The government reported that per capita income rose to $8,300 in 1994, and forecasters expect it to reach at least $9,700 in 1995 and break the $10,000 barrier in 1996.[6] In making these economic strides, Korea is moving from a foundation of heavy manufacturing industries toward more diversification. In 1993 Korea was the world's largest producer of semiconductors and a leader in chemicals, machinery, ships, and high-technology consumer goods.

Rapid industrialization in Korea has left its mark on the landscape, and the results of this environmental neglect are easily found.[7] Although no nationwide epidemiologic research has been conducted (many local studies do exist), chronic respiratory ailments and the incidence of environmentally linked cancers are assumed to be rising steadily. Concerns about environmentally associated diseases are further aggravated by the heavy consumption of tobacco and alcohol products. Over 73 percent of Korean males smoke the relatively cheap and government-subsidized Korean tobacco. Only 7 percent of the female population use tobacco, but that percentage is rising rapidly. This use of tobacco in Korea compares to 61 percent of Japanese and Chinese males, 47 percent of Thais, and 28 percent of American men.[8] Drink, too, is cheap and widely and heavily used in all social and business interactions, with the national liquor, *soju*, costing about 800 won ($1) per half-liter bottle.

The urban areas of Seoul and Pusan have become heavily congested by growing populations and millions of vehicles. Even cities with populations of less than one million are feeling the effects of uncontrolled urbanization due to centrally directed industrial development. In 1994 it was estimated that Korea had over seven million automobiles on its streets, and hundreds of thousands of new vehicles are being added annually. Moreover, the incessant construction of housing, office complexes,

Table 1.1

Average SO$_2$ Level in Major Korean Cities (ppm)

City	1984	1986	1990	1992
Seoul	0.066	0.054	0.051	0.035
Pusan	0.050	0.042	0.039	0.033
Taegu	0.040	0.043	0.041	0.040
Kwangju	0.026	0.020	0.017	0.017
Ulsan	0.024	0.032	0.031	0.031

Source: Korean Ministry of Environment, Seoul, *1993 Report on Environmental Status of Korea.*

roads, subways, and factories adds tons of large particulates to the nation's airsheds. Air pollution levels, therefore, are high by world standards in all major Korean cities. Although some progress has been made in recent years, the citizens of Seoul suffer air pollution levels slightly below those of Mexico City, which has long been known for having the most polluted air of the world's major urban centers. On most days in Seoul, the lovely mountains that serve as the city's backdrop are shrouded by smog created by auto emissions, the burning of carbon fuels, construction and municipal wastes, and suspended dust particles (see Table 1.1).

The high levels of air pollution have produced serious acid rain problems. A recent two-year survey of rainfall pH in Seoul, conducted by the Ministry of Environment and the Korea Meteorological Administration, revealed that the situation in the nation's capital was critical. Of thirty-eight measurements, four were below pH 3.6, thirty-two ranged between pH 3.6 and 4.6, and two exceeded pH 5.6, which is the level of unpolluted rainfall. The higher range (lower pH) of these acidity levels is one hundred times the official Korean government limit.[9] In addition, the acid content of surface and ground water resources and of the thin soils of Seoul and the nation's mountainous areas has increased sharply. Buildings, clothing, and cars are severely affected by these elevated levels of acid rain, and the economic costs are incalculable. Acidification of soils and water resources and industrial development have also either eliminated or severely reduced the amount of habitat available for animals. Since 1960, it is estimated that more than one hundred animal species have disappeared, and Korean urban areas

Table 1.2

Total Suspended Particulates in Major Korean Cities
(micrograms of particulate matter per cubic meter of air)

City	1984	1986	1988	1989	1990
Seoul	210	183	179	149	150
Pusan	228	194	214	178	149
Taegu	224	140	155	128	133
Kwangju	132	133	100	116	109
Ulsan	177	172	238	165	122

Source: Korean Ministry of Environment, Seoul, *1993 Report on Environmental Status of Korea.*
Note: Significant declines between 1984 and 1990 are largely the result of the reduction of coal burning and the increased use of natural gas, oil, and nuclear energy.

are approaching sterility. Even hardy species such as squirrels and pigeons are finding it difficult to survive.[10]

The most evident air pollution problem is the restricted visibility in most major Korean cities. The incessant construction dust, traffic jams, and industrial emissions have led to high levels of suspended particulates in the atmosphere, earning Seoul the ranking of the second-worst urban airshed in the world in 1990 (see Table 1.2).

If air pollution is the most visible environmental problem in Korea, surface-water pollution is the most critical (see Table 1.3). The majority of the nation's freshwater and coastal water resources have been subjected to moderate to high levels of municipal, agricultural, and industrial contamination. Nationally, only 37 percent of the population is served by sewage treatment facilities: The water quality of the Han River in Seoul rarely exceeds the poor international water-quality standard of third grade.[11] This has caused many Koreans to suspect the safety of their tap water and to rely on bottled water or private wells for drinking supplies.[12] A recent survey sponsored by a firm selling bottled water revealed that just 0.6 percent of Seoul residents drink untreated or unboiled tap water.[13] (The booming bottled water industry was largely illegal until 1994. Only foreigners could legally buy bottled water, though, in fact, it was widely available to anyone willing to pay for its delivery. Not surprisingly, independent tests have shown that the quality of some bottled water is below that of the untreated tap water.[14])

Coastal waters, especially along the semi-enclosed west coast of the

Table 1.3

Biological Oxygen Demand in Major Korean Rivers (mg/l)

River	1982	1985	1988	1989	1990	1991	1992
Han	5.4	4.7	4.3	3.4	3.4	3.4	3.6
Naktong	3.7	3.7	3.9	3.6	3.0	4.0	3.3
Kum	2.4	2.5	3.2	3.5	3.1	3.1	3.2
Yongsan	3.9	5.2	7.0	6.6	6.7	5.6	5.6

Source: Korean Ministry of Environment, Seoul, *1993 Report on Environmental Status of Korea.*

Yellow Sea (West Sea), fall below Korea's own water-quality standards. Chinhae Bay, site of a large naval base on the south coast, has been severely polluted since the early 1980s by heavy metals, cadmium, copper, lead, and zinc from the large industrial complexes of Masan, Changweon, and Chinhae City.[15] As a result, harvests of shellfish and production of near-shore fisheries have been greatly reduced. The number of fish species has declined from 141 to only 24 in recent years, a direct result of wholesale contamination of near-shore sediments and rising levels of heat pollution from power plants and industrial activities.[16] According to the World Watch Institute, the environmental condition of the Yellow Sea has reached crisis proportions, and the sea will soon "die" due to continued Korean-produced environmental contamination and the rapid industrialization of China along the sea's western shore.[17]

Underground there has been significant contamination of soils and groundwater due to the widespread improper storage, handling and disposal of industrial chemicals such as industrial solvents and dyes.[18] In the rural areas, heavy use of chemical pesticides, fertilizers, and herbicides and uncontrolled runoff from cow and swine farms have caused dramatic damage to the soils and aquifers. This was recently revealed by the preliminary report of the first national survey of Korea's groundwater supplies.[19] This three-hundred-sample study, conducted by faculty and students at Yonsei University's Institute of Environmental Research, estimates that fully 20 percent of the nation's aquifers have been contaminated. This includes mountainous areas where acid rain has seeped into underground water supplies, supplies that are being looked to by local governments to replace already contaminated surface-water resources.

Construction wastes and runoffs from building sites are also major sources of non-point-source pollution. The handling of these is largely unregulated, and the filling of wetlands with construction wastes is a common practice. Open burning of scrap combustible material is a widespread means of disposal throughout urban areas, thus adding to the generally poor air quality. The urban environment is further degraded by excessive noise and vibration, which take their toll on the health and emotional well-being of citizens living in Korea's cities. In a recent study, the city of Seoul found that the residents of apartment buildings near roadways suffered noise levels as high as 70 decibels; the international standard for urban centers is 55 decibels.[20] Noise and vibration are increasingly becoming problems in rural development zones as well.

Korea has had difficulty keeping up with the demand for managed solid-waste disposal sites and the enforcement of disposal regulations. In 1985 Koreans generated 2.2 kilograms of waste per day, compared to 1.3 kilograms in the United States, 1.0 kilograms in Japan, and 0.9 kilograms in the United Kingdom. In 1994 the average Seoul per capita waste production was still 1.48 kg, compared to the average New Yorker's waste of 1.3 kg and that of Tokyo's residents, which stood at 1.1 kg.[21] Today, the generation of solid wastes per capita in Korea is among the highest in the world, and it is estimated that the total volume of waste produced may be growing by as much as 8 percent per year. This sheer mass of material is swamping the small nation's limited landfill capacity. Of Korea's 601 legal landfills, only 4 were equipped with sanitary facilities as recently as 1994. The huge generation of waste material has also created a significant illegal dumping problem. The unfortunate result of this all too common practice is that hazardous chemical and animal wastes, nontoxic industrial byproducts, and domestic wastes are freely commingled and unmanaged in both urban and rural sites.[22]

The poor quality of the environment in Korea is more than a health problem. It is related to the competitiveness and productivity of the national economy and may prove to be a severe limitation on continued Korean economic expansion. Korea is no longer a cheap-labor economy, and the cost of labor is a growing factor in the nation's ability to compete globally. Gridlock in the nation's transportation system is estimated to account for 20 percent of all production costs. The declining water quality is forcing companies in need of clean water to install their own expensive prefiltration and treatment plants. And it is already too expensive to have legions of unskilled laborers devoted to cleaning and repairing environmentally fouled machinery and facilities.[23]

One of the most insidious and widespread costs of environmental pollution is the damage that airborne particulates do to sensitive electronic machinery. Although the cost of this has not been calculated, anyone who has tried to use a computer in Seoul quickly finds that the dirt and grime make constant cleaning and repair a necessity. Multiplied by millions of machines and millions of lost hours, the burdens imposed by pollution on the national economic capacity are enormous.

Still, perhaps the best barometer of Korean pollution is the challenge faced by the average Korean housekeeper. Despite some recent improvements in air quality due to the reduction of anthracite coal burning, an average apartment in Seoul must be cleaned twice a day just to keep even with the relentless rain of microscopic airborne pollution. The cuffs of white business shirts must be scrubbed to clean off the ring of black soot acquired by a salaryman at his desk, and draperies and bedding turn gray after only a few months of use.

Korea now faces an immense, unprecedented public and private challenge. For thirty years it has polluted its environment with abandon. Economic planners have failed to account for the environment in their planning or calculations. Pollution abatement and control expenditures, for example, increased from 0.011 percent of GNP in 1974 to 0.25 percent in 1992. Between 1985 and 1992, those expenditures in OECD countries ranged from 0.5 percent to 1.6 percent.[24] Korea has underinvested in the environment, partly out of the belief that prosperity and modernization could be achieved in a small country without concern for air and water pollution. These could be attended to in the future, after industrialization was complete.[25]

The problem of cleaning up Korea's environment, though, is not just one of changing course when the nation has achieved full industrialization. It will involve new ways of thinking and doing to undo the cumulative effects of the nation's poisoned prosperity. Little in the headlong rush toward development has prepared Korea for this challenge. The structures of its government institutions have not modernized as quickly as its means of production. As a result, the minds of Korea's people remain securely anchored to old patterns of behavior that make it difficult for them and their leaders to creatively come to terms with the unintended byproduct of their remarkable industrial success. Nonetheless, Koreans are coming to terms with their environmental problems, and what follows is an examination of the limits and possibilities of their thinking and actions.

Notes

1. Despite the rapid rise of Christianity in Korea, the country remains solidly wedded to its Confucian and Buddhist past. An excellent study of these cultural underpinnings can be found in Martina Deuchler, *The Confucian Transformation of Korea: A Study of Society and Ideology* (Cambridge, MA: Harvard University Press, 1992).

2. Mark L. Clifford, *Troubled Tiger: Businessmen, Bureaucrats, and Generals in South Korea*. Armonk, NY: M.E. Sharpe, 1994.

3. Andrew C. Nahm, *Korea: Tradition and Transformation—A History of the Korean People*. Seoul, Korea: Hollym, 1988.

4. Cho Lee-Jay and Kim Yoon-Hyung, eds., *Economic Development in the Republic of Korea: A Policy Perspective*. Honolulu, HI: East–West Center University of Hawaii Press, 1991.

5. "Korea Ranks 13th in Terms of GNP in 1992," *Korea Times*, March 17, 1994. The official numbers in the growth of personal income in Korea are impressive, but they, too, may be a good illustration of the unreliability of statistical evidence in assessing Korean affairs, from the economy to the environment. There is widespread speculation in Korea that the real level of personal income may actually range from $12,000 to $15,000. Korea remains a strongly cash-based economy with active gray commercial markets. Moreover, Korean workers, from university professors to factory laborers, receive annual "bonuses" that can be as high as ten times their reported annual salaries. The result is that reported incomes for statistical purposes are hugely suppressed. This underground banking economy, complete with savings clubs, curbside lenders, and money changers, is vibrant and largely unaccounted for by government economic estimates. See also Cho Jae-Hyon, "Average Household Savings Hit W11 Mil.," *Korea Times*, May 26, 1994.

6. "Controlling Growth for Stability Is '95 Goal," *Korea Herald*, January 10, 1995.

7. There is an abundance of statistical source material highlighting Korean environmental conditions. However, the accuracy of these measurements and the methodologies on which they are based are widely suspected, both in and out of government circles. As a result, all official statistics must be treated with great care. Unfortunately, few other outside measures are any more reliable. As a result, statistical evidence used in this monograph is to illustrate trends only.

8. In early 1995 the government announced its intention to launch antismoking programs in schools. In addition, the creation of smoke-free areas is a growing trend, and the government has announced that it intends to ban smoking from public places by the end of 1995. See "Expansion of No-Smoking Areas," *Korea Times*, January 11, 1995. Also see Philip Shendon, "Asia's Having One Huge

Nicotine Fit," *New York Times*, May 15, 1994. The Korean Ministry of Health and Social Affairs recently announced that it would ban smoking in its buildings. This is the first time that any government agency has put forward a smoking prohibition as a step toward curbing smoking and improving the indoor environmental quality for workers. "Health Ministry Prohibits Smoking in Its Work Areas," *Korea Herald*, May 31, 1994.

9. "Rain in May Found Most Acid," *Korea Times*, May 20, 1994. Some of this increase, perhaps up to 70 percent, is due to the rapid and very dirty industrialization of China.

10. Han Sang-Wook, "Environmental Issues and Projects in Korea," unpublished manuscript, 1994. Kim Jong-Won, "An Ecological Strategy for Conservation and Rehabilitation of Korean Biological Diversity," *Journal of Environmental Science* (Kyungpook National University), vol. 7, 1993.

11. Ibid.

12. "Foul Odor Detected Again in Tap Water in E. Seoul," *Korea Times*, March 25, 1994.

13. "1 in 5 Seoulites Buys Bottled Water, 0.6 Pct Drink Tap," *Korea Times*, March 17, 1994.

14. In May 1994 the Korean Broadcasting Service presented a nationally broadcast television documentary reporting that the bacterial counts in independently sampled bottled water were higher than those in tap water.

15. Lee Soo-Hyung, "Heavy Metals in the Surface Water of Chinhae Bay during 1970–1983," *Bulletin of KORDI* [Korean Ocean Research and Development Institute], vol. 6, 1984.

16. Anne E. Platt, "Dying Seas," *World Watch Magazine*, vol. 6, no. 1, January–February 1995. See also "The Dying Yellow Sea," *Kyunghyang Shinmun*, January 7, 1995.

17. Kim Jung-Wk, "Environmental Cooperation in North-East Asia," *Proceedings of the Conference on Political Economy of Development and Cooperation in North-East Asian Rim*, June 30–July 2, 1993, Changchin, China. Kim Jung-Wk, "Environmental Aspects of Transnational Corporation Activities in Ulsan/Onsan Industrial Complexes, Republic of Korea," Japan Environmental Congress, 1991. Dr. Kim is a long-time activist in environmental issues. He is a member of many environmental groups and once ran for a local council in the Kangnam area of Seoul. He lost by a large margin. See also "Pollution in China Reaches Dangerous Levels," *Korea Herald*, May 16, 1994.

18. Lee Chan-Won, "Metal Distribution and Contamination in Sediments from Estuaries of Masan Bay as a Potential Source of Ground Water Quality Deterioration," *Ocean Resources*, vol. 12, no. 2, 1990, pp. 97–104.

19. Kwon Sook-Pyo, "Study on the Standards of Ground Water Quality and Setting of Evaluation Standard of Ground Water Pollution," Interim Report submitted to Korean Research Council on Environmental Sciences, Seoul, Korea, August 1993.

20. "Woes of Noise Pollution," *Korea Herald*, January 15, 1995.

21. "Garbage, Old Furniture Dumped in Back Streets," *Korea Herald*, January 5, 1995.

22. This statistical information is dated, but it illustrates the scope of the problem, which has grown worse with time. Kim Jung-Wk and Jeon Eui-Chan,

"Strategies for Developing Responsive Solid Waste Management in Seoul City: Institutional Arrangement," *Journal of Environmental Studies* (Seoul National University), vol. 28, 1991.

23. Korean wage rates have climbed rapidly since the middle eighties. Today Korea "imports" cheaper labor from the Philippines and other Southeast Asian nations, but the economy is plagued by its increasingly high-cost, low-efficiency industrial system. "KIEP Stresses Need for Economic Dynamism," *Korea Herald*, May 12, 1994.

24. Korean Ministry of Environment, "National Report to the Secretary General of the United Nations to Be Reviewed by the Commission on Sustainable Development," unpublished report, Seoul, 1993.

25. Kim Jung-Wk, "Current Environmental Problems and Policies in the Republic of Korea," unpublished paper, November 1994.

2

The History and Structure of Environmental Administration in Korea: A Brief Overview

Although the broad outline of statute and regulation of Korean environmental law is well known, its political and social history cannot yet be written. Access to government documents is restricted, and many of the problems, motivations, and even the actors themselves are still hidden under a thick national security blanket.[1] However, the general structural development of the legal and regulatory measures taken since the 1960s that form the backbone of environmental administration in Korea are evident. These can be found in the government's own official reports, within the Korean academic community, and in the media and larger public.[2] In addition, a wealth of information exists in the growing body of detailed information presented to the United Nations, World Bank, and other international bodies.[3] A brief outline of the main themes of the still-developing body of Korean environmental law will suffice to provide the necessary foundation for a discussion in chapter three of the realities of environmental administration and its limits.[4]

The history of Korean environmental law originates with the development of the 1961 New Forest Law, which began a major national reforestation program.[5] This law called for the planting of hundreds of millions of trees to reestablish Korea's woodlands, which had been abused by the Japanese occupation, the Korean War, and a fuel-starved population in the 1950s. Until the 1980s these efforts were largely controlled by the government, but more recently they have come to enjoy wide public support and participation. Today, tree planting is ongoing and is pointed to with pride by Koreans as a sign of their commitment to maintain and restore their country's natural environment.

The early efforts at reforestation were complemented by the nation's first antipollution law. Enacted in 1963, the Anti-Public-Nuisance Control Law sought to set a tone for maintaining the nation's environmental integrity. However, while it did establish general goals for reducing and controlling pollution, it did not create any administrative or enforcement mechanisms to ensure compliance with the broad national goals outlined in the statute. Rapid industrialization and single-minded government support of economic expansion simply overwhelmed this early legislation.

The seeds of Korean official government action to come to terms with environmental degradation were more firmly planted in 1973. At that time, the national government established the Pollution Control Division within the Bureau of Sanitation of the Ministry of Health and Social Affairs (MoHSA). As an independent agency under the administrative control of MoHSA, this small unit was charged with overseeing public efforts to address health-related concerns due to declining air and water quality. However, the agency had no real direct enforcement power, and its responsibilities were limited by its own narrow public health perspective on environmental issues.

Throughout the 1970s, environmental problems increased in Korea, largely as a result of rapid industrialization and urbanization in Seoul, Pusan, Masan, and Ulsan. During the early stages of economic expansion, oversight of industrial environmental practices was almost completely ignored. Rather, policy makers almost always viewed clogged roadways, inadequate sewers, and smog-shrouded mountains as positive reflections of economic growth. They believed these secondary problems, associated with rapid economic expansion, needed only time and good engineering to solve. Most important, they could be addressed well in the future when prosperity allowed for such luxuries. Other environmental hazards, such as toxic chemical wastes and pesticide contamination of food and water supplies, received little or no attention from government officials or the public until late in the decade.

In 1978 the Korean government enacted Korea's first comprehensive environmental protection legislation, the Environmental Preservation Act. This was modeled on similar innovations in the developed world, especially in Japan, and sought to create a single comprehensive environmental management policy and strategy. The act covered most aspects of environmental concerns and established environmental standards for emissions and waste discharge. It also outlined the creation of waste-disposal and monitoring programs as well as various administrative sanctions for violations. In 1979, the law was amended to implement a nationwide system of environmental assessment as a way of assuring environmental quality.

In a related action, the Korean government passed the Marine Pollution Preservation Act in 1978. This legislation recognized, for the first time, the importance of the coastal marine environment and sought to protect Korea's fragile coastal zones. The Marine Pollution Act classified the nation's seas into three classes and made designations according to their existing and anticipated uses. Water-quality standards were subsequently established based on those evaluations. Under this act, Korea implemented relatively strict regulation of pollution from urban areas and discharges from ships (waste water, oil, and solid wastes) and established a system for monitoring sea water quality. Also under authority of the act, the Korean government created a network of dockside vessel and marine facilities capable of safely handling hazardous cargoes. It sited protective equipment and chemicals in coastal areas to cope with hazardous chemical and oil spills. Finally, the government established a system of marine environmental impact assessment and established special protected zones.

In 1980 Korea's government and business patricians still faced weak public and international pressure to substantially improve efforts to address environmental problems. As a result, the new constitution ratified that year recognized environmental needs. Article 35 stated, "All citizens shall have the right to a healthy and a pleasant environment: the state and all citizens shall endeavor to protect the environment." The laws of the late 1970s and the new constitution laid a legal foundation for environmental activity, but the administrative structure necessary to ensure compliance was at best extremely feeble and usually nonexistent. Even so, the Korean government continued to experiment with environmental administration by consolidating environmental programs. The Environmental Administration was established in 1980 and placed under the control of a vice minister within MoSHA who was given responsibility for implementing the nation's environmental laws and overseeing their enforcement.

Shortly after its creation, the Environmental Administration in 1986 opened Korea's first environmental regional offices to monitor environmental conditions and identify problems, which represented a dramatic expansion of official government activity. The structure was roughly analogous to the U.S. EPA's regional office structure, but there was a significant difference. In Korea, regional offices lacked the authority and technical capability to engage in independent problem identification and remediation. This lack of capability was further accentuated by the general Korean bureaucratic tendency to "exile" the least accomplished and most junior bureaucrats to regional offices outside Seoul, the center of everything important in modern Korean life.

The major environmental legislation of the 1980s also came in 1986, when the Korean government adopted the Solid Waste Management Act. Interest in solid waste was directly linked to growing economic success. As wage and living standards rose steadily through the decade, refuse became a national crisis and its disposal an administrative obsession. The 1986 law addressed disposal of refuse, sludge, ash, excreta, waste oil and acid, and animal carcasses. The law did not, however, govern the disposal of radioactive wastes generated by public and private activities; oversight of those was and is the responsibility of the Ministry of Science and Technology.

Despite the developing environmental legislative and planning frameworks, regulation, enforcement, and certainly compliance lagged well behind the establishment of public policy. In the name of economic prosperity, the national government consistently refused to impose environmental controls on either existing industry or new development.[6] Also, government investment for environmental preservation such as the construction of waste-water treatment plants remained minimal. Nonetheless, the national government did take steps to address the broader environmental needs of a growing consumer economy. For example, it required catalytic converters on all new Korean automobiles in 1988 and subsequently banned leaded gasoline in 1992. In the early 1990s public environmental education programs were launched, and public participation in household-waste separation and reduction was widely promoted through the media.

The National Assembly made major revisions to environmental laws in 1990. The Environmental Preservation Act was superseded by a number of specific actions designed to tackle the growing complexity of environmental problems. Six separate laws were passed dealing with environmental policy, environmental preservation, water quality, noise and vibration control, hazardous chemical substances, and environmental-pollution damage-dispute mediation. These were complemented in 1992 by the adoption of the Natural Environment Preservation Act and the Resource Recycling Act. To date, Korea has adopted eleven major environmental laws, and the process of developing additional law is ongoing.[7]

Elevation of the environment issue to ministerial rank by creation of the Ministry of Environment (MoE) in 1990 lent political punctuation to the growing importance of the environment within Korea. Still, securing actual compliance with the law remained a nagging problem. Partly in recognition of that, the first action of the MoE was to establish a five-year master plan for environmental improvement between 1992 and 1996. Its main goals were to upgrade Korea's most visible environmental problems by:

- improving water quality so that the safety and reliability of the water supply in every part of the country would be ensured;
- increasing the sewage treatment rate in Korea from 37 percent to 65 percent by 1997 through the construction of seventy-five additional sewage treatment plants;
- improving air quality through a reduction of ambient SO_2 from an annual average of .05 to .03 ppm by 1993;
- promoting waste reduction and recycling; and
- implementing programs and regulations to systematically manage the environment and reduce pollution.

The total investment necessary to carry out this plan was estimated to be more than $12 billion, which on an annual basis accounted for approximately 1 percent of Korea's current GNP. The plan estimated that 55 percent of the cost would be borne by government, with the balance coming from the private sector.

MoE also developed a ten-year master plan to promote the development of environmental technology. This is, of course, based on assumptions of the growing global importance of industrial technologies designed to reduce or remediate environmental problems. It was estimated that the total investment necessary in the ten-year national environmental research and development plan will be $1 billion.

Korea has secured several loans from the World Bank to pay for this program.[8]

The ten-year plan also outlined programs for low-interest loans and tax reductions to stimulate the development of Korean environmental technologies for both domestic application and international sale. Additionally, the master plan outlined a program to identify and purchase environmentally safe products. It further stressed greater public education about environmental issues such as energy conservation, waste reduction and elimination, and citizen involvement in environmental management questions. Finally, the ten-year plan proposed to establish several environmental research institutes to support the cleanup of industry and promotion of environmentally clean technologies to small and medium-sized companies.

As Korea has moved onto the international stage as an industrial power, it has sought to acquire legitimacy as an international partner through broader global participation. In 1989 Korea agreed to join the Basel Convention (on international transport of hazardous wastes) by the end of 1993. In 1992, the Korean government adopted a national Declaration on Environmental Conservation. This consisted of internationally recognizable environmental principles designed to ensure a cleaner environment. In summit meetings with Japan and China, development of regional strategies for cooperative environmental action has been discussed, but few meaningful achievements have been observed.[9]

Early in 1993, Korea joined the executive board of the Commission on Sustainable Development (CSD). This international body is responsible for the implementation of policies and plans adopted at the earth summit in Rio de Janeiro. Despite the nation's prominence in CSD affairs, its delegation to the Rio summit expressed concern about the primary agreements at the meeting. Like the governments of many industrializing and newly industrialized nations, the Korean government saw stringent environmental controls as a threat to continued economic progress. Nevertheless, Korea signed the two most important Framework Convention documents: biodiversity and climate change. The Korean government has also set the country on the road to becoming a full member of the United Nations Conference on Environment and Development (UNCED). It has done so with the full understanding that UNCED participation will make demands on Korea and shape its efforts to improve environmental protection.[10]

The evolution of environmental law in Korea is usually held up by

Korean authorities as evidence of the nation's commitment to environmental quality. To be sure, the laws themselves and the standards and plans they support compare quite well to international norms. Yet, the existence of law, regulation, and long-term plans are not enough to protect the environment. The Korean environmental reality is that the administration of national laws, regulations, and qualitative environmental standards has generally been lax, subject to corruption and heavy-handed pressure to ease the way for industrial development. Any understanding of the value of Korea's legal structure of environmental regulation must include the knowledge that, for most of industrial Korea's short history, environmental laws and regulations have meant very little. At every turn, passionate pursuit of economic security and an end to the nation's impoverishment simply pushed all other concerns aside. However, the environmental bill for unbridled economic expansion is now coming due in a nation that, nearly three decades after the passage of its first environmental legislation, still lacks the experienced personnel, policies, methodologies, and practical strategies to promptly and prudently come to terms with its immense environmental problems.

Notes

1. Government documents prepared by the Korean bureaucracy are notoriously incomplete, misleading, and at times inaccurate. This is not a new phenomenon in Korean civil administration, which often prizes consistency and perceived loyalty to authority over accuracy. Given this, all public documents in Korea should be approached with a cautious eye.

2. The most current and complete review of Korean environmental law is Hong Joon-Hyun, *Environmental Law* (Seoul: Hanwool Press, 1994; Korean). Another excellent discussion of the administrative legal culture of Korea is Hahn Pyong-Chon, *Korean Jurisprudence: Politics and Culture* (Seoul: Yonsei University Press, 1986).

3. Korean Ministry of Environment, *National Report to the Secretary General of the United Nations to Be Reviewed by the Commission on Sustainable Development* (Seoul, 1993), is perhaps the most recent survey of environmental management issues in Korea. See also Korean Ministry of Environment, *National Report of the Republic of Korea to UNCED* (Seoul, 1992).

4. The Korean government has published a complete compendium of its enacted environmental laws, translated into English. Korean Ministry of Environment, *Environmental Acts of the Republic of Korea*. Seoul: 1993.

5. Park Tai-Shik, "Forest Planning and Management Policy in Korea," *Research Bulletin of Seoul National University*, vol. 21, 1985.

6. Hong Joon-Hyun, "Abandoned Environment, Unkept Promise," *Law and Society*, vol. 9, September, 1994.

7. Korean Ministry of Environment, *National Report of the Republic of Korea to UNCED*. Seoul: 1992.

8. Korean Ministry of Environment, *Korea Report to the World Bank*. Seoul: 1993.

9. Kim Jung-Wk, "Environmental Cooperation in North-East Asia," *Proceedings of the Conference on Political Economy of Development and Cooperation in North-East Asian Rim*, sponsored by UNDP and UNESCAP, Changchin, China, June 30–July 2, 1993.

10. In this regard, Korea's leaders and policy makers are well ahead of the Korean public. This is illustrated by the widespread concern over the linkage of trade and environment questions that surfaced in late 1993. "Environment Day Points to Future of Earth," *Korea Herald*, August 19, 1993.

3

Realities and Limits of Environmental Law and Management in Korea

Korea has rapidly developed a framework of law to assist it in reaching broadly stated environmental goals. Nonetheless, the establishment of these goals has not been sufficient to deal with the economic and social implications of developing environmental concerns in Korean society.[1] As a result, pollution and its effects on the natural environment and human health have progressively become more severe, until today conditions have reached crisis proportions.

However, in 1995, there is hopeful evidence that Korea has finally begun to develop the will and expertise to address the problems of environmental administration and regulation. The nation's bureaucracy and its political masters still have a long way to go, and there is a significant gap between public rhetoric and the realities of effective environmental administration. Many difficult challenges lie ahead. Coordination among responsible entities, public and private, is at best ragged; lines of authority are unclear. The necessary talent and expertise for effective environmental administration are in short supply. The nation is just beginning to struggle with establishing policies that will better align the demands for continued development with the growing realities of the political, social, and economic costs of environmental damage. These limitations and barriers to effective environmental administration and management are substantial and cannot be overstated. Yet, despite all the difficulties, what is emerging is a picture of environmental administration in transition. It is rising from relative obscurity and ineffectiveness to a greater degree of importance in Korea's public life.

Law and the Environment

The Korean legal system is based on traditional Asian concepts of law and governance and blended with continental European legal traditions. As befits a long Confucian tradition, emphasis is placed on social harmony, consensus, and the authority and power of the central government. As a result, Korean law does not allow for civil actions as commonly understood in the United States. Moreover, the nation's legal tradition does not recognize concepts of punitive damages or class standing, although the Ministry of Justice is studying the question. Currently, as part of an effort to modernize legal institutions, damages are often defined very narrowly, as are questions of standing in general. At the same time, although it is possible for an individual or corporation to sue the government, there is little real possibility of winning such cases. Similarly, one level of government cannot sue another, and civil disputes are most often resolved through the use of arbitration panels appointed by the government. The panels generally are empowered to investigate complaints as well as render decisions. Independent discovery is also not an accepted part of the Korean system. Therefore, lawyers representing private clients generally are forced to rely on evidence gathered by arbitration panels or by government officials.

The implications of this tradition of civil procedure for environmental administration are obvious. Citizens are usually denied litigation as a remedy for settling disputes, if not in theory, then in reality. In order to successfully gain a legal remedy, a litigant must prove immediate and personal damage. Epidemiological and other statistical evidence is usually disallowed by the courts and arbitration panels. If a judgment is made in a citizen's favor, damages can be awarded for loss of present and future income and for payment for medical treatment and medication. However, the amounts are usually quite small, and there is little incentive for attorneys to represent clients claiming environmental harm to themselves or their property.[2] Appeals of arbitration rulings can be made to the civil courts, but in practice the rulings are rarely overturned. This system serves as a substantial barrier to all aspects of litigation, but especially to litigation that might be viewed as having adverse economic consequences or posing a challenge to the established order.

In recent years, the government has increased its level of prosecution for environmental offenses, but the rate of prosecution is well below that of other industrialized countries. Administrative fees and fines can be levied upon violators. The charges are determined according to the amount and period of emission and the type of pollutant released. But, so far, administrative fines, when levied, are commonly thought to be much smaller than the cost of improved process or control technologies, other prevention measures, or cleanup. This is as true in the case of individual violations of environmental laws as it is in cases of corporate malfeasance. For example, in 1991 the national government banned cookstoves in national parks and imposed a 10,000 won ($12.50) fine on violators of the ban,[3] but the law is universally ignored by campers. Similarly, the amount of trash left in national parks grows every year; it is estimated that for every ton of trash disposed of by visitors in the Mt. Puksan area, north of Seoul, another fifteen tons have to be collected by park employees after a busy weekend.[4] More seriously, in 1989 four Korean food processors were found to be using industrial beef tallow in their production of soup noodles. The prosecutor of the case further accused the four firms of using "sewage water" and demanded a fine of 2.339 billion won ($2,923,750) as well as long prison sentences. The four were convicted, but the court suspended the convictions and eliminated the fines.[5] In addition, until 1994, government-owned and -operated facilities could not be fined by the courts. This changed in mid-1994, but the military, an unknown but potentially major source of environmental pollution, remains exempt from civil and criminal environmental judgments.[6]

The gross violation of environmental laws can lead to criminal charges in Korea. Although the law allows up to lifetime incarceration, the common practice has been to impose fines on plant managers and company presidents in response to major or repeated violations. Another major failing of current Korean environmental law is its silence on damages due to past practices, which leaves unresolved many potentially serious environmental problems ranging from historic abuses to abandoned materials. This limits government at all levels in efforts to clean up historic sites and to assess fines and criminal penalties when ownership is not clear. MoE has not ignored this problem, and officials have had preliminary discussions about the development of a national law that would allow for the cleanup of previously contaminated sites for which ownership cannot be determined.

It is important to recognize that the entire body of Korean environmental law is understood quite differently from similar law in the Western industrialized nations. Most Koreans, government officials and citizens alike, widely see all bodies of law as goals rather than strict standards that demand immediate compliance. Naturally, this has given rise to a good deal of confusion and variability in enforcement and compliance.

Ministerial Jurisdictions

Today, at least ten national ministries are active in environmental affairs (see Table 3.1).[7]

In 1994, progress was made toward delineating the responsibilities of each ministry in an effort to rationalize ministerial responsibilities. However, in practice, the interests of one ministry are often pitted against another, and their bureaucracies remain very competitive. Examples of this bureaucratic infighting are hard to document, but they are widely discussed by participants and close observers with a passion that rivals support for local baseball teams. In most cases the struggles resemble the fight between the Ministry of Environment and the Ministry of Trade, Industry, and Energy (MoTIE) in 1990 over the phasing out of diesel fuels for light trucks, buses, and vans. At the time, about 45 percent of all vehicles used diesel fuel, and the MoE asked that the fuel be eliminated from use by 1995. MoTIE, speaking for industrial interests, though, advocated continued use of diesel fuel. In the end, MoTIE prevailed after Korean industry, most notably the Sangyong Group, objected in order to protect an agreement it had just signed with Mercedes-Benz AG to produce diesel-fueled light commercial vehicles.[8]

In another example of the lack of ministerial coordination, the Ministry of Foreign Affairs called off what was seen as a draconian MoE regulation regarding the disposal and recycling of glass and plastic bottles. If enacted, the proposal would have had an adverse effect on trade relations and reduced the level of activity with Korea's major trading partners. In its complaint against the MoE proposed regulation, MoFA noted that MoE officials had not consulted them about the

Table 3.1

Agency and Ministerial Environmental Responsibility in Korea

Ministry/Agency	Environmental Responsibility
Ministry of Finance	To exert influence through policy coordination and the establishment of economic strategies and goals.
Ministry of Foreign Affairs	Diplomatic policy for environment-related issues.
Ministry of Home Affairs (including local government)	Environmental regulation, supervision, and nature protection.
Ministry of Justice	Penalties for environmental crimes.
Ministry of Trade, Industry, and Energy	Promotion of environmental industry (shared responsibility with Ministry of Education).
Ministry of Agriculture, Forestry, and Fishery	Regulation of agricultural pesticides and forest conservation.
Ministry of Public Health and Social Affairs	Regulation of pesticides for human health and safety.
Ministry of Construction and Transport	Management of freshwater quantity resources and construction of waste-water treatment plants.
Ministry of Science and Technology	Environmental research and technology development support.
Ministry of Energy and Resources	Development of environmentally sound energy resources and energy conservation strategies.

impact of the regulation on foreign trade and investment.

The emergence of environmental interests within the bureaucracies of the most powerful Korean ministries and agencies should be interpreted as a positive sign of progress. It stands as an acknowledgment that the right to set environmental policy and administer its implementation is worth fighting over. In 1993 the central government allocated 38.08 billion won ($47.6 million) to environmental administration and conservation across all national government agencies. This represents a 21.6 percent rise over 1992 and is the highest percentage increase of any activity funded by the national government. These funds now amount to 0.5–1.0 percent of GNP. Despite this growth in expenditures, most environmental programs remain severely underfunded, given the daunting tasks of environmental management and regulation.[9]

Ministry of Environment and Its Related Agencies

The legal center of Korean environmental administration is the Ministry of Environment. The role of the MoE is to oversee the implementation and administration of the National Basic Environmental Pollution Law. In order to assist it in evaluating environmental problems such as the toxicity of hazardous wastes, the Ministry of Environment operates the National Institute of Environmental Research (NIER). This institute was founded in 1978 and currently has a research staff of about two hundred professionals who carry out environmental research and development. NIER's major role is to test and monitor health, air, and water quality throughout the Korean peninsula. It also seeks to develop control technologies for pollution prevention and abatement and serves as the national manager for INFOTERRA, the international environmental resource database.

However, NIER is currently housed in an old and inadequate building, and its laboratories and equipment are far from state of the art, thus undermining its research effectiveness. Discussions are now underway to act on a plan for modernization, but the necessary funding is not in place. However, perhaps the most significant problem facing the institute is that its professional personnel often lack sufficient training and experience to carry out the institute's mission.

The MoE also oversees the Environmental Officials Training Institute (EOTI). This institute was established in 1981 under NIER, but in 1992 it became an independent organization under the MoE, although it still shares a building with NIER. The role of EOTI is to be an independent training and education center for meeting the nation's environmental personnel needs. It provides mandated certification training to local and national government officials as well as to employees of private companies. Since 1981, more than 27,000 students (15,000 from government and 12,000 from industry) have participated in technical and nontechnical programs. In 1995, the institute will provide training to approximately 5,500 public and private environmental managers.[10]

The curriculum for public officials includes two- to three-week core short-course offerings that introduce managers to the basic principles and goals of environmental administration and management. Environmental managers also are required to take special one- to two-week courses to improve specific skills. Currently, there are thirteen of these courses, including hazardous-waste management, motor-vehicle emission testing, and environmental impact assessment. Privately employed environmental managers are offered a choice of ten one-week seminars. These range from marine pollution prevention and sanitary treatment facility design to programs designed to introduce new technology and analytical methods.

The educational programs sponsored by EOTI are limited by the inability of the institute to integrate laboratory and field experience into its curriculum. Moreover, the short amount of time devoted to courses covering the most complicated aspects of environmental control and management gives students only rudimentary knowledge. There are plans, though, to address these problems in the future. The institute also has plans to move to a new and more modern facility near the city of Inchon, where it will expand its capacity to provide more comprehensive training and will have access to field sites, such as the Kimpo Landfill, for some hands-on training. Additional plans call for the establishment of analytical training laboratories, but commitments for funding have yet to be made by senior MoE officials for that purpose.

The Ministry of Environment has also established a policy analysis institute known as the Korean Environmental Technology Research Institute. Created in 1992, KETRI has been given the role of linking technology capabilities and trends with the development of national environmental policy. As the ministry's "think tank," it is building a database of foreign and domestic environmental technology resources, and it currently has studies underway in air pollution, global environmental issues, and ways to link development to improved environmental management. KETRI has recently undergone leadership changes. In 1994 a new director, Dr. Chung Chin-Seung, an economist previously with the influential Korea Development Institute (KDI), came to KETRI. Dr. Chung began to make significant changes in the focus of the institute by strengthening its ability to do environmental economics. However, Chung left KETRI in early 1995 to take overall responsibility for program planning in the Ministry of Environment. This has left the future direction of KETRI in doubt.

Finally, the ministry maintains informal contact with dozens of university research centers, professional organizations, and government-sponsored institutes that have been established to conduct research and policy studies in environmental science and engineering. This formal and informal academic network is extensive and plays an important role in assisting MoE to shape policies and programs to improve environmental management in Korea.

Unfortunately, the Ministry of Environment and its institutions are still far from effective environmental management agencies. There is no overriding sense of policy direction, nor is there a clear understanding of even how to begin to develop methodologies and strategies to implement consistent environmental regulation and expectations of compliance by industry, government, and the public. Although a lack of money and cooperation from other organs of government is a significant part of the problem, MoE professional staff also lacks experience and training. As a result, the public perception of MoE is of a ministry that lurches from one crisis to another, falling victim along the way to aggressive and relentless political and economic pressure.

The structure of Korean environmental administration is highly centralized. In environmental administration, as in all other areas of government activity, decrees emanate from the president and prime minister, and control is exercised at the ministerial level. In practice, however, responsibility for environmental management is widely spread across government, with local government having significant responsibility for implementing the national environmental regulations. The principal result of this diffusion of authority is that no one agency has been given sufficient power to demand compliance with regulations and standards (as in the case of the U.S. Environmental Protection Agency) from either sister government bureaucracies or the private sector. This has meant that the enforcement of standards is erratic, and environmental concerns are not yet effectively integrated into national development decision making. Finally, many tools of environmental management, such as well-defined methodologies and strategies to improve compliance levels, enforcement, and public participation, are partially or wholly missing.

In late 1994, however, a cabinet shuffle increased the status of the minister of environment to the number eight ministry.[11] The most important aspect of this change was that with full cabinet rank, the minister of environment was given the ability to independently issue decrees, as well as greater latitude in enforcement. This change has cleared the way for the serious consideration of much stronger pollution control and regulatory systems and given rise to new respect for the power of the ministry. Although it will be subject to approval by the National Assembly, MoE is preparing to introduce a total pollution discharge system similar to the total maximum daily load system for water and airsheds that is widely used in the United States. If adopted, the effect would be revolutionary, as highly visible environmental milestones and a regulatory methodology would be firmly fixed as the foundation for all future regulation and enforcement. This would be a radical change from the total density standards that generally have been used by the government and industry to measure levels of contamination. Thus, it is highly unlikely that a decision to adopt a new system will come anytime soon.

Still, even without this kind of sweeping regulatory change, there is ample evidence that environmental enforcement actions are increasing throughout the country. One of many illustrations of the effect of this changing attitude occurred in May 1995. The city of Seoul's environmental office announced that they were issuing a reprimand and improvement order against the Hilton Hotel which is owned by the wife of the chairman of the Daewoo Group. The city cited the hotel for exceeding the 0.003 parts per billion limit for dry cleaning solvent in wastewater despite a test result that showed that the amount, although greater than the allowable ceiling, was less than 0.004 parts per billion. In years past this kind of violation would have never been detected, let alone acted upon.

Environmental Assessment Process

As part of its core function, the MoE is responsible for evaluating the environmental impact of all proposed development and other human activities with a potential effect on the natural environment. To accomplish this, it oversees the environmental assessment statement (EAS) process, which is based on the U.S. environmental impact statement model. This system was put in place in 1978, but it was not implemented until 1981. Even today, the EAS process remains a rather loosely applied administrative tool that is widely thought to be ineffective and has been the cause of much conflict between environmental groups and the government. In a case involving the approval of a pumped-power storage plant in Kyongsangnamdo, Korea's largest environmental group threatened to physically obstruct construction unless the EAS system was properly used to evaluate the environmental consequences of the facility. Those demands, though, were unilaterally dismissed when the minister of environment asserted that opponents to the new plant were "ignorant . . . and senseless people."[12]

Under current practice, environmental assessments are required only where a construction or manufacturing site covers more than 150,000 square meters. In addition, if construction is to occur at a preexisting industrial complex, no EAS is required. Government and private developers are required to submit environmental assessment statements when a project is covered by the EAS law. There are seventeen project types that demand EAS evaluations. These include urban development plans, such as the building of new towns, landfills, or solid-waste handling sites; harbor, road, and water resource construction projects; leisure development such as golf courses, stadiums, and gymnasiums; and energy projects. Environmental assessment statements are also required for projects that may affect mountainous zones and national parks. The president may unilaterally order the preparation of an environmental assessment statement or suspend the requirement for one if a project is declared a "national priority."[13] It is that latter aspect of presidential power that reduces the effectiveness of the EAS system as a tool for habitat preservation and environmental monitoring.

All EAS documentation is prepared under procedural guidelines developed by the Ministry of Environment. Once the documents are prepared, they must first be submitted to all relevant government agencies (in the case of a private developer) and responsible local officials. After the government accepts a draft of the EAS, the developer must make the EAS available to the public for inspection for at least twenty days. This may take the form of a public notice in a local newspaper or a posting in a public building. If a local official thinks it necessary, a public hearing may be held. The law requires that the developer must account for public sentiment in the final EAS documents. Once complete, all EASs are submitted to MoE for final review and approval. If the ministry finds that the plans present some danger to the environment, it has the power to ask the developer to take remedial measures.

From their introduction in 1981 through 1991, 869 EASs were submitted to MoE.[14] In many cases, the documents were prepared after all the important decisions were made, and they were often "cookie cutter" documents, copied from previous filings. In practice, permits are seldom held up by the absence of a completed evaluation, and many EASs are filed after ground is broken. Finally, follow-up inspections to ensure compliance with EAS guidelines and proposed plans are rare. In large part, this is a direct result of the absence of conditional permitting as a management and quality assurance tool. There is no significant process for tracking the environmental impact of projects, once approved, and little post-construction inspection to assure compliance with EAS plans.

The Korean EAS process is clearly not yet an effective planning or regulatory tool for environmental management. Even beyond weak enforcement, the current system has a number of liabilities. There is no certification process for those producing EASs. Since Korean environmental law largely focuses on measurable physical qualities, there is not significant consideration within the current EAS system for water and air contamination, preservation of natural habitat, open space, or the remediation of sites disturbed by construction. There are also no generally mandated testing or sampling methodologies for EAS evaluations. Thus, although there are those in Korea who produce quality evaluations based on careful scientific analysis, it has become common for untrained moonlighting university professors to churn out the necessary paperwork for developers. As a result, many EASs are little more than biological surveys of the plants and animals thought to inhabit sites slated for development.

Even if current regulation and enforcement were stringent, the above factors have imposed severe practical administrative limitations on the utility of EASs. In 1993 the MoE called for a review of the environmental assessment system, establishing a committee to suggest modifications to make the system more effective. The working group issued a report to the MoE in December 1993 that outlined a process for improving the effectiveness of the EAS system.[15] Important recommendations were made regarding timing and improvements of methodology, as well as accreditation standards for those who produce the environmental evaluations. Most of those were accepted, and implementation began in 1995. The reforms, however, will likely carry the EAS process only part way toward real integrity in environmental evaluation and planning. The ability to independently monitor land development remains weak, and environmentalists fear that the new procedures may increase the rate of rural development for leisure activities, such as golf courses, ski areas, and marine resort areas.

The failure of the EAS system as an effective agent for environmental management is symptomatic of the position of the MoE in general. Both inside and outside the ministry, there is broad consensus that it is disadvantaged in its dealings with other more powerful ministries. As a result, development projects have yet to receive the kind of environmental supervision that has become common in the United States and Europe. This is true for both government and private programs. To date, no private or government construction project in Korea has ever been stopped solely due to negative environmental evaluations by the MoE.

National Standards, Local Control: A Failed Experiment

Although the Ministry of Environment has general responsibility for overseeing environmental laws, local government is the locus for everyday management. In 1991, local governments were made responsible for all effluent monitoring and all enforcement activities for nonhazardous urban and industrial wastes. This devolution of environmental control and regulation to local government was part of a larger experiment in Korea to reinvigorate local autonomy. However, in the environmental arena, local autonomy worked to limit the development of strong administration and enforcement. Local government officials simply lacked the money, expertise, technical facilities, and staff to accomplish the tasks given to them. Thus, the gulf between printed regulations and actual environmental conditions was further exacerbated by the division of labor and administration between national and local governments.

The localization of environmental management produced a failure of regulatory control and compliance. The problem is not simply one of oversight or willful pollution by individuals, companies, or even governments themselves, although the reliance on local government made it easier to circumvent environmental regulations. Many companies desiring to meet environmental standards report that their way to compliance is often blocked by inexperienced local officials. This makes it difficult for responsible firms to operate within a predictable regulatory environment. This situation is further aggravated by widespread suspicions of corruption and preferential treatment among business leaders and the public at large. By 1994, though, change was clearly visible. Although statistical evidence is not available, it is apparent that the government is increasing its attention to at least the most obvious violations of environmental standards. Evidence for this can be found in the rising number of appeals for relief from regulation and exemptions to environmental laws and the frequency that these are being denied by authorities.[16]

Despite improvements in enforcement, Korea remains a long way from full compliance with its own environmental laws. An example of this inconsistency can be found in Seoul and Pusan, where the national government has sought to preserve green space through the creation of urban green zones. In these zones, which surround the two cities, development is supposed to be kept to a minimum. However, encroachments upon green spaces are common. Variances from zoning regulations have been easily obtained due to the pressure for additional housing and other development activities. As a result, the few remaining green spaces in Korea's crowded urban centers are being rapidly fragmented. Ironically, the major developers of these green zones are local and central governments. Understandably, there is rising concern among urban planners and environmentalists that the increasingly rare open space in Korean cities will soon disappear.

In large measure, encroachments into precious green spaces occur because of the tremendous pressure to develop. The few local officials who might like to preserve open areas do not have the necessary planning expertise, monetary resources, or experience to understand and manage environmental problems. In addition, municipal and provincial governments have often been even less willing to enforce environmental regulations than their national counterparts. This is especially true in Korea's rural areas and smaller cities, where local and regional officials find it impossible to resist the real or imagined pressures of local developers who promise new jobs (and freely provide gifts) in exchange for precious building permits.

A similar pattern is evident in city planning; Korean cities, although they clearly have a certain irresistible vitality, have become a jumble of unplanned mixed uses. This is understandable in the older city cores, but the same lack or failure of urban design is found in newly developed areas across the country. One such example is Shillim-Dong, an area south of the Han River, near the base of Mt. Kwanak. This neighborhood was originally populated by low-income residents, and its initial development was in line with Seoul City's General Plan of 1970, which sought to reduce congestion by redistributing the population from north of the Han to its south shore. The 1970 plan allowed for only low-rise development in Shillim-Dong and established Seoul's first "setback" regulations. As Shillim-Dong has evolved, those regulations have been largely ignored due to steady housing pressures. Twenty-story, high-rise apartment buildings have been allowed to proliferate along the base of Mt. Kwanak. Visual access to the surrounding mountains is now destroyed, and, as in many neighborhoods throughout Seoul, local street and traffic patterns have been permanently altered and overwhelmed by increased vehicle use.[17] Shillim-Dong and nearly every other Seoul neighborhood are a planner's nightmare; they represent a curious laboratory in which everything that could go wrong has gone wrong.

There are many examples of poor environmental planning in Korea, and not all of them are the result of ineffective local government. In many instances, weak planning is a direct result of the national government's inability to coordinate its own development projects among its various ministries. The classic example of the lack of effective planning and oversight in Korea is in the Naktong River basin in the southern part of the country. Massive industrialization has occurred in the watershed, and millions of metric tons of water are diverted from a principal tributary for use in agriculture and major industries, such as steel production in Pohang, on the east coast. As a result, stream flows have fallen well below natural levels. The result has been making the high levels of point- and non-point-source pollution in the Naktong much harder to address.

In 1991 the Naktong became the lightning rod of Korean environmentalism when thousands of gallons of phenol were accidentally spilled into the river by the Doosan Corporation.[18] In January 1994 Korea suffered a second major industrial spill in the Naktong River. Nearly ten million people in southern Korea, including the southern port city of Pusan, the second-largest city in Korea, had their tap water contaminated by benzene and toluene. The Korean media and environmental activists protested as they had done after the earlier accident. A boycott of water bills was led by activists, and both political parties sent teams from the National Assembly to the Naktong to "investigate the situation."[19] The public, civic activists, and nearly all political leaders insisted on improved water-quality management and pointed to the lack of management coordination as a primary cause of the problem that produced benzene levels 1.8 times higher than the World Health Organization's standard.[20] An independent 1992 study prepared by the Pusan Institute of Environmental Research that came to light during the 1994 crisis revealed the stark realities of the Naktong. Its authors charged that they had discovered 307 pollutants in the Naktong, 9 of which were U.S. EPA priority pollutants.[21] The report only served to underscore the public perception that the national government's actions fell far short of their rhetoric.

The Crisis in Drinking Water

Water quality has been a particular problem in Korea. Although Korea receives 1.3 times the world rainfall average, most rain comes during the midsummer monsoon season.[22] Seven multipurpose dams and four estuary dikes have been built on the nation's large river systems to manage water, but until recently there has not been a comprehensive water management authority or plan. As a result, water quality has declined precipitously under the impact of urbanization and industrialization. Today, for example, only 33 percent of the water released from municipal systems into the Naktong basin is treated. In the Han River the level stands at 69 percent. The rate of sewage treatment in the Kum is 31 percent, and the level in the Yongsan is 48 percent.[23] However, these numbers are not the real waste-water rates. Rather, they represent waste-water capacity divided by the total waste-water discharge. This means that the real rates of water treatment are much lower than official government statistical reports indicate.

Improvements are being made in controlling biological and organic contaminants, but in every corner of the nation, Korean public water supplies are hard-pressed to meet anything other than minimally acceptable health and safety standards. Making matters worse is the lack of a consistent national program for monitoring of water quality for organic and inorganic chemicals and heavy-metal contamination. Spot sampling at water treatment plants is conducted, but there is widespread suspicion about the utility and accuracy of that testing. In 1988 suspicion about water quality and the government's assurances of safety led to demands by the International Olympic Committee that bottled water be used in the Olympic Village. The water-quality situation is not much better six years later. Not only has the Naktong River remained an embarrassing problem, but there are daily press reports of foul-smelling and contaminated water throughout the country. In reality there is little chance for rapid improvement of this situation, in large measure because the problems are so large, the human and committed financial resources are inadequate, and construction of new treatment plants cannot be completed overnight.

In 1994 there were ten large bulk-water purification plants in operation and five under construction. Korea has 585 independent water districts that are managed at the local level. If a local government desires to build a new facility, it must gain the approval of the Ministry of Construction (MoC), which sets the specifications for all drinking-water purification plants. Local governments can also apply for financial and educational assistance, but these funds and resources are in short supply. As a result, many treatment and purification plant personnel are poorly trained and certainly underpaid. This makes skilled operators a valued commodity in the private sector, where such capabilities are in growing demand. The result is that local authorities are often unable to properly maintain and operate waste treatment plants at peak efficiency.

In April 1994 the national government, embarrassed by repeated water-quality problems, reformed its management of the nation's water resources and waste-water treatment plants. The Ministry of Environment, which already held power over the water and sewage delivery systems (sewers and pipes) was given supervision of waste-water facilities. This completed a consolidation that began in 1990. The Ministry of Construction, which had held this portfolio, was made responsible for planning, building, and operating large regional bulk drinking-water supply facilities. In late 1994, President Kim Young-Sam reorganized his government and merged the MoC with the Ministry of Transport to form a new unified Ministry of Construction and Transport. This change, though, did not alter the existing division between water quality and supply, and the newly combined Ministry of Construction and Transport continued to hold the portfolio of the MoC, which includes the maintenance and operation of rural water purification and delivery in areas where population densities and government capabilities are low.

The source of Korea's water-quality problems are not found just in the nation's municipal systems. The production and treatment of industrial waste water is a chronic and dangerous problem. Industrial effluents are treated in both public and private treatment facilities, and, in the case of government facilities, actual operation can come under either municipal or national management. Since 1984 the national government has financed the construction of fourteen waste-water treatment plants in six large industrial zones and another eleven in areas of significant but less concentrated industrial development. These plants are operated by a quasi-public corporation known as the Environmental Management Corporation (EMC), which functions under the authority of the Ministry of Environment. The industries at each of the six industrial sites cover the costs of operation by paying user fees to the EMC. In addition to management of industrial waste treatment facilities, the EMC has landfilling operations, three incinerators for burning hazardous materials, and three other plants for collecting and preparing toxic wastes for placement in landfills. A recent independent audit of EMC practices, though, revealed that its staff is chronically undertrained in the proper management of its waste treatment facilities. Dangerous materials are often mishandled, and widely accepted emergency, maintenance, health, and safety precautions are not always properly implemented. EMC also has a low-interest loan program (pegged at 7 percent in 1994) that makes funds available to small and medium-sized companies seeking to improve their ability to reduce and treat waste. However, critics have pointed out that the loan period, set at three years with a three-year grace period, is too short a time for most firms in need of long-term capital-improvement financing.[24] In 1994, the legislative mandate of the EMC was altered to allow the corporation to design and build treatment plants for operation by municipalities and county governments.

Non-point-source contamination of surface and groundwater supplies is another pressing environmental concern, with long-term consequences. The problems in Korea are typical of and pervasive in most developing countries.[25] Illegal dumping and burial of wastes have littered the rural landscape and resulted in the creation of both toxic and nontoxic runoff and leachates. The modernization of agriculture has further introduced fungicides, pesticides, and petrochemical-based fertilizers and herbicides into the rural ecosystem.[26] Fortunately, after two decades of rising application rates, recent government statistics show that reductions in the use of these chemicals may be occurring. The widespread and largely unregulated use of fertilizers and pesticides has been only part of the pollution problems created by modern agriculture.

There has also been a tremendous growth in national meat production due to rising living standards (see Tables 3.2, 3.3, and 3.4). The increase in meat production has, in turn, produced high levels of biological runoffs into the nation's watershed and estuaries. Recently the national government has sought to mitigate this problem by installing nineteen collective treatment facilities in the upper Han River basin. By 1996, thirty-two additional facilities are planned. These steps will lead to some improvement in the problems associated with livestock production, but they are barely adequate to catch up with the growth of

Table 3.2

Use of Pesticides

	1980	1985	1990	1992
Total use (tons)	151,000	167,000	191,000	188,000
Total use per hectare (kg)	69	78	91	—

Source: Korean Ministry of Agriculture, Forestry, and Fishery.

Table 3.3

Use of Fertilizers

	1975	1985	1990	1993
Total use (tons)	1,941,000	1,618,000	2,364,000	2,074,000
Total use per hectare under cultivation (kg)	867	755	1,121	—

Source: Korean Ministry of Agriculture, Forestry, and Fishery.

the demand for meat in prosperous Korea.[27] What makes matters worse is that these meat production farms are mostly small scale and are widely scattered throughout every watershed in the country.

As in meat and farm production, Korea's small-scale industry makes significant contributions to environmental problems. In every city and neighborhood, Koreans have created small-scale manufacturing and other economic activities that when combined produce a significant source of non-point-source pollution, from waste oils to solid wastes. Automobile mechanics' shops are one of the most vexing problems. There are more than eighteen thousand registered repair shops nationwide (and an unaccountable number of unregistered shops) that pour an estimated fifty thousand metric tons of waste oils and antifreeze solutions into urban sewer systems and rural waterways. This situation exists despite government sponsorship of fee-based waste-oil collection trucks. In 1995 the MoE began an effort to educate shop owners about how to properly store and dispose of waste materials. Actual regulation and control, though, will be difficult, and large quantities of oils will continue to be spilled on soil and hard surfaces and into sewers. In recognition of this, MoE has taken, in April 1995, the practical step of ordering the Korea Water Resources Development Corporation to install double oil-prevention fences at intake points for

Table 3.4

Cattle, Swine, and Poultry Production in Korea
1981–90 (units: 1,000 head)

	Cow	Pig	Poultry
1981	1,570	1,830	43,000
1984	2,650	2,960	45,480
1987	2,390	4,280	59,320
1990	2,150	4,570	71,500

Source: Korean Ministry of Agriculture, Forestry, and Fishery.

water supplies and at sewer outflows. The ministry estimates that about 64 percent of all water sources will be protected in this manner while it works to develop more effective programs to improve its regulation of waste oils and other non-point sources of pollution.

Despite the important efforts now underway, it remains to be seen whether the new waste-treatment-facilities building program and management regimes can actually improve the protection of the nation's water resources. Improving the treatment of pollutants through technical innovations, comprehensive monitoring, and enforcement of water-quality regulations will be helpful. However, in the end, sustained environmental improvements will come only from a reduction in the release of pollutants into the environment. Certainly, many Koreans remain cynical about the prospects for the future. They have good cause.

In 1989 the government undertook a 3.5 trillion won ($4.375 billion) plan to address the nation's water-quality problems. However, in 1993 the MoE admitted that not only did the plan fail but conditions have grown worse.[28] As part of its overhaul of water management in the spring of 1994, the government announced a massive new infusion of capital for the construction of new water and waste treatment plants and infrastructure development. Over a five-year period it will spend 15 trillion won ($18.75 billion) or about one-third of the nation's current annual budget on new waste treatment and water-delivery system infrastructure. Still, the plants and other facilities will take time to build, and improvements will take several years to be gained. If the Ministry of Construction and Transportation meets the government's 1997 goals, new capital construction will bring the rate of treated municipal sewage in the Han and the Yongsan into the mid-90 percent range, with the Kum and Naktong brought only to the 60 percent level. But again, because of the way the government has chosen to calculate its current treatment measurements, the actual water-quality levels will almost certainly remain below the public's expectations.

Because of this, Koreans will continue to purchase bottled water or collect water on weekend trips to the mountains (as is very common) even after the crash building program is completed. It is a sad commentary on public confidence in Korean environmental management that in exasperation at least one senior official has recently concluded that the best way to solve the problem is to abandon the concept of tap water for human consumption. Instead, the official has argued that the government should subsidize the delivery of safe bottled water to every household, thus allowing tap water to be purified to a lower standard and reserved for cleaning and other non-drinking purposes.

Solid Waste: Too Little Land, Too Much Production

While water quality is clearly the single most important environmental issue in the public mind, just as complex are the challenges posed by the disposal of solid wastes. Korea ranks among the world's highest producers of solid wastes.[29] From construction wastes to ordinary domestic wastes, the small, crowded nation has had difficulty in finding landfill space. Landfills come under the management of local municipalities, but as often happens in Korea, the national government has had to step in and settle disputes about siting and management.

Landfill capacity has been a chronic problem in Korea, especially in the major metropolitan areas.[30] Seoul, of course, has the largest and most complex solid-waste problem, and in Seoul, solid-waste disposal has reached crisis proportions. The city has a mixed private and municipal waste collection system, with the private collectors being heavily subsidized by local and city governments. In 1989 the government collected fees for waste disposal that amounted to only 26.4 percent of the total cost. Thus, solid waste is a major economic burden to the civic governments. Even with this government subsidy, illegal dumping is a chronic problem, as private haulers seek to maximize profits by avoiding landfill fees. Private citizens have also sought to avoid paying fees and have contributed greatly to the presence—throughout Seoul, its surrounding countryside, and all of Korea—of unauthorized and environmentally damaging waste disposal.

Seoul's longtime landfill at Nanji-do was located in Makpo-Ku, north of the Han River directly west of the center of the central city. After nearly three decades of operation, it reached a height of 40 meters above the surrounding terrain in 1989. By the time it was closed in the early 1990s, the landfill had grown to roughly 100 meters tall, covered an area of 1,755,600 square meters, and contained some 77 million tons of material. The situation in Seoul was, of course, the most immediate in the country, but by the mid-1980s the increasing rates of production of solid wastes and the lack of land resources to devote to disposal produced similar situations for local governments all over Korea. Because of this, the Seoul government led the way in the mid-1980s by developing Korea's first modern solid-waste management strategy.

Seoul's city government sought to reduce land filling by encouraging recycling and separation of reusable household materials. To accomplish that, the city proposed to build new enclosed waste-transfer stations throughout the city. Planners chose this strategy to eliminate the existing practice of small-scale neighborhood-level open-space (street) consolidation of trash. However, there was little that planners could or can do to improve urban sanitary conditions created by the need to use hand carts to collect trash in the 30 percent of Seoul that is inaccessible to modern garbage collection trucks. These problems, though, pale by comparison to the looming crisis in landfill space. Seoul needed to find more land to deal with its trash, which by 1985 was 40 percent of the nation's total production of wastes. To tackle this, the city launched an all-out effort to identify land suitable for waste-transfer stations and, most important, a major new landfill capable of accommodating the city's needs for the next several decades.

By 1986 Seoul had built two trash-transfer buildings to facilitate the collection and centralization of waste separation for recycling. But due to public protest, neither one was opened. As a result, much of Seoul's domestic waste continues to be separated by hand on city streets behind movable metal barriers. The city government also selected seventeen potential landfill sites for feasibility studies and finally decided to construct three waste facilities in Kyunggi Province, which surrounds Seoul. Citizen protests stopped all three projects as they had done in the case of the transfer stations. By 1990 the search for greater landfill capacity was brought under the control of the MoE, which developed a regional agreement between Seoul, Inchon, and Kyunggi Province to place a new landfill near the site of Kimpo Airport with a capacity of 410 cubic meters. This decision, too, was marked by controversy, which still continues. The new 21-million-square-meter landfill had been designed and opened without installation of a bottom liner to prevent leachate seepage onto soil and into groundwater near the dump site. Massive community protests were launched, and the regions' governments were forced to install monitoring devices and pay compensation to local residents.[31]

In order to address the problems of capacity and regulatory control, the Ministry of Environment launched several rate-based trash-collection experiments in which, instead of flat fees for hauling and disposal services, householders were charged for volume. These small-scale experiments were turned into a massive national program on January 1, 1995, when a volume-based system was introduced with enthusiastic participation, confusion, and much higher garbage removal costs for the average household. The government unleashed the campaign with a tremendous burst of public service advertising on radio and television, and news media coverage was widespread. Under the newly implemented effort, homeowners and apartment-dwellers alike are required to purchase plastic trash-disposal bags that are distributed by local government authorities.[32] (Ironically, the bags are not made of biodegradable plastic.) Residents are charged a separate fee for large items such as major appliances and discarded furniture. Revenues from the sale of the bags are designated to pay the costs of hauling, disposal, and recycling programs.

Under the new system, segregated paper, metals, glass, plastics, and other recyclables are placed in ordinary containers or bundled. Trash and segregated materials are picked up together, usually at curb side, by haulers. In order to ensure compliance with the new system, the government announced a 100,000-won ($125) fine on all those who violate the new law. The government claimed that nationwide the volume of trash (defined as only those materials now placed in the required bags, thus not counting items thought to be entering the recycling stream) fell by 31 percent during the first five days of the program in January 1995. Anecdotal evidence of public acceptance and participation could be found all over the country. Almost instantly, wayside highway rest stop receptacles for glass, plastic, and paper wastes appeared. Residents of large apartment buildings found that recycling bins materialized overnight, and apartment guards took on the chores of self-appointed recycling police. The new plastic bags, filled and often piled high, are found every few paces along the roads and alleyways of all city neighborhoods. To enforce the demands for public compliance, local governing authorities deputized apartment-house and public employees and neighborhood volunteers to make sure that bags were properly used. It has become common for these trash inspectors to sort through abandoned trash looking for evidence of its source. Those cited for violating the new volume-based collection system are increasingly found listed in local newspapers, a social stigma that all but guarantees wholesale public obedience and heightened environmental awareness.

In implementing this strategy, the government hopes to bring more efficiency to the collection of recyclable materials, encourage the growth of viable recycling and reprocessing enterprises, and change consumption patterns. In order to reduce the flow of waste into the waste stream, MoE also announced a number of other steps shortly after the implementation of the new volume-charge system. In February 1995, the government even proposed to ban toothpicks and wooden chopsticks from restaurant use, but public outcry turned the order into a recommendation. Supermarkets and grocery stores were prohibited from using plastic bags and wrappings on all products, with the not inconsequential exception of meats, poultry, and fresh vegetables.[33] Unfortunately, the system was undertaken in the absence of a large-scale commercial or government-subsidized recycling industry. The government, for example, announced only after the new system was in operation that there would not be enough plastic recycling capacity to meet the nation's need until June 1995, when recycling plants were scheduled to be opened by the government in seven cities.[34] As a result, the efforts of the nation's households and businesses would be thwarted, at least in the short run, as segregated materials found their way into scarce landfill space or were simply illegally dumped or burned in back alleys or the countryside. Still, the implementation of the volume-based solid-waste charge system is a significant event for Korea and Koreans. No industrial country has attempted such a sudden shift in policy and practice, and despite the initial confusion, the system holds great promise for slowing the flow of trash to landfills and jump-starting a recycling industry through the creation of massive supplies of raw materials.

In addition to restructuring fees for disposal and collection, the government has embarked on a program to build trash incinerators. In Seoul alone, incinerators able to dispose of ten thousand tons a day were planned in the mid-1980s. Construction began on the first of these incinerators in the early 1990s, and in addition to domestic funds, the government has sought international financial assistance to meet the capital costs for the proposed building program. The effort has not been without public controversy, and the government has had great difficulty in siting the new incinerators due to widespread public suspicion and resistance. In the Seoul district of Songae, plans were made for a facility with a capacity of sixteen hundred tons per day. Public protest forced the downsizing of the plant to a capacity of only eight hundred tons. Similar reductions were made throughout Seoul and other cities as angry communities complained about being forced to take trash from others. As much as anything else this compelled the government to look to novel ideas about waste reduction, which led directly to the creation of the volume-disposal charge program launched in January 1995 as well as the reduction in the size and number of planned waste incinerators.[35]

Industrial and Chemical Wastes

Industrial chemical and solid wastes are regulated by the national government under the Toxic Chemicals Control Law and are also under the administrative authority of the MoE. The law regulates the manufacture and importation of chemicals harmful to human health and requires that associated waste products be disposed of properly and safely. The MoE requires the registration of all such materials unless the amount is below 240 tons annually or the materials are used for research purposes. There are a few exclusion zones for the ownership, handling, and storage of hazardous chemicals, but generally permits to purchase and use hazardous materials are easily obtained.[36]

About fifty chemicals are barred from entry into or use in Korea. Prior to manufacture or importation of new chemicals, the MoE is required to perform a toxicity test to determine the safety of the material. Like other aspects of current Korean regulatory practice, application of the regulations varies widely and is complicated and made inefficient by the lack of cradle-to-grave hazardous-materials tracking systems.

The physical disposal of chemical and hazardous wastes is the responsibility of the Environmental Management Corporation.[37] The EMC builds and manages hazardous-waste disposal sites, which include incineration and landfill facilities. Three such sites were in operation at the end of 1994. The operations of these facilities are financed through a system of fees charged directly to industrial waste generators. Although the system is in place, the capacity of the existing EMC plants is too small relative to the national need. Currently, it is estimated that only 1–3 percent of Korea's hazardous wastes are being treated by the EMC facilities.

The balance of the "treated waste" is handled by private corporations that have built their own facilities. There is no reliable information about how much hazardous waste is produced and how much of this is properly disposed of through incineration and sanitary landfills. Estimates by experts inside and outside the responsible government agencies suggest that the amounts of treated chemical wastes range from 10–30 percent of the nation's total output. The remainder is deposited in landfills, stored on industrial sites, or disposed of illegally.

Regulation, Monitoring, Inspection, and Compliance

Under the Basic Environmental Policy Act, the government is responsible for the establishment of all regulation and standards of environmental quality. The standards are set by presidential decree, although the mayors of Seoul, Pusan, Taegu, Taejon, Kwangju, and Inchon, as well as provincial governors, have the power to establish special standards in their domains. In practice, the Ministry of Environment is responsible for overseeing this work. It provides advice to the president based on its own technical evaluation and those of scientists and engineers scattered throughout industry, universities, and research institutes.

The law stipulates that proposed regulations and standards must be released to the public twenty days before they are implemented. Public hearings are required. Thus, disputes over the promulgation of regulations by groups outside government or industry are uncommon. Environmental standards in Korea are not binding on government agencies, but they do set up criteria for measuring industrial activity. Moreover, the emission standards set by the Korean government are based on a medium-specific density measurement basis and place no importance on the aggregate totals of released materials. Under this system, industrial and municipal polluters have historically been required to keep only qualitative records by the MoE. The weakness of this data collection system is twofold: Records are often incomplete and inadequate for careful environmental trends analysis, and polluters are allowed to discharge as much material as they want into the environment (air, water, soil) so long as densities of released materials are within the allowable limits.

The monitoring of industrial emissions and effluents is largely dependent on self-monitoring by the waste generators under a combined voluntary/polluter-pays policy (all equipment is paid for, operated, and maintained by those emitting pollutants into the environment). To supplement this system, the Ministry of Environment has installed sixty-eight automatic ambient-air-quality monitoring systems. Some of these are equipped with large reader boards for purposes of public information.[38] The MoE also operates acid-deposition monitoring systems throughout the country. In general, though, the ministry relies heavily on data collection at major industrial sites. It requires that all large pollution-emitting smokestacks have monitoring equipment installed. Information from this equipment is collected by the operators of the facilities and transferred to regional MoE managers for analysis and evaluation. Water-quality sampling follows the same model, with industrial polluters required to submit qualitative assessments of their discharges into rivers and streams.

There are two principal complaints about this mixed responsibility system. The first is that the pollution data are not necessarily secure from corruption and can easily vary in quality and trustworthiness. The second is that, although requirements are strict, inspections and outside independent calibrations of equipment are lax. As a result, suspicions about broken or unmaintained equipment are widespread, as is the widely held belief that national environmental statistics are unreliable. When coupled with the generally inadequate training of MoE inspectors, it is clear that Korea's monitoring and data collection as a regulatory and enforcement tool must be greatly sharpened and strengthened.

The weaknesses in the national system of environmental data collection are evident in the poor official national records of inspection and compliance. The MoE reported that nationwide only 130,093 inspections were conducted in 1993. During those inspections, only 12,965 violations of Korea's minimum emission or discharge quality standards were discovered. Given the easily observable environmental conditions in Korea and some independent analysis, this seems a very low level of inspection and fined violations. The average fine levied on violators was a little more than 1,200,000 won ($1,500). Thus, current fines are mere inconveniences, although they do serve to embarrass those found guilty of violating the environmental standards. It is only in the "publicly sensitive" cases—like the Doosan Group's phenol spill in the Naktong—that fines rise to significant levels. This pattern is apparent in the official MoE records of inspection activity and the number of fines levied. Although the number of inspections has risen since 1988, the officially reported rates of violations have not significantly changed over the past several years (see Table 3.5).

Until recently, government efforts to enforce compliance with environmental laws bordered on gross negligence. However, that is not the full story of the patterns of government activity to enforce environmental laws and regulations. As usual in Korea, there is a need to look beyond formal structures to the way things actually work. Although imposed fines for violations of environmental standards (loose as they are) are small, it is estimated that for every 1 won paid in official fines, 100 won are made available for nonjudicial compensation to "victims." This kind of informal, honor-driven system reflects the ancient Confucian values that still hold sway in Korea. When a harmful environmental accident occurs, for example, the responsible firm or individual usually feels bound to make some payment to the injured party as an honorable settlement. Damages to property and even health become matters of a personal debt to be settled to the satisfaction of all. These private transactions are rarely reported to the government, and only if the compensation is paid by the government are they accounted for in official statistics. This ethics-based system has a certain attraction for the litigious West, but it is an inadequate basis for resolving modern environmental disputes. Among its many obvious shortcomings, it fails to recognize the long-term harm that environmental abuse can cause, and it is certainly not a substitute for improved environmental standards and their consistent enforcement.[39]

Most senior experts and government officials understand that the national environmental inspection and monitoring program remains feeble. Its limitations reflect the inadequate personnel and lack of technical sophistication of government at all levels. They also stand as a testament to the continuing uncertainty about how stringently environ-

Table 3.5

Environmental Inspection/Violation/Compliance in Korea, 1988–93

Year	1988	1989	1990	1992	1993
Inspections (national MoE)	56,940	65,392	108,205	121,024	130,093
Violations	8,127	11,500	16,705	11,083	12,965
% out of compliance	14.3	17.6	15.5	9.2	10

Source: Korean Ministry of Environment, *1993 Report on Environmental Status of Korea*.

mental laws and regulations should be enforced at this stage of national economic development. This lack of national clarity, money, and training leaves ample room for incompetence, abuse, and corruption. Any serious quantitative evaluation of regulatory compliance records is impossible given the combination of distributed management and unreliable and nonstandardized measurement procedures.

The effectiveness of these regulatory programs is further reduced by the complexities of regulating small and medium-sized firms. In practice these companies are almost free of significant government oversight, although some limited progress is being made in sensitizing them to environmental problems. This general attitude toward small firms is a practical expression of Korean realities. Small enterprises are chronically short of working capital and are a long way from acquiring either suitable control technology or the necessary personnel to oversee environmental management. In contrast, the large industrial and trading groups in Korea, such as Samsung, Daewoo, and Hyundai, are expected to make and have made substantial efforts to meet and exceed minimal national environmental standards. But here, too, there is little statistical or other evidence capable of independently establishing compliance levels across the country. Finally, nonpoint sources from small-scale industry and agricultural activities, while recognized as a significant problem, are completely unregulated and unmanaged.

Perhaps the best indication of MoE frustration can be found in its efforts to accommodate its regulatory programs to the realities of Korean life. In 1995, the Ministry of Environment began to experiment with voluntary environmental management systems. It announced its intention to adopt a self-regulating improvement program that asked all firms to submit waste reduction and control plans to the ministry. Corporations whose plans satisfy the standards set by MoE may be offered tax and finance benefits and may be allowed to implement their plans and engage in self-evaluation. Participants are further promised that MoE will, in exchange for voluntary cooperation, ease oversight and inspections.

Infrastructure Planning

Korea has undergone rapid urbanization as a result of industrialization. Not only Seoul but Taegu, Pusan, and the areas around the large industrial zones of Ulsan, Masan, and Onsan have grown dramatically. Korea was unprepared for this urbanization and its related infrastructure and environmental problems. As a result, the role of urban planning has been to catch up with the vast changes that have so altered the lives of average Koreans. For the most part, planners have by necessity responded to these challenges by focusing on infrastructure: housing, roads, and urban services such as drinking water, sewage treatment, and solid-waste disposal. There does not seem to be any effective planning yet for conservation and preservation with the exception of the previously noted green zones.

Nationally, infrastructure planning is the responsibility of the Ministry of Construction and Transport, which brings its builder's mentality to every planning exercise. In 1992, Korea adopted its third ten-year Comprehensive National Development Plan. This, as those before it, outlines an aggressive strategy of building the necessary infrastructure for national economic growth: housing, transportation, industrial and civic infrastructure development. Environmental goals were not part of previous plans, but the current national planning document, accepted and signed by the president, has a chapter dealing with the environment.[40]

The first-ever adoption of environmental goals within an important economic policy and planning document is a significant, if symbolic, step forward for Korea. The ten-year plan anticipates raising Korea's investment in environmental activities from the current 0.15 percent of GNP to 1.0 percent by the year 2001. In order to pay for this, the plan proposes new market-based tax systems on polluting industries and an expansion of the fund deposit system for waste generation. In addition to taxation, the plan advocates the division of the nation into three environmental management zones. Within these, comprehensive management strategies will be implemented to:

- broaden use of the Environmental Assessment process;
- improve the quality of drinking water supplies;
- reduce the volume of waste material;
- continue the progress in improving air quality;
- address the problems of soil contamination;
- establish natural preserves for forests, tidelands, and bird habitats;
- improve energy efficiency and conservation measures; and
- manage forest lands for multiple use.

The section devoted to the environment in the Third Comprehensive National Development Plan identifies many important issues for future environmental management and concern. However, its impact and effectiveness are weakened by a failure to integrate its elements with the rest of the highly aggressive development plan. Moreover, the environmental sections of the plan are circumscribed by qualifying language about availability of funds and other, perhaps more important, national priorities. This conflict between Korean environmental concerns and the urge to develop at all costs has made coordination and integration among ministerial authorities one of the most significant problems barring the path to improved environmental administration in Korea. Recently, efforts have been made to address this problem through the establishment of interministerial committees to develop common environmental management plans. Still, autonomy and at times animosity among individual ministries and agencies of national and local government are deeply ingrained and repeatedly prove to be a high barrier to improvements in environmental management.

This often intractable difficulty has too often led to situations such as that in the Shi-Wha area, on South Korea's northwest coast. In that case, the Korea Water Research Corporation, a quasi-government corporation under the authority of the then Ministry of Construction, planned and began building a retaining barrier in an estuary in June 1987 to reclaim land and to create a freshwater reservoir. After the project was fully designed and committed, an environmental assessment statement was completed, which recommended that the scheme should be modified by the construction of a bypass water system to carry upstream industrial effluents outside the planned barrier. The recommendation was ignored, however; the barrier was built, and no bypass system was installed prior to its completion in January 1994. The predictable result has been the unnecessary contamination of the newly created freshwater reservoir and a significant economic loss of value—exactly the opposite of the project's goals.[41]

In another example of poor coordination and inadequate environmental planning, a dam was built in Hapchon, in the southern part of the country. Although the rural residents were offered new land downstream from the dam, they simply established new homes near their old homes and ancestral grave sites on the shore of the newly constructed reservoir. The rebuilt community's human, animal, agricultural, and small-scale industrial wastes are now flowing freely into the nearby lake because no level of government had anticipated or adequately planned for that predictable outcome.

Conservation, National Parks, and Rural Development

The Ministry of Environment is responsible for the overall management of nature conservation programs throughout Korea. The main duties of the MoE with regard to preserving the nation's green spaces are to designate green preservation and ecosystem conservation areas, and to identify wild animals and plants within those areas. To accomplish this, the MoE carried out a national ecosystem survey between 1986 and 1990 and subsequently published a green map of Korea in 1992. From that process, three natural ecosystem areas have been designated in order to preserve habitat and protect their cultural assets (temples, etc.) from vandalism. In practice, responsibility for conservation is fragmented across several agencies and ministries, ranging from Construction and Transport to Agriculture, Forestry, and Fishery to Environment. The different management philosophies of each have made consistent management of natural resources difficult at best and impossible at worst.

Korea has an established system of national parks and marine reserves, which contain some of the country's most important national treasures, such as monasteries, historic sites, and undisturbed or relatively undisturbed natural habitat. However, the park preserves are coming under increasing human pressure as urbanized Koreans seek the solitude of their remaining natural environment. This is severely straining the parks and their ability to sustain their ecosystems under the weight of millions of feet, thousands of picnic fires, and tons of litter.

The parks are also not immune to development, and there are many examples of contamination due to nearby industrial or commercial activity. This is true even in areas protected by government to maintain water quality for urban populations. For example, the Paldang Reservoir on the Han River is a primary source of drinking water for the city of Seoul. Development around its shores has long been illegal. However, any visitor to it will find all kinds of commercial development without any significant infrastructure to maintain the reservoir's water quality. As a result, while Seoul residents can sample restaurants and recreational opportunities in the Paldang area, their enjoyment adversely affects the quality of their tap water at home.

Forestry and forest health is another significant problem area for Korean environmental managers. Although Korea can point to significant reforestation since the early 1950s, many of those new forests are largely unmanaged. As a result, they are often harvested or more typically cleared when they stand in the way of development. The situation is further complicated by Korean patterns of public and private land management. For example, in a 1989 survey of private land owners, 60 percent of private forest owners did not know of government silviculture assistance programs and 61.2 percent had not made any effort to acquire information about forest management techniques. Those factors and the harmful effects of acid rain have combined to greatly endanger forested areas of Korea, where wood densities are only 33 cubic meters per hectare, versus 120 in Japan and 150 in Germany. The world average is 88.[42]

On a larger scale, the issues of land-use planning, conservation, and preservation too often fall victim to divided and competitive responsibilities in the national and local governments. The Ministry of Construction and Transport, for example, has most of the nation's significant land-use planning responsibilities. The Ministry of Environment, in contrast, has none. In February 1994 the Ministry of Construction completed a reevaluation of its national land-use plan and submitted it for approval to the National Assembly, which quickly adopted the changes. The primary outgrowth of this new plan was the reduction in the number of defined land-use zones from ten to five and the identification of 41 percent of the nation's land as open for development. In addition, the ministry has established three hundred mixed industrial and agricultural zones for current and future intensive development. This in a nation in which roughly 70 percent of the land mass is composed of steep mountainous terrain and in which arable land is in short supply. This kind of situation is repeated all too often in Korean government circles. It is another illustration of a general lack of critical and imaginative thinking about the all-too-real linkages between land use, water and air quality, and many other aspects of environmental problems.

Few areas of Korea have been untouched by human activity and modern development. As a result, preservation in the sense of preserving wilderness is certainly not at issue. However, the question of preserving long-protected military zones has arisen and gained some interest in government circles. Those areas, especially around and inside the demilitarized zone, have often been allowed to return to a relatively natural state, largely through inattention. The government has recently decontrolled some of those areas and is considering setting some of the land aside for natural areas. However, the definition of preservation is far from clear. The soon-to-be-opened military preserves will be an interesting test of the new importance of environmental ideas and their relationship to the heretofore irresistible drive in Korea for economic development.[43] Similarly, the Korean government will face the challenge of how to ensure the reach of its environmental regulations to the military, which in late 1994 established its own planning group to evaluate the Korean army's environmental responsibilities and to consider environmental programs.[44] The Korean military will have its work cut out for it as nearly all its camps and bases lack even minimal sewage and waste treatment capabilities, and soldiers lack training in the proper handling, storage, and disposal of hazardous materials.

Conservation and Recycling

The Korean people have shown themselves willing and even eager to participate in environmental programs ranging from recycling to waste reduction. It is here that government action has had its most notable success. Korea's Waste Management Law requires firms to engage in waste-reduction programs to cut discharges into the national waste stream. Under the authority of the 1986 law, Korea has developed a waste deposit system as its primary strategy for national waste reduction.[45] With this, the government requires all companies that manufacture materials such as packaging and containers to take measures to assist in the collection and treatment of those materials after they have been used. The same is true of companies that import or produce materials that will become waste (bottles, cans, oils, tires, and paper goods).

To promote participation in industrial recycling efforts, the MoE requires all regulated firms to pay a per-item deposit. For example, companies producing plastic products pay 0.7 percent of total sales. Tire manufacturers pay a deposit of 150 won per unit for automobile tires, 500 won for large tires, and 50 won per unit for two-wheeled vehicle tires. The deposit law covers household and electronic appliances, batteries, pesticides and poisons, and containers for food, beverages, and cosmetics. Manufacturers of nonrecyclable items, such as disposable diapers, are also charged a fee based on their output for domestic sales. Some or all of the deposit is returned to the affected companies based on a formula that calculates their rate of recycling. Unclaimed funds are used to finance the government's recycling programs.[46]

During the first six months of 1992, the Ministry of Environment collected 13.3 billion won ($16.6 million) under the deposit program. However, the rate of return has disappointed many of the program's advocates. In the same 1992 period, only 30 million won ($3.75 million) was returned to manufacturers who had successfully recycled products covered by the program. Without a doubt, this is a reflection of the real economics of recycling. Korean manufacturing and importing firms find that although disposal is expensive, it is far cheaper to send waste materials to landfills than to work to collect what is in practice a rather insignificant deposit. What's more, the deposit is easily built into product costs, thus effectively becoming a hidden waste tax that is passed along to consumers.[47]

Today, there is wide discussion about increasing the level of deposit fees or reforming the system to make the industrial sector more responsive to recycling needs. Still, fees alone will not make the program effective. The Korean government, in alliance with industry, will have to build a functioning waste-recovery and recycling infrastructure. This will have to be firmly coupled to appropriate economic incentives that are capable of diverting materials from the nation's fast-filling landfills to alternative uses within industrial sectors.

In 1980 the Korean government established the Korea Resources Recovery and Re-utilization Corporation (KRRRC). As a nonprofit, quasi-government organization, it was charged with establishing a national recycling effort to collect and recycle scrap metal, plastics, waste paper, and used pesticide bottles from industry and the public. The creation of the KRRRC was complemented by a government commitment to large-scale public information campaigns about the necessity of public participation in waste reduction and the importance of curtailing the growth of household refuse. These efforts have been successful in terms of growing public sensitivity to environmental problems and the need to reduce wastes and recycle. In 1995, this recycling program was expanded in order to support the development of a national recycling industry. MoE created a 15 billion won fund to provide financial assistance to recycling companies. Of this, 13 billion will be lent at 7 percent with up to a ten-year payback for the expansion of facilities, and the remaining 2 billion ($2.5 million) will be reserved for recycling technology development loans, which will carry an interest rate of 5 percent. Loans will range from 100 million won ($125,000) to 500 million won ($625,000) for recycling facilities and up to 100 million for technology development.

Despite this, the failure of the government to provide adequate infrastructure for collection and conservation of materials as well as incentives for reuse by industry have severely limited the ability of all recycling programs to reduce wastes. In turn this has led to the public's growing disenchantment with voluntary recycling and waste reduction efforts.

Energy Conservation

Korea consumes power voraciously, though its energy efficiency is poor by international standards. Eighty-two percent of all fuel used in Korea comes from fossil resources, and in 1993 the nation's energy consumption grew 2.66 times faster than the GNP. The rapid growth in consumption has made Korea the world's eighteenth-largest producer of greenhouse gases, such as carbon dioxide and sulfur dioxide. The Korea Energy Economics Institute estimates that by the year 2000, the country will become the world's tenth-largest generator of gases that adversely affect the atmosphere.[48]

Korea has very limited domestic energy resources; therefore, its development and management of power supply is at the center of national economic planning. During the last several decades the government has generally relied on taxation strategies to depress consumption and encourage efficiency. The most successful aspect of Korea's energy-efficiency/conservation and pollution-reduction program has been the introduction of clean liquefied natural gas (LNG) to replace high-sulfur anthracite coal, which has been traditionally used for heating and cooking as well as for large-scale industrial energy needs. All of the major cities have been named LNG-using areas, and by the year 2000, all heating will be done with the gas. To reduce fuel consumption by private vehicles, the government has also built desulfurization facilities to reduce the sulfur content of bunker oil from 1.6 percent to 1.0 percent and light oil sulfur from 0.4 percent to 0.2 percent.[49]

The national government has invested massive amounts of money in public transportation as well. Seoul's subway system will soon be one of the world's largest, with two new lines now under construction. A new high-speed rail corridor is being built from Seoul to Pusan, and within two years a new multilane beltway will be completed around Seoul. This latter capital project will relieve some of Seoul's inner-city congestion by diverting traffic, but, as demonstrated elsewhere in the world, it will also serve to further encourage automobile use. In late 1994, Seoul's municipal government began to plan for bus-only lanes on many of the city's major thoroughfares. This will free up surface mass transit, which has heretofore been prisoner of Seoul's nightmarish traffic congestion. Finally, as a consequence of the tragic collapse of Seoul's Song-Su bridge on October 21, 1994, the city has implemented a "leave-your-car-at-home day" for all drivers. Car owners are barred from driving every ten days (determined by the license plate numbers) in order to reduce road congestion while the fallen bridge and others across the Han River are repaired.[50] This measure has successfully reduced traffic levels in Seoul, but the system will be abandoned once the bridge is repaired.

Still, despite high gasoline, fuel, and electricity costs, Korea remains a grossly energy-inefficient nation. The new infrastructure investments will eventually make a difference in environmental conditions in Korea, especially in the nation's air quality, but these will take time to bring on line.[51] Despite the impressive construction projects, the national strategy still is dominated by an unrestrained drive to increase production and marked by an almost compete absence of efforts to conserve.[52] Even with a headlong rush to develop electrical energy capacity, Korea can barely keep up with demand. Between 1989 and 1994, the demand for power increased by 9.2 million kilowatts. During the same period the Korea Electric Power Corporation (KEPCO) expanded its power generation capability by only 3.06 million kilowatts.

To make up for this ever-rising demand, the Korean government has become unalterably committed to nuclear energy as its technology of choice (ignoring the complaints of antinuclear activists). In all, Korea has a total of nine nuclear plants in operation and seven more on the drawing board. By the first decade of the next century Korea expects to have a total of twenty-one nuclear power plants on line. In 1992 KEPCO's nuclear plants produced 43.4 percent of Korea's electrical energy, yet the national construction program has consistently lagged behind incessant demand.[53]

Energy conservation has not entered significantly into the government's long-term energy management plans. However, due to a lack of electrical energy capacity in peak seasons, conservation programs have been implemented as temporary, stop-gap measures. During the summer months the government asks that buildings be cooled only to eighty degrees, and many elevators have been reprogrammed to stop only at alternate floors. Much attention is placed on curbing the use of nonessential industrial and home air conditioners. Building owners are encouraged to convert to gas-operated air conditioners, and homeowners are urged to use only minimal air conditioning during the stifling Korean summer. During the most recent summer Olympics (1992), the state-run Korean Broadcasting System suspended coverage of events between two and four o'clock in the afternoon after being criticized for unnecessarily raising consumer demands for electrical power during peak consumption time.[54]

Conservation, Education, and the Public Imagination

Throughout Korea, citizens have been subjected to public information and education programs urging them to reduce wastes. In these "Don't Waste Wastes" information campaigns (the environmental slogan of Seoul and nearly everyplace else), public service advertising, bumper stickers, posters, and television and radio are used to communicate the importance of environmental protection directly to the public.[55] The government has also encouraged private organizations to get involved in advocating recycling and conservation through informal education. On the first World Environment Day, June 5, 1992, the Seoul committee of UNCED initiated a nationwide one-day campaign to reduce waste production. Over five hundred churches and three hundred industrial companies were involved. Citizens were exhorted to finish all of their food so leftovers would not be thrown away, and to refuse to purchase goods that come with excessive packaging.[56] In 1993 the Taejon Expo, Korea's first world's fair, adopted the environment as its theme. During the Expo's late summer and fall operation, over twelve million visitors (mostly Koreans) toured pavilions illustrating environmental technology and planning on a global scale.[57]

Since the late 1980s, the Korean Ministry of Education has been active in developing new approaches to environmental education in Korean public schools. Initially those efforts focused on specific issues of recycling and individual environmental awareness. However, in 1990 Korea received funds from UNESCO to undertake planning for a model curriculum,[58] and as part of a general trend in curriculum reform, the ministry began to explore the potential for incorporating environmental education into the highly structured and test-dominated Korean school curriculum. An initial seminar was held, and it produced a four-year planning effort that sought to introduce comprehensive environmental studies into all levels of Korean public education— kindergarten through twelfth-grade—in 1995 and 1996.

Under the new curriculum guidelines for primary schools, children will learn the importance of environmental responsibility and participate in recycling and waste-collection programs. Environmental education will be coordinated with other aspects of primary-grade social studies programs. In middle school, students will be allowed to select among several electives; at least one will be environmental studies or environmental science. In those classes, students will participate in programs designed to highlight the types of pollution problems facing Korea and the world today and learn about the interrelationships among all life. There will also be an emphasis on field experiences, and a strong theme in the program will be the attempt to bridge science and social studies subjects.

The high school program moves students from general environmental studies to environmental science. In taking this approach, the ministry has developed core curriculum materials that integrate environmental issues with the teaching of hard sciences and social sciences. In addition, under the newly enacted Sixth National Curriculum Reform, schools will be able to select environmental science from a new list of pre-college electives.[59] In the material prepared and adopted by the Ministry of Education, students taking the elective course will be encouraged to think broadly about environmental problems and to approach them in an interdisciplinary manner. This is a noteworthy innovation and one that is symbolic of the slow but important changes that are more broadly underway in Korean public education. Comprehensive thinking skills are now recognized as an important aspect of educational quality, although rote learning still dominates the school day.[60]

Korea is one of the first countries in the world to create a national environmental curriculum for use in its public schools.[61] The Korean government has recognized that to implement this curriculum, it needs qualified teachers. The ministry, therefore, has instructed the nation's teachers' colleges to expand environmental studies for future teachers and to offer in-service programs to train the current teacher corps. Approximately thirty colleges and universities had instituted such programs by 1995. The government has not yet approved a standard teacher's certificate program in environmental studies, but it is expected to do so soon.

Although Korea has made significant strides in establishing the foundation of environmental education in the public schools, it is widely recognized that it will take a long time to see any real impact. This is an understandable and unavoidable limitation. The Ministry of Education has been slow to insist that all teacher training programs be adjusted to accommodate the new environmental programs, thus making it likely that for the foreseeable future there will be a shortage of well-trained teachers to provide high-quality instruction to primary, middle, and high school students. However, the real impact of the soon-to-be implemented national curriculum will be determined by how Korean parents and students perceive the importance of the new environmental programs to college admission. For example, although Chinese characters will also become an elective under the reform plan, it is widely thought that a student's proficiency in that classical subject is important to assure entrance to a good university. In the same regard, computer science will soon be offered as another standard elective course in Korean high schools. It is easy to imagine the competition classical and computer science courses will present to environmental science programs in a nation where educational background is closely associated with achieving social and economic status. Thus, it remains to be seen if education-crazed parents allow their sons and daughters to take elective courses that may not be perceived as vital or even helpful when applying to the nation's top universities.

The remarkable thing about the planning and introduction of environmental education to date is how free of controversy it has been, even though the curriculum asks teachers to encourage students to talk openly about the political, social, and economic causes of environmental pollution. Environmental activist groups and industry alike seem to have left the issue alone. To be sure, there have been academic turf struggles as university and college departments fight over the right to teach the new "hot" topic. There has also been resistance from those who see that demand and therefore funding for their own subjects may be weakened. Nonetheless, if such a significant curriculum reform had been introduced in the United States, complete with teaching materials and texts that speak openly of environmental damage, it would have become a bloody political battleground of special interests. That this hasn't happened in Korea may be partly a reflection of the lack of environmental and political sophistication there, where many are just beginning to understand the implications of adopting environmental education programs. At the time of the plan's adoption, then Minister of Environment Whang Sang-Sung claimed that the reforms would help overcome the NIMBY (Not in My Back Yard) syndrome rather than make it more serious, as might be feared by opponents in the West.[62]

Public Involvement and the Environment

In addition to public education and recycling efforts, the Ministry of Environment has sought to involve the public in environmental matters in other ways. The ministry sponsors an Honorary Guard for the Environment program. In this program, ordinary citizens are registered as "official" agents of the ministry. After they complete some training, they are given an identification card, organized into groups, and asked to monitor and report daily environmental problems directly to ministry officials; it is not unusual to find quite senior people as card-carrying members of this public action program. The program is limited, though, by the general public's long-standing and deep suspicion of all government-sponsored programs.

Public involvement has led to some limited innovation and experimentation. In 1993 a group of volunteer technical experts approached the ministry and asked for seed funds to launch a small-scale composting station. The ministry agreed to pay 10.4 billion won ($13 million) for the construction and operation of the pilot program, which will begin operation as an independent community corporation in 1995. This decision by the MoE was the first action of its kind. Although this does not signify the bureaucracy's willingness to support small-scale, community-based innovation, it is at least a small acknowledgment of the role that neighborhood programs can play in environmental management.

The Ministry of Environment has recently adopted a hearings process for public comment on environmental policy and development plans. It is further required by law to give notice of all proposed regulatory changes.[63] This public process has been widely used in the area of solid-waste landfill siting decisions and the building of waste incinerators. However, the input remains rather formalized and is not yet fully mature and integrated into the decision-making process. Moreover, the efforts of the MoE are limited by the fact that it is the only ministry that holds such hearings. Other ministries, such as Construction and Transportation and Trade, Industry, and Energy, have yet to adopt this approach, even though many of their decisions have major environmental consequences.

Citizens' Environmental Education

The nongovernment public information efforts aimed at improving public participation in recycling and waste reduction in Korea take many forms and have many sponsors. The YMCA and YWCA have been long-time leaders in this area, but public environmental education is not restricted to large mainstream organizations. Today it can be found in every corner of Korean life, from churches and community volunteer groups to civic and business organizations.

One example of the range of informal environmental education can be found in a church-based organization known as the Korea Church Research Institute for Peace and the Integrity of Creation. This small organization is the most direct descendant of Korea's first environmental activist group, the Korea Anti-Pollution Organization, which was established in 1982. Its founding members were largely an ecumenical assembly of Buddhists, Catholics, and Protestants. In 1989 the organization was renamed the Korea Anti-Nuclear, Anti-Pollution Research Center for Peace, and in 1992 it was again reformed under its current name. The institute is now supported by its Protestant founders alone and propounds a strong antimaterialist and anti-American (Western) point of view. Although the institute works with other more secular environmental organizations, it seeks to combine evangelicalism and fundamentalism with environmental education and action.

As of 1994, this institute was led by a council of ministers and had developed especially strong ties to the Korean Methodist church. Bishop Chang Ki-Chun, who has a long history of social and antinuclear activism, serves as its chair. Other participants include representatives from the Korean Presbyterian church, the Salvation Army, the Episcopal church, and various evangelical congregations. The Catholic church left the coalition and is pursuing environmental issues through its own organizations. The current director of the Korea Church Research Institute for Peace and the Integrity of Creation is Reverend Im Myung-Jin, and the day-to-day environmental program operations are managed by Kim Jong-Hwan, who studied engineering at Seoul National University. Kim did not participate in political activity while at SNU, and after graduation he took a job with one of Korea's major chemical manufacturers as a chemical engineer. It was only later that his particular blend of Christian piety, social radicalism, and concern for the environment took shape.

The Korea Church Research Institute for Peace and the Integrity of Creation promotes the "Christian" view that God created the world and entrusted its beauty to humans. Materialism, secular modern life, and big business (and their supporters in the mainline Korean churches) have largely ignored this responsibility and instead sought to greedily exploit nature. The institute believes that only through religious-based reformation can human and nature again come into the balance that God intended. The institute provides teaching materials to participating congregations and runs a six-month correspondence and lecture course on environmental issues. The course draws on numerous case studies with titles such as *The Industrial Pollution Situation at Panwol Industrial Estate, Bando Electronics Co. Where Three Employees Died of Lead Poisoning*, and *The Safety Status of Kori Nuclear Power Plant*. The institute has also published tracts and books such as *My Land Is Dying*; *Life or Death?*; *Yankee Go Home*; and *The Peasant and Agri-*

cultural Chemicals.[64] These course materials teach a mix of scriptural justification for environmental concern, condemnation of Western consumer lifestyles, and suspicion of the ability of civil government to address the core environmental issues facing Korean society. Approximately two hundred church-based activists had completed the curriculum as of the spring of 1994.

A different kind of informal public environmental education is sponsored by the Institute of Environmental and Social Policy. This organization is led by a former National Assembly member, Ms. Park Young-Soo, and until the end of 1994 was directed by her one-time legislative assistant, Ms. Lee Sang-Duk.[65] Lee attended Ehwa Women's University and has a long history of social and political activism. Unlike the religiously motivated institute above, the Institute of Environmental and Social Policy is secular in outlook. Although it sees itself as having an educational mission, it is avowedly political in its approach, and it combines environmental awareness with feminism and demand for social reform through a mix of activism and education.[66]

In seeking to educate and mobilize women for environmental and social action, the institute sponsors educational activities such as public seminars through an education center. It also publishes papers that seek to highlight the abuses to the environment and the people by government and industry. Through these they disseminate government reports and other information that their members have managed to secure about the reality of environmental and other social conditions in Korea.

The one-time radical activists who form the core of the Institute of Environmental and Social Policy see democratization as an important tool for social change. They advocate and even seek out participation in the electoral process by identifying candidates with strong pro-environmental views. They do so without regard to party affiliation. Nonetheless, in practice, the institute's leaders are generally aligned with the opposition Democratic party and favor candidates with impeccable social activist pedigrees. For the institute, political action now includes winning one vote at a time. The hoped-for result is not only public enlightenment, it is, more critically, the creation of allies on every city and provincial council as well as in the National Assembly. If the Korea Church Research Institute for Peace and the Integrity of Creation is creating witnesses for the environment, the Institute of Environmental and Social Policy hopes to capture the political system by using the weapons of secular democracy.

These are only two examples of the hundreds of informal education and civic activist groups in Korea today. Most are very small, and some are no more than an individual or two with a desire to write a newsletter or engage in neighborhood-scale organization. Still, when combined, they make a lot of noise and constantly remind the public of the environmental crisis facing Korean society today. When added to the increasing attention the environment is receiving in the public schools, it is not hard to imagine the establishment of a durable basis for a broader and more comprehensive environmental public consciousness—one that links middle-class concerns with those of environmental and social activists and political leaders whose interests converge on the need to come to terms with the contamination of the nation.

The Limits of Public Policy and Environmental Administration: Public Attitudes, Private Thoughts

This survey of the scope and limits of environmental law, regulation management, and education has focused on some of the major themes that are evident in Korean environmental administration today. Many of the trends, such as those in the area of public education, recycling, and capital construction projects, will make a difference over the long term.[67] To date, though, the government has largely failed in its most elementary environmental responsibility: to develop effective management systems for addressing environmental problems.[68] Korea has environmental laws and programs in place, but the government has yet to develop a clear policy or comprehensive strategies capable of meeting and reversing the nation's all too apparent environmental decay. Many of the reasons for this can be found in the inadequacies of the Korean legal system, the structure of Korean government and bureaucracies, and the failure to consider environmental consequences inherent in the Korean industrial and economic development model. When coupled with the nation's rigid political and social stratification, the contradictions in environmental policy, planning, and enforcement will be difficult to overcome. The reasons for this are enormously complex, but insights can be found embedded in Korean society itself, in the interaction between public attitudes and private thoughts about the environment and its importance.

Korea has moved from the ranks of developing countries to become a newly developed economic power. Its leaders have stated their intention to continue its progress toward joining the so-called G–7 industrial nations and to enter as a full member in 1996. Many in Korea, and certainly the dominant forces in government and society, still reject the idea that realistic, balanced development that respects the environment is possible or even desirable. For many politicians, civil servants, and industrial leaders, environmental problems remain a costly and complex political inconvenience because of their apparent intractability and conflicts with the deeply ingrained Korean faith in industrial development. The result is that the environment earns lip service and little else. Given this attitude, it is easy to understand why the application of law and regulation remains severely limited in practice to immediately visible problems. Similarly, it is apparent why long-term environmental planning and its integration with all other social and economic goals has not yet established firm roots in the Korean administrative psyche.

The second factor limiting Korean environmental management is the traditional view of government and administration in Korea itself. Generations of centralization and thirty years of authoritarian rule in Korea have raised inflexible and bureaucratic government administration to an art form that leaves little room for innovation or change in any aspect of government activity. This inertia is aggravated by the long-held Confucian tradition of senior administrators frequently moving from one position to another. As a result, responsible managers have little opportunity to develop the necessary technical, planning, and political expertise necessary for modern environmental management.

Furthermore, it has been common for ministers and their senior staff to be forced to resign in the wake of environmental accidents, such as those on the Naktong River in 1991 and 1994. Since the MoE became a full-fledged ministry in 1990, three ministers (including one of Korea's few women cabinet members) have served in the post. While personal responsibility is an important cornerstone of Korean governance, the traditional reflexive blaming of officials for industrial accidents, which are epidemic, does little to improve environmental management. Korea needs commitment, stability, and increased professionalism in its environmental management and administration. At the moment it has too little of each across and within its bureaucracy.

Another major inhibitor to modern environmental administration is the prevailing narrow view of environmental management. Almost without exception, the focus of public concern and government officials is on the "end of pipe."[69] As recently as January 1995, in announcing the creation of the Environmental Vision for the Year 2005, the minister of environment, Kim Zoo-Wei, stated that MoE "will place a greater burden of ensuring water quality on users than on those who actually create pollution to cope with the seemingly worsening water conditions." With the notable exception of air-quality management, there is an absence of systemic approaches toward environmental problems. Waste reduction and prevention are in their infancy, and the difficult decisions to modify development in the face of environmental concerns implied in the current environmental assessment process are rarely made with any real integrity. As a result, there is little consistent anticipation of the environmental consequences of any given private or public action. Thus, in most cases, environmental administration remains almost exclusively an exercise in crisis management.

For example, the national government announced in 1994 that it was considering building large bypass systems to transport and dump industrial wastes in the open sea.[70] Although this plan sought to improve inland freshwater quality, it would do nothing to reduce the actual pollution problem, only shifting the unwanted effluents to another locale. In another case, the government is planning to build new and badly needed water-treatment plants throughout the country. However, the plants will be connected to the existing water-delivery system, which often contaminates otherwise clean water supplies. To be sure, the costs of addressing this issue are enormous, but no comprehensive national plan to replace this part of the nation's infrastructure has surfaced.

In a similar vein, the national government has failed to establish consistent national sampling, testing, and measurement regimes that can be used to assist in the design of the new water-treatment facilities. This means that no one in or out of the government knows, for example, how much mercury is used in Korean industry and how much of it finds its way into the nation's drinking water. The story for chromium, cadmium, other heavy metals, pesticides, and solvents is much the same. Without this information, it will be difficult for the government to plan and build a water-delivery system capable of providing Koreans with safe and clean drinking water in the future.

Another barrier to dealing effectively and imaginatively with

Korea's environmental problems lies with the Korean people. Although most, if not all, declare their concern for the environment, the prevailing common concern is about the immediate personal health consequences of polluted air and water. This is important, of course, and it is surely a powerful motivator, but for Koreans to truly accept the environmental challenge, a more expansive view is required. Sales of household filtration systems and bottled water are soaring, but these are not a replacement for large-scale public action to clean up the environment through communal action.

This points to an important and notable hole in Korean environmental thinking. Preservation of resources and the aesthetic values of environmental integrity are barely visible ideas in Korean law and administration. Similarly, they are not evident in public attitudes, where private aesthetics are held in high esteem and community aesthetics have little value. This is rooted in ancient Confucian values and Korean concepts of individualism and has been accentuated by the single-minded attention paid to creating an industrial economy over the past thirty years. During this period, construction of all kinds became the measure of success, and smog and pollution were visible reminders of increasing industrial capacity and a rising standard of living. Unfortunately, this view has now trapped and limited Korean government and the political imagination of its leaders. As a result, the many officials who now feel pressured to take action on environmental problems are doing little more than grasping for immediate ideas of how to come to terms with the nation's environmental needs.

All the inadequacies of environmental management and administration share a common thread, and the problem stretches to every corner of Korean industrial and civil society. All have become mired in impenetrable bureaucracies whose power is held in place by social custom and habits of authority and conformity. These bureaucracies have taken on a life of their own that often checks even the best intentions of government officials. This is no secret to Koreans, who have to live with the daily frustrations of dealing with the immovable structure of public life that strangles all efforts to bring about administrative reform, innovation, and management efficiency. One result of this barrier in public life is that Koreans have learned that the only way to get things done, in business and government, is to apply massive energy, time, and labor to every problem. This has created a particularly Korean kind of national frenzy to achieve immediate results and a nearly complete lack of appreciation for planning, scheduling, efficiency, and quality, to say nothing of health and safety considerations. Now that Korea is facing an unprecedented environmental crisis, many are seeking to apply the same ceaseless level of activity to overcome degraded air and water quality. However, the restoration of nature will demand more than frenzied activity. Environmental management takes time, strategic planning, and patience to achieve meaningful results. Most important, it demands a consistent and vigilant eye for quality. Without these, no amount of commitment can hope to produce a less toxic environment.

Notes

1. There are few resources in English to describe Korean administrative principles and culture, which are often founded on Confucian ideals and ill-suited for modern public administration. This issue is widely discussed among Korean scholars. Two recent English-language examinations of the Korean bureaucracy are: Ro Chung-Hyun, *Public Administration and the Koreans' Transformation* (Seoul: Kumarian Press, 1993); and Paik Wan-Ki, *Korean Administrative Culture* (Seoul: Korea University Press, 1991). Neither book deals with environmental questions, although many of the problems in Korean environmental management are endemic in the government bureaucracy.

2. Contingency fees are unknown in Korea. This severely limits the ability of poor plaintiffs to engage in risky legal suits. The system of arbitration was borrowed from the Japanese, as is most of Korean civil law, and created under the Environmental Pollution Damage Dispute Act of 1991.

3. For purposes of consistency, the won-to-dollar conversion rate is calculated at eight hundred won to the dollar.

4. "Proper Hiking Culture," *Korea Herald*, January 15, 1995.

5. Kim Byong-Kuk, "Realistic, Equitable Law Enforcement," *Korea Times*, February 2, 1994. "Cabbies Earn Extra W260,000 Monthly from Joint Rides, Tips," *Korea Times*, May 15, 1994.

6. Although there has been discussion in Korea about the advisability of creating CERCLA or RCRA-like laws on the U.S. model, these have been rejected to date as too expensive for Korean industry and society to afford at its current level of development. See Nam Il-Chong, "Using Price Mechanism in Waste Management," Korea Development Institute, Seoul, unpublished proceedings, 1993.

7. Korean Ministry of Environment, *Environmental Protection in Korea.* Seoul: 1993.

8. "Two Ministries in Korea Clash on Diesel Use," *Automotive News*, June 10, 1990.

9. Korean Ministry of Environment, *National Report to the Secretary General of the United Nations to Be Reviewed by the Commission on Sustainable Development.* Seoul: 1993.

10. Environmental Officers Training Institute, *Program Guide.* Unpublished internal document, Seoul, Korea, 1994.

11. Korean ministries, like everything else in Korean society, are ranked according to importance. Power and influence are directly tied to how close to the president the minister of the day stands at official functions, for example. In the case of MoE, the ministry moved up four rungs on the cabinet ladder as a sign of the new importance of the environment to the Korean government and public.

12. "Environment Min. Whang, KFEM Clash over EIA Filing Libel Suit," *Korea Times*, November 12, 1993.

13. Ho Nam-Hyun, *Report of the Asia Pacific Environmental Management Institute to the Ministry of Environment on Environmental Assessment Process*, Seoul, Korea, unpublished report, December 1993.

14. Korean Ministry of Environment, Seoul.

15. Ho Nam-Hyun, *Report of the Asia Pacific Environmental Management Institute.*

16. There are now statistics on this trend, but lawyers report a brisk business among those who specialize in securing waivers from regulations.

17. Josh Moreinis, "Zoning Policy and Neighborhood Transformation in Seoul: The Case of Shillim-Dong," *Interplan*, no. 49, December 1994.

18. Clayton Jones, "Water Shocks Rouse South Korea," *Christian Science Monitor,* May 29, 1991.

19. "Benzene Found in Naktong River," *Korea Herald,* January 14, 1994

20. Kim K. C., "Water Pollution of the Naktong River–(II)," *Korea Times*, January 30, 1994. "Naktong River Scandal: Citizens Refuse to Pay Tap Water Bills," *Korea Herald*, January 24, 1994. "Level of Benzene in Naktong River 1.8 Times Higher Than WHO Standard," *Korea Herald*, January 15, 1994.

21. "Naktong River Contamination Identified in Oct.," *Korea Times*, January 20, 1994. As in many environmental groups, the methodology and skill of the volunteer samplers are suspect, but their work did underscore the serious water-quality problems in the Naktong basin that plague the river daily.

22. Korean Ministry of Environment, *National Report of Republic of Korea to UNCED.*

23. Korean Ministry of Environment, *National Report to the Secretary General of the United Nations to Be Reviewed by the Commission on Sustainable Development.*

24. Chung Chin-Seung, "Origin and Development of Environmental Problems and Awareness in Korea," unpublished manuscript, 1994.

25. They are also a persistent problem in industrialized nations, and they are among the most intractable of environmental issues. "The Environment in Asia," *Far Eastern Economic Review Focus*, November 17, 1994.

26. "Ground Water Contamination Found at Dangerous Levels," *Korea Times*, November 12, 1993.

27. Chung Chin-Seung, "Origin and Development of Environmental Problems and Awareness in Korea."

28. "W3.5 Trillion Water Quality Plan Seen Failed," *Korea Times*, September 19, 1993.

29. Korean Ministry of Environment, *National Report of the Republic of Korea to UNCED.*

30. Kim Jung-Wk and Jeon Eui-Chan, "Policy Responses towards Improving

Solid Waste Management in Seoul City," *Journal of Environmental Studies* (Seoul National University), vol. 25, 1989.

31. Ibid.

32. "New Garbage Disposal System: Everything You Wanted to Know about It," *Korea Times*, January 7, 1995. The bags come in packages of ten and twenty and are available in several sizes. The price of the bags varies from neighborhood to neighborhood, the cost determined by a formula that accounts for factors such as the distance of the neighborhood to the landfill sites. Because of this price differential the bags, which are of uniform size, cannot be used outside of the zone in which they are purchased. See also "Garbage, Old Furniture Dumped in Back Streets," *Korea Herald*, January 5, 1995. Predictably, the week prior to the implementation of the new law the volume of trash arriving at Kimpo landfill, west of Seoul, rose to an estimated 18,214 tons, or 13,000 tons higher than the usual daily average.

33. "Toothpicks to Disappear at Restaurants Next Mo.," *Korea Times*, January 18, 1995.

34. Nho Joon-Hun, "Plastic Recycling Plants Due by June," *Korea Times*, January 11, 1995.

35. In another aspect of this story, several large apartment developers announced in January 1995 that they intended to build small household waste incinerators to service tenants in their housing projects. While this is clearly a response to market forces, the air-quality impact of thousands of small trash incinerators will only shift the waste problem from land to air unless adequate environmental controls are imposed.

36. Park Sang-Yeol, "Environmental Law in Korea," *Journal of Environmental Law and Practice*, no. 3, November 1993.

37. Environmental Management Corporation, *Annual Report*, Seoul, Korea, 1994.

38. The program has greatly improved the consistency and quality of sampling methodology in Korea, which has been notoriously poor. The government intends to continue the expansion of this automated testing system as funds become available with each year's new budget. The reader boards are especially liked by the public, many of whom closely follow air-quality conditions.

39. This system goes to the heart of the Korean gray economy, where debts of all kinds are settled immediately. It is common practice, for example, for automobile accidents to be settled on the side of the road through an immediate cash payment.

40. Republic of Korea, *Third Comprehensive National Development Plan*. Seoul: 1992.

41. "Waste Water to Be Funneled into Sea," *Korea Times*, April 3, 1994.

42. Yoo Byoung-Il, "The Case Study of Private Forest Management Activities in Korea," *Bulletin of the Forestry Research Institute* (Seoul), no. 39, 1989.

43. "Decontrolled Military Protection Areas to Come under Ecological Preservation," *Korea Times*, May 25, 1994.

44. The environmental condition of land under the control of the Korean military is shrouded in secrecy, and only rarely has the military come under scrutiny for its environmental impact. Perhaps the most significant case was when the army proposed a new exercise and firing zone in Kangwon Province in South

Korea's rugged northeast corner. Several nongovernment organizations led protests in 1992, but they were unable to obstruct the military development plans.

45. Kwak Il-Chyun, "Reconciling Free Trade and the Protection of Global Commons: The Tasks for Korean Environmental Policy Makers," *International Symposium on Trade-Environment Issues and Korea's Alternatives*, Seoul, Korea, April 22, 1994.

46. Chung Chin-Seung, "Origin and Development of Environmental Problems and Awareness in Korea." For a more enthusiastic view of the deposit system, see also Lee Sun-Yong, "Economic Incentives to Control Pollution: A Case Study of Korea's Non-Compliance Charge System," Indiana University dissertation, 1992. Dr. Lee is now a senior official responsible for policy development in Korea's Ministry of Environment.

47. Ibid.

48. Choi Sung-Jin, "Korean Firms Play Catch-up in Race for Green Market," *Korea Herald*, May 19, 1994.

49. Ministry of Environment, *National Report of the Republic of Korea to UNCED*.

50. The collapse of the fifteen-year-old Song-Su bridge across the Han River killed thirty-two people. The failure of the bridge (apparently due to poor materials, welds, and maintenance and excessive loads and vibration) sent shock waves through the Korean establishment and led to recriminations over the quality of Korea's industrial output and government oversight. The mayor of Seoul resigned due to the lack of significant inspection, and several large lawsuits against contractors are in the courts. Following the disaster, Seoul residents were told that several other heavily traveled spans linking the city's north and south sides were at risk and would need repairs. Seoul now faces several years of snarled traffic as bridges are closed for safety inspection and retrofitting. See also "1994: A Year to Forget," *Maeil Kyungje Shinmun*, December 31, 1994.

51. A simple reduction in all the digging and movement of earth would reduce the massive amount of dust that plagues every urban center in Korea. However, it is unlikely that any less earth will be moved in the coming years as Korea's building boom continues.

52. Rhee Deok-Gil, "Environmental Challenges in the 1990s: A Korean Context," *Energy & Environment*, vol. 2, no. 4, 1991.

53. KEPCO, *Annual Report*, 1993. In 1994 Korea had over 10 percent of all of Asia's nuclear power plants in operation. Chuan Wen-Hu and George Wolfe, "Nuclear Power Development in Asia," *IAEA Bulletin* (International Atomic Energy Agency), April 1993.

54. Three of four Korean TV stations do not broadcast at all between 10:00 A.M. and 5:00 P.M. on weekdays, and one is off the air from 10:00 A.M. to 2 P.M., which means that the 2:00 to 4:00 coverage was unusual and perceived as expendable.

55. The symbol of the Don't Waste Wastes campaign is a green and blue line drawing of mountains, a river, and a rising sun. It was first developed by the *Chosun Ilbo*, Korea's largest newspaper. In an interesting commentary on the uniformity in Korean society, the symbol has been taken over and used widely by citizen action groups, including Korea's largest environmental advocacy coalition, which uses the symbol on its pins, canvas carrying bags, and other products. It is also used in advertising everything from soap to soju.

56. Korean Ministry of Environment, *National Report to the Secretary General of the United Nations to Be Reviewed by the Commission on Sustainable Development.*

57. "Environment Day Points to Future of Earth," *Korea Herald*, August 19, 1993.

58. Korea Educational Development Institute, *Environmental Education in Korea, Final Report to UNESCO*, Seoul, Korea, 1990.

59. In the Korean public education system, schools—not students—choose elective courses that will be offered and taken. Parents play a strong role in the selection of those courses.

60. Korean Ministry of Education, *The School Curriculum of the Republic of Korea.* Seoul: 1994. Discussion of this issue has become something like conversations about the weather. Everyone argues that vast reform is needed, but the educational system and its highly structured system of rote learning remain in place.

61. Choi Suk-Jin, "Curriculum of Environmental Subjects in Korean Middle School," *Journal of the Korean Society for Environmental Education*, no. 4, 1992.

62. "Environmental Education Needed at Pre-School Age," *Korea Times*, June 5, 1993.

63. Korean Ministry of Environment, *National Report of the Republic of Korea to UNCED.* Seoul: 1992.

64. The Korea Church Research Institute for Peace and the Integrity of Creation, *Informational Brochure.* Seoul, 1994.

65. Lee departed to take a post with a women's crisis hotline. She was replaced at KIEP by her sister Lee Sang-Young.

66. For an evaluation of women in Korean public and political life, see Soh Chung-Hee, *The Chosen Women in Korean Politics: An Anthropological Study.* New York: Praeger, 1991.

67. There are, of course, many other elements that could be highlighted, but a discussion of these would add only detail not additional analysis.

68. "Environment Policies Make No Progress," *Korea Times*, June 6, 1994.

69. "Users to Bear More Cost for Clean Water," *Korea Times*, January 17, 1995.

70. "Waste Water to Be Funneled into Sea," *Korea Times*, April 3, 1994.

Seoul, Korea's capital city of 11 million inhabitants. The city is ringed by rugged mountains that trap dust and airborne pollutants, making blue sky a rarity.

The symbol of the new Korea. Thousands of new cars are added to the nation's clogged roads every year.

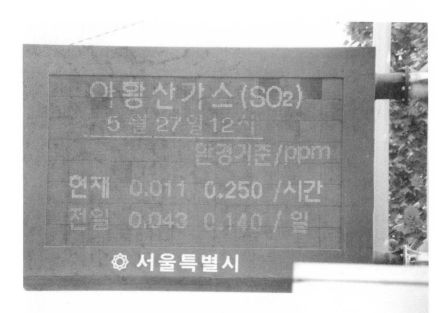

Electronic reader board in central Seoul announcing SO₂ concentrations in city air.

Trash bins and bagged refuse are now common sights in every Korean city.

Sewer overflow. A chronic problem during the rainy season in Korean cities.

Rural dumping of wastes is a chronic problem in the Korean countryside.

Mixed wastes stored near industrial site.

Cement and brick factory located on the bank of a shallow river without any barriers to protect water quality from runoff.

Expressway construction and sewer outflow on the banks of the Han River in central Seoul.

Trucks hauling construction wastes are a common sight throughout Korea. Some go to legal landfills but often material is dumped in the countryside or used as fill for wetlands or on construction sites.

Some of the 2,500 trucks per day waiting to dispose of trash outside the gate of Seoul's solid waste landfill.

The smell and sight of Korean prosperity at sunset.

Greenpeace arrives to internationalize Korea's domestic environmental movement.

Washing rocks after a coastal bunker oil spill.

Don't Drive on Saturday! Don't drive on Saturday!

Dr. Yoo, Jae-Hyun, Secretary General of Citizens Coalition for Economic Justice.

4

The Forces for Change: Prosperity, Democratization, and Internationalization

It is easy to be pessimistic about the prospects for Korea's natural environment. The sheer scope of the scientific and technical problems and the institutional and financial barriers to grappling effectively with them are enormous. Nonetheless, there is room for cautious optimism that Koreans are turning their legendary energy to address their environmental crisis. The forces driving this change, such as rising middle-class demands for improved quality of life, democratization, and internationalization, are still in their infancy. Yet, they are seeping into every aspect of Korean life and becoming powerful motivators of public opinion. The result has been the rapid rise of the environment as an important domestic political and social issue. In turn, this widespread environmental concern holds the potential to modify the primary tenet of the modern Korean state: unbridled economic expansion.

In a 1982 survey of Korean public opinion, only 14 percent of the respondents said that preserving environmental quality was an important issue in the world. Similar surveys conducted in 1987 and 1990 revealed a strong growth in environmental consciousness among Korean adults. In 1987, 40 percent of the surveyed population thought that environmental quality was a serious problem, and in 1990 the number jumped to 64 percent. In the same series of polls, in 1982 only 6 percent of Koreans thought that the environment was a serious problem warranting government attention. Environmental decay ranked well behind war and peace, housing, social welfare, and education. By

1987 the number had grown to 17 percent, and by 1990, 22 percent asked that the environment be a high priority for the government. This put the environment ahead of transportation, housing, social welfare, and education. The polls also sampled public confidence in the government's ability to effectively solve the problems identified. When asked in 1982 if the government was working for the environment, 68 percent of the respondents answered positively. By 1987 this dropped to 57 percent, and in 1990, only 24 percent of those questioned said they were confident in the government's ability to solve environmental problems.[1]

Patterns of Public Environmental Attitudes

Foreign visitors to Korea often are amazed by how quickly and dramatically the physical character of the country is changing. After only three decades of development, Korea has climbed the economic ladder to relative prosperity. This prosperity is evident today in Seoul, Pusan, Taejon, and nearly every other Korean city. In less than a generation a thriving middle class developed and turned Korea into a classic consumer society. New cars, designer clothing, and expensive nightclubs are the most visible evidence of how far Korea has come from its recent past of abject poverty (see Table 4.1)

As the middle class has expanded and its position solidified, new social demands have emerged. No longer are most people concerned only about having enough food, clothing, and housing. Instead, the talk around Seoul's booming middle-class neighborhoods and satellite suburban communities is about the quality of life and educational prospects for children. No issue is spoken of more often than the condition of Korea's natural environment. In numerous opinion polls and academic studies, the public has identified clean water and clean air as the most important public issues. The class that owes its existence to recent industrialization and prosperity is now asking that it be able to savor the fruits of its labor more fully.

Demands for improved environmental quality are reflected and at times led by press attention to environmental issues. News coverage of environmental issues was first undertaken by the *Chosun-Ilbo*, Korea's largest newspaper, which launched an independent environmental campaign in 1989. In 1994, the paper won a United Nations Global 500 award for its long-standing efforts. By that time, every major

Table 4.1

Socioeconomic Indicators: Korea 1961–92

Indicator	Unit	1961	1992	Change Rate, Times
GNP per capita	US$	82	6,750	82
Export (amount)	10^6 US$	41	76,631	1,869
Energy consumption	10^3 total output energy	9,750	116,008	11.9
Electricity consumption	Gigawatt hours	1,470	115,244	78
Population	10^3	25,012	43,663	1.75
Population density	People/km^2	254	440	1.73
Urban population	%	28	79	2.82
Motor vehicle registration	10^3	29	5,231	180 +

Source: Han Sang-Wook, "Environmental Issues and Projects in Korea," unpublished manuscript, 1994.

newspaper had at least one reporter dedicated to the environmental beat. Few newspapers lack a daily story about some aspect of the environment, including Seoul's two English-language papers. In 1982 there were only 479 environmental stories in major newspapers, whereas by 1992 there were 8,884, and the number has risen rapidly since then.[2] In addition to the dailies, there are several weekly newspapers entirely devoted to environmental concerns around the country and dozens of broadsheets produced by local environmental groups. The *Environmental Industry Weekly* is a new commercial venture that highlights environmental technology.

All of this media coverage, which is increasing daily, creates a constant drumbeat of publicity that few Koreans can avoid. In January 1995, two major Korean-language dailies began massive campaigns to heighten public environmental awareness. The *Dong-A Ilbo* launched the Green Scouts Movement, in which daily environmental tips are given to readers. Considerable coverage is also given by the *Hangook Ilbo*, which is conducting its campaign in cooperation with the Hwan-Kyung Un-dong Yeon-Hap (Korea Federation of Environmental Movements, or KFEM). KFEM has lent four full-time staff members to assist the newspaper in its coverage, and KFEM activists will write many of the published articles.[3] The environment has also become widely discussed in academic circles. Dozens of new institutes and professional organizations have sprung up to address one or more aspects of Korea's damaged environment, as well as to study the broad range of public policy, social, and economic consequences of environmental damage.

Perhaps the best measure of this environmental interest is the increasing use of environmental consciousness in mass marketing. Koreans are bombarded with statements about environmentally friendly products from manufacturers and advertisers of everything from paper cups to computer monitors. Samsung introduced a new bio-video display recently that its makers claim is less harmful to the eyes. For its part, the Ssangyong Group is distributing ten thousand videotapes and books about the natural environment to schools and "educational groups" in an effort to associate Ssangyong's commitment to environmental programs with its products.

The most prominent effort in this regard is in the highly competitive beer market, where for the past two years, Korean beer makers have tripped over themselves to introduce new products made from "clean spring water." The first of these products, Hite Beer, has captured 16 percent of the nation's beer market for Chosun Brewery. In commenting on that success, the Korea Management Association noted that Hite's introduction in 1993 as the first "clean beer" was perfect timing. The beer came to market at a time when the Korean public began to seriously worry about the contamination of drinking-water resources.[4] Although marketing campaigns are not environmental programs in themselves, they are another (albeit superficial) indicator of public interest and concern. Marketers know that their job is to reinforce public perceptions, and in the case of environmental theme advertising, they are clearly reflecting public acceptance of the need for a clean environment. Nowhere is this more apparent than in the "green insurance" now being offered by several enterprising insurance companies. This product's advertising promises to compensate policy holders for physical harm, injury, or death caused by the pollution of Korea's environment.

The rise of environmental consciousness must be treated with care. It is at a rudimentary stage and is strongly self-limiting. Neither the majority of the public nor many of those at the most senior levels of government have learned to take a broad view of environmental issues. A majority of Korean citizens have yet to understand that environmental quality is not an isolated problem that can be addressed in a piecemeal fashion as each crisis arises. Rather, it is an issue that is connected to every facet of Korean life. Because of this lack of understanding, demands for environmental quality will challenge the nation's collective political, social, and economic imagination in ways that are only now beginning to be revealed.

Elements of Korean Environmental Consciousness

The most pervasive theme in Korean environmental thinking today is that environmental issues are important but are a secondary concern when weighed against development needs. Repeatedly in Korea there are expressions of the opinion that Korea simply needs more time to develop its economy, and that in the future, when the nation has reached a stable economic position, it can shoulder the burdens of addressing the needs of the environment. In the meantime, Korea must accept environmental degradation as the cost of prosperity and modernization.

A second strain of contemporary Korean environmental attitudes is pessimism. Many Koreans believe that it is already too late for their natural environment because it has been irreparably overwhelmed by the forces of industrialization. While some improvements might be possible, the best Koreans can expect is stabilization of environmental conditions at a relatively low level. There is even a stream of thought (admittedly a minority view) that Korea's environmental condition is a natural state ordained by God and not redeemable by human action. In contrast, there are many church-based activists interested in the environment who are motivated by their interpretation of God's commandments to care for the earth.

An equally strong theme in Korean public attitudes holds that the way to address environmental problems is through personal and public education and individual action. As in other countries, there has been significant growth in the demands for organic food and related environmentally sound personal products. At the same time, there is a great emphasis placed on public education through the media, churches, and schools. In fact, for those who adopt pro-environmentalist views, one of the major shortcomings of the government is its failure to adequately inform the people of the real state of the environment.[5] Environmental advocates assume that once people are informed of the problem, they will feel the necessity of communal participation in an appropriate solution. Advocates also hold that this expression of public willpower might motivate the government to act responsibly to stem the tide of environmental degradation. However, this view is self-limiting in that no amount of personal education and action will be capable of addressing the staggering environmental problems of Korea today. To be sure, hiking trails might become a bit less littered with paper and cans. But in the end, personal action is no substitute for strong, centrally managed waste minimization programs, regulatory control, and enforcement of environmental standards. And, at its worst, such thinking can actually allow government bodies and industry a handy smoke screen for continuation of environmental degradation.

Another major theme in Korean environmental thinking is pro-environmentalist and draws heavily on the antigovernment social and political traditions of the 1970s and 1980s. Environmental problems are seen as a visible expression of the failures of capitalism and Western consumerism. According to this view, Korea is the victim of Western plundering of natural and human resources and must search for its own pathway to a less polluting society. Within this attitude lies a wide range of opinion and thought, from those advocating a return to a primitive, preindustrial past to those who see in the environment evidence of the failure of capitalism and colonialism. Proponents of this view range from social activists to Luddites to those who envision replacing the current heavy-industry-led development model with the foundations for a green sustainable economy.

It is not uncommon for individuals to draw on ideas from all four patterns of environmental thought. Still, there is a strong tendency among all those shades of opinion to see environmental questions far more narrowly than in Western industrialized countries. For example, when questioned about water pollution, a group of graduate students in a university environmental science program agreed that the best answer to the problem of poor drinking water was to reduce their use of soap and shampoo. Such individual actions are of course beneficial, but none of the students seemed aware that water-damaging phosphorous soaps are no longer sold in Korea.

When the same group of students was asked about industry's contribution to the water pollution problem, none said that it was significant or that if it was, much could be done to stem its tide. This once again illustrates the deeply held cynicism and resignation to the fact of environmental decay. The sole exception was in the case of accidents such as those in the Naktong River basin, where the students strongly demanded and believed in government action to reduce the harmful effects of widespread pollution. Moreover, in contrast to European and American environmental views, the interviewed students (and almost everyone else in Korea today) express a strong faith that technology can overcome environmental contamination.[6] One repeatedly hears that the primary challenge is to build enough treatment plants, not to stop or reduce pollution at its source before it has to be treated or is allowed to flow into the nation's rivers, air, and soils.

Many Koreans also have built an emotional and political barrier between domestic and international environmental problems. There is great concern about pesticide and fungicide residues on imported foodstuffs. Stories about the poisoning and unhealthful nature of foreign food products circulate freely in Korean society. However, there has been little or no comparative concern about the contamination of the domestic food supply, though pesticide use in Korean agriculture is widespread and until recently largely unregulated.

In another example of this kind of selective environmentalism, the YMCA launched a boycott of foreign-made cigarettes in 1990. In its boycott, which lasted nearly three years, the YMCA activists stated that they were motivated by concerns about the effects of the advertising and marketing prowess of large international firms. This, they suggested, would lead to an increase in smoking, especially among women and children. The irony, of course, is that Koreans are among the world's heaviest smokers. Having exacerbated the fear of foreign tobacco, the leaders of the YMCA boycott all but ignored the overriding health effects of smoking any tobacco, including that grown in Korea. At the same time, few people realize that many domestically produced cigarettes are actually blends of domestic and foreign-grown tobacco. This is typical of the many ironies of contemporary life in Korea.

Today in Korea there is also great concern about the environmental consequences of Chinese industrialization. One of China's primary industrial zones is situated upwind of the Korean peninsula. The prevailing winds carry chemical-laden air the short distance across the Yellow Sea, adding to the acid rainfall across the Korean land mass. Moreover, the quantity of effluents flowing into the Yellow Sea from the Chinese mainland is rising, threatening an already badly polluted shallow sea. The worry about increased levels of Chinese pollution is properly placed, but among Koreans it has led to a growing tendency to blame the Chinese for their country's pollution problems and to overlook the domestic problem. This certainly regionalizes the environmental problems of Northeast Asia, but it also provides a handy excuse for those not seriously committed to addressing Korea's own problems. The result could be to move responsibility one step further from practical action and to play on traditional themes of xenophobia and international isolation.

Thus, while the demands for a higher-quality environment are widespread and insistent, they are at times severely limited in scope, consistency, and depth. Environmental thinking is also linked to a significant degree of pessimism and a lack of confidence that the government and its officials can deal effectively with environmental issues. In large part this environmental pessimism reflects a larger historic pattern in Korean public life and tradition. Greatly influenced by Confucianism, Koreans intuitively and instinctively surrender to authority and adhere to strict formalistic social codes of behavior. Expressions of Confucian social patterns are found in the smallest details of daily life and the grandest public events, and they are the foundation of concepts of social order and continuity.[7] In this system, government is viewed as responsible and powerful but ultimately corrupt and helpless in the face of serious and complex problems. Politicians are seen in much the same light and widely regarded throughout society as nothing more than self-promoters. Few Koreans perceive any substantive differences between their political parties and politicians, and except for the ideological left wing, most see politics as an extension of individual power, without significant ideological content or intent.

In many ways these attitudes have been amplified by industrial development, which for many Koreans has become an irresistible supernatural force. The individual cannot stop or even alter the process even if it were desirable to do so. Thus, while it is clear that there is great public concern about environmental degradation, few Koreans express much confidence that the government or the public can or will come to terms with the daunting challenge of addressing environmental problems.

Democratization and Political Modernization and the Rise of Environmental Politics

The development of democracy in Korea is an unlikely story. Once free from the Japanese in 1945, Korea found itself divided between the great powers of the United States and Russia and at the front line of the Cold War. In 1950 the Korean War began, and with it all practical hope for either reunification or democracy disappeared. During the next decade, Korean life was dominated by a national-security dictatorship, which in 1961 gave way to the military dictatorship of Park Chung-Hee.

During the late 1960s and for the next two decades, Korea's military leaders committed the nation to rapid industrialization and modernization. Using a strategy of heavy industrial development and export-led growth, Korea set an unmatched pace for gross national product growth. This period witnessed rapid income growth and the concentration of industrial power in the hands of large integrated industrial groups known as chaebol. These groups, such as Hyundai, Daewoo, Ssangyong, Samsung, Lucky-Goldstar, and Lotte, were granted critical concessions by the government in the form of capital, protection from labor activism, and other ingredients of unimpeded business growth. This placed an inordinate amount of economic influence in the hands of the large business groups. In 1994 over 70 percent of all business activity was connected to the chaebol. In exchange for allowing the government to set the pace and direction of their business development the chaebol provided financial support for the political leadership. For the Korean public, though, the benefits of prosperity came at the price of repression and an epidemic of corruption.[8]

Korea was an inhospitable place for dissent in the early 1980s. With power highly centralized in the hands of the military command and economic oligarchy, a sweeping national security law was used to stifle all domestic voices of political and social opposition. The plainclothes police, Korean Central Intelligence Agency, military, and other arms of government were ever present, and they used torture, terror, and censorship to sustain the power of the military dictatorship. This cozy power relationship held social forces in check while commanding national economic growth. It also led to significant corruption as absolute power and growing prosperity were used to line the pockets of generals and their bureaucrats. The result was the institutionalization of corruption at all levels of Korean society.[9]

In 1987 the authoritarian establishment was shattered by a popular uprising in the streets of Seoul and other Korean cities. Student rioters, demanding an end to political repression, were joined by members of the new middle class who demanded reform and an end to the favoritism and corruption that plagued government. The government of President Chun Doo-Hwan lost control of the situation and was forced to promise reform and a free election.

Over the next five years, under President Roh Tae-Woo, Korea's path to ending authoritarianism was slow, disjointed, and sometimes painful. Resistance by the old guard, though, was met with commitment and an unwillingness to bow to personal repression by reformers and social progressives. Expansion of free speech and political action was occasionally stalled, but by the early 1990s, liberalization was well under way and supported gingerly by the United States. Although conservatives resisted and worked to undercut change, the collapse of the Soviet bloc and the end of the Cold War made their security-based demands for social order increasingly anachronistic and untenable.

In December 1992, Korean political history was turned on its head with the election of President Kim Young-Sam. A political reformer who had spent years in the wilderness of dissent, Kim launched a major reform drive shortly after taking office.[10] He pushed for expanded liberty and sought to open up the government to the light of public scrutiny. High-level corruption was exposed, and politicians and bureaucrats of all parties were dismissed from office due to the discovery of large fortunes in real estate and secret false-name bank accounts. Liberalization efforts were not restricted to politics. In 1993 President Kim began to free up the Korean economy by selling off government financial holdings in large corporations and insisting that the stock market and banks be freed from the limitations of government control and regulation.[11] Most important, in August 1993 he issued an executive order that immediately banned false-name bank accounts, which are estimated to have accounted for about 4 percent of all bank assets. This single act ended the all-too-common practice of hiding money and made it far more difficult for public officials to shelter bribes and extra income from public view. Audit committees were established at all levels of government to judge the disclosures of thirty-four thousand local and national officials. By 1995 hundreds of bureaucrats and politicians and six members of the National Assembly had been fired or driven into early retirement.[12]

The cornerstone of Kim Young-Sam's presidency has been democratization of Korean society. This was confirmed when he pushed his own party, the Democratic Liberal party, to support many of the opposition's electoral reform demands. In March 1994 the National

Assembly passed a landmark electoral reform legislative package.[13] This sought, for the first time, to reduce the amount of secret money in Korean politics and to break the back of political corruption by placing limits on campaign expenditures.

Under the new law, candidates for the National Assembly must strictly account for all campaign spending. At the same time, the new law limits the money that can be spent by political parties on presidential campaigns. The new presidential campaign limit has been lowered from 36 billion won to 16 billion ($44.6 million to $20 million) and assembly candidates will be limited to no more than 53 million won ($66,250). At the same time, the reform measure did away with the requirement that big contributors identify which parties they are funding. Under the previous system, contributors were often intimidated by fears of offending ruling party officials and therefore chose to support only the existing government's candidates. Moreover, large contributions were often made in secret and through third parties. This led to spending well above the legal limits that were placed on all candidates. To address this and other problems the electoral law reform raised the state subsidy for electoral management from the previous 600 won to 800 (75 cents to $1.00) per voter and outlawed independently paid campaign workers. (The total political capitation fee is divided among competing candidates.) Moreover, under the new reform system, campaign finances must be reported to a Central Election Management Committee, which is obligated by law to fully disclose all information to the public.[14]

The March 1994 electoral reform legislation was more than a fiscal measure; it turned Korean campaign law inside out and upside down. Before the reform measure was enacted, campaigning was severely restricted by the requirement that candidates could act only with government permission and within very constrained limits. Although the law was not always enforced, it always could be and therefore had a chilling effect on opposition candidates and their parties. With reform, candidates for office were no longer restricted to approved settings for campaign speeches and were free to print and distribute campaign literature to their constituents during the campaign period. Door-to-door campaigning has been created from whole cloth in Korea.

Legal and institutional change has left much of the interlocked Korean political and business elite reeling. President Kim has been criticized for trying to reform too much too fast, while others eager for reform have been quick to accuse him of abandoning the cause of greater democratization and reform. This tension points to perhaps the single most important reality of Korean life today. Political liberalization and democratization are incomplete and clearly an evolving process. Electoral law reform alone will not be enough to alter age-old Korean political habits. The public remains widely suspicious of their leaders' true understanding and commitment to democracy, as well as of the integrity of their newly formed "open" political institutions and political parties. This has accentuated the prevailing tradition of social cynicism. Nonetheless, the problem is not just one of the civil leadership. Many average Koreans still expect to benefit from democracy and see little wrong with receiving "gifts" from those seeking their votes. The result has been that roots of democracy remain weak and only shallowly anchored to the soil of ancient Korean culture.

Nonetheless, the results of democratization efforts can be found in the most surprising corners of Korean life. The Supreme Court is a case in point. Historically, Korean law and the judiciary have been used as tools of repression, not only by military dictators but also by the Japanese and Korean monarchies before them. This goes a long way to explain the almost universal public reluctance to resort to the courts for redress or dispute settlement. However, today the Korean court and legal systems, like other elements of Korean civil society, are being redefined. In the process, the court is becoming more assertive and expansive in its rulings in support of civil liberties and the public's right to exercise long-stated but rarely enjoyed constitutional rights.[15] Citizens are filing more court cases, and it is significant that in 1990, a separate Constitutional Court was created specifically to rule on questions of constitutional importance.

Shortly after the election of Kim Young-Sam, the Korean Supreme Court ruled on an important case involving the Kukje Corporation. In the mid-1980s the corporation was forced to the brink of bankruptcy when its chairman, Yang Jung-Mo, refused to cooperate with ruling party requests. Eventually, he was forced to sell his 1.19 million shares in the Hanil Business Group, the holding company for Kukje, and lost control of Kukje to Hanil. Shortly afterward, he filed suit to regain his lost wealth, valued today at 10 billion won ($800 million). In its 1993 judgment, the nation's Supreme Court held that the previous government had no right to economically "punish" individuals or corporations who did not submit to demands for political contributions and obedience. This landmark decision sent strong shock waves through Korea's corporate community since it set a precedent for other business enterprises, including newspaper companies, which had relinquished their management control under heavy government pressure.

In May 1994, an appellate court issued a new ruling that the shares did not have to be returned to Kukje's previous chairman, Yang. In examining the Supreme Court's ruling, the lower court held that the constitutional ruling did not pertain to the current government because there was no evidence that it had participated in the forcible seizure of the shares. The case will now return to the Korean Supreme Court, but according to press accounts, Yang's chances for restitution may now be "ruined."[16]

Another example of growing legal activism is a ruling about the decade-old ban (only foreigners were exempt) on the sale of bottled water in Korea.[17] The ban rested on two sociopolitical judgments by the government, which ironically were supported by several leading radical social activists. The first was that approval of bottled-water sales would implicitly acknowledge the low quality of public tap water, which is mostly treated by municipalities. By definition that admission would embarrass both local and national governments, which have long maintained the fiction of safe water supplies. The second issue was a concern by the national government that approval to sell private water would aggravate class differences: Those too poor to afford bottled water delivery would be forced to drink from the public water system, while the middle and upper classes bought their way out of the problem. However, like many Korean laws, the ban was not enforced and bottled water became a staple of Korean domestic life long ago. In the spring of 1994 the newly invigorated Supreme Court struck down the government's unenforced ban on the sale of bottled water, saying that the government had no right to interfere in the rights of individual citizens to choose.[18]

The transitional nature of Korean institutions can be seen in both the Kukje case and the decision that disposed of the bottled water ban. Throughout the country there are similar examples of change, inconsistency, and gridlock. In looking at Korea's movement away from authoritarianism and repressive rule, it is apparent that the nation has much further to go. Perhaps the best example of this is the ongoing controversy surrounding the publication of a multivolume work of historical fiction by noted Korean author Cho Chung-Rae, titled *Taebaek*

Mountain Range, in which the author offers a revisionist view of Korea in the 1940s and 1950s. Right-wing organizations in Korean society, including the Korean War and Vietnam War Veterans Association, have charged in a lawsuit that the novel violates the National Security and Libel Laws and is a "socialist revolutionary textbook." The controversy, which has been fueled by the conservative media, including the *Chosun-Ilbo* (Korea's largest daily paper), has pushed sales of the book to over 3.5 million copies, making it the best-selling book in Korean history.[19]

The debate surrounding *Taebaek Mountain Range* is interesting in that the book was first published ten years ago, and only now has it become the focal point for ideological debate. The furor over the book is widely interpreted as a reaction by the most conservative elements in Korean society against liberalization and democratization. It is also likely a reflection of the growing freedom of political discourse. But certainly one cause of the delayed controversy is that political and social conservatives have found their position repeatedly eroded since the election of Kim Young-Sam. As a result they are using a literary debate to strike back at those who are undercutting the social order as they perceive it. Nonetheless, there is a widespread sense that despite some recalcitrant elements in society, the liberalization process will not be reversed.[20] Moreover, the local elections held on June 27, 1995, were a major step toward establishing greater local and regional autonomy from the central government. At the same time the elections signaled the reemergence of significant regional divisions and hostilities that seem destined to shape the future of Korean democracy.[21]

One of the principal effects of democratization has been to change the political rules of the road. In the past, party sponsorship and personal patronage were everything in politics. While these factors are still crucial, they are beginning to break down, as candidates and their parties adjust to a more demanding and prosperous electorate. To paraphrase one moderate Democratic Liberal party politician with over a decade of experience in the National Assembly, "I won't be able to just go and bow to my constituents anymore. Now I will have to tell the people what I stand for and what I will do to fix the nation's problems when they return me to the assembly." The member was not sure what he would say, but he recognized that politics in Korea has fundamentally changed, and he must adjust to be successful in this new business. Old personal and regional loyalties won't fade away easily or quickly, but over time, substantive political issues may become important determinants in voter opinion.

The other important aspect of democratization is generational change. Kim Young-Sam has surrounded himself with a cadre of aggressive young officials who are moving into positions of power and influence in the Blue House (the presidential residence and seat of power in Seoul) and the bureaucracy. These people (almost all male and in their mid-thirties to forties) are well educated, and many wear their history of dissent as a badge of honor. They are the first generation with significant international experience and are eager to take control of the levers of government power. Most lack hands-on administrative experience, but they seek to make up for that with principle, energy, and enthusiasm for the challenges ahead. This pattern is repeated today outside of government, where the young and well educated are moving steadily upward into positions of influence in Korean society. This phenomenon is widely discussed within Korean society, contemporary literature, and the press.[22] Commentary is often marked by a mix of optimism, deep pessimism, and abiding cynicism. Will this new generation successfully navigate its way to greater power and influence while maintaining its reformist ambitions, or will it surrender to the very real seductions of prestige, social standing, and, of course, money that are afforded private and public leaders within Korea's vertical social order?[23]

These forces affecting the practice of Korean politics can be seen in the developing importance of environmental issues as political tools and electoral weapons. Nearly every Korean elected official today is acutely aware of the power of popular concern about the environment. As a result, they are seeking to position themselves as advocates for environmental improvement.

The National Assembly has established a special committee on the environment, and both current major parties are competing for public recognition as the party of the environment. During the spring of 1994, President Kim Young-Sam spoke repeatedly about the importance of environmental cleanup and insisted on administrative reorganization in the government's efforts to deal with environmental problems.[24] He also made a point of publicly ordering his minister of environment to immediately address the pressing problems of water quality in light of repeated water contamination problems in the Naktong River basin. In the language of Korean politics this was a strong and unambiguous message about the importance of the environment as a public issue and a strategic political concern.

It is the Democratic party opposition, though, that has most completely grasped the political potential of environmental issues in Korea. The DP is free from the responsibilities of power and can take political potshots at will. Still, the environment is serving a more subtle political cause for the Democratic party. Since the breakup of the opposition in 1990 (as a result of the alliance between Kim Young-Sam and Roh Tae-Woo), DP leaders have been hard pressed to find a distinctive voice for their progressive agenda. At every turn they have found themselves "out-reformed" by President Kim Young-Sam.[25] This has made it difficult for the DP to differentiate its positions from the ruling party's popular reformist policies. Environmental pollution gives them a platform for criticism, an appeal to broadly held public sentiment, and the ability to articulate a vision of improved quality of life for all Koreans. When combined, these make for an irresistible political strategy.

In order to breathe life into the environment as an effective political issue, the leadership of the Democratic party established the Group for Environment and Life (GEL). This parliamentary group, chaired by National Assembly member Kim Sang-Hyun, was established in March 1993 and is composed of fifty-eight DP members (about half of the party's seats in the National Assembly). The avowed purpose of the GEL is to "seriously delve into environmental affairs and prepare legal and other policies that could assist in addressing the nation's environmental needs." In this way the group's leadership council has sought to raise the environmental consciousness of the Korean people while using it for their own political advancement.

As part of this strategy, the GEL produces a substantial quarterly magazine called *Environment and Life*. In 1993 the group launched so-called environment schools, where ordinary citizens were invited to attend meetings sponsored and led by the group's assembly members. These meetings presented the importance of action at all levels of Korean society to reduce pollution. In May and August of 1993 over 1,700 people participated in these schools. By early 1994 the GEL had planned and was conducting a series of national seminars on the environment, which were given broad coverage in the Korean media. The first program was opened by a speech by former Soviet president Mikhail Gorbachev on March 30, 1994, in Seoul. Following that, four seminars were presented around the country that focused on the issue of water quality in the country's major river basins—the Han, Naktong, Yongsan, and Kum.[26]

The GEL openly discusses the political potential of their activities. The environment is seen as a kind of political binder that might be capable of building "organic" cooperation within the National Assembly and within the various political communities in Korea. What the DP politicians have intuitively grasped is that under the influence of democratic change, the deft use of public issues such as environmental concern can etch away at the old personal and geographic loyalties that form the bedrock of Korean politics. The ability of such issues-driven political dialogue to change voting patterns will not be dramatic, but over time this thoroughly modern approach has the potential to draw votes. The first evidence of this potential came during the 1995 local elections, when candidates for municipal and provincial office moved quickly to establish their environmental credentials and enunciate their concerns.

At the municipal level, other DP politicians have worked to become identified with environmental issues. One of these, Kim Young-Geun, is typical. Kim was elected to the Seoul City Council in 1991 and represents a mixed middle-class, young professional, and working-class district. He is a former university professor who was expelled from his job due to his on-campus political activity. He holds a Ph.D. in geology from the University of Iowa and has sought to develop neighborhood-scale environmental programs. Through a private institute he publishes a newsletter every other month that highlights the environmental problems of his district: traffic congestion, recycling, and pollution caused by the area's small businesses. Councilor Kim has two unpaid staff members and personally contributes up to half of the monthly cost of his programs; the balance comes from approximately two hundred contributors. Environmentalism is important to Kim Young-Geun, but he also recognizes the political power in the issue. He knows that by walking and working his district and by talking about environmental problems, he is playing a new game in Korea—the politics of democracy.

Kim Young-Geun is in the vanguard of an important trend in Korean politics that will become even more evident as new rounds of local elections are held. In these, numerous candidates will seek seats on city and provincial councils by speaking about their region's environmental problems. These candidates will come from all political parties. To be sure, not all of these pro-environment candidates will win. But as the winners take their places in local government, they will begin to act on their environmental views and work to see them reflected in local policies toward development and preservation. This may lay the foundation for a new dynamic in Korean environmental management: local autonomy and diversity in establishing regulations and standards. In some cases, local autonomy may produce less supervision, but in others it could produce more, especially in those areas that have already been heavily impacted by environmental degradation. The expected result will be more official local pressures on the national government for improvements in environmental quality.

The Democratic party, like its young member Kim Young-Geun, has been working to "pre-position" itself to use the environment as a political weapon in Korea's national political struggles. In April 1994, the DP leadership found its chance to use its new capability when a large fish kill occurred in the Yongsan River basin in the extreme southeast corner of Korea. The discovery of dead fish forced the Mokpo municipal water system to cease service to sixty-three thousand households and to begin water rationing while authorities looked for clues to the obvious contamination. Immediately after the problem became public, the minister of environment, in a standard political ploy, traveled to Mokpo to personally survey the situation.[27]

When asked about the cause of the crisis in Mokpo, the Ministry of Environment's director general for water quality declared that the cause of the fish kill was "not due to any discharge of industrial waste or other forms of pollution but a natural phenomenon" created by the washing of existing pollutants downstream by heavy rains after months of severe drought conditions. Unfortunately, the MoE officials had not consulted the official records of the Ministry of Construction, which show that the water quality in the Yongsan River is well below acceptable standards at all times of the year due to the inflow of untreated municipal, agricultural, and industrial effluents. The drought only made a bad situation worse, and the consistently low quality of Yongsan River water did not escape the notice of the City of Mokpo. In an aggressive and unilateral action revealing the intensity of environmental concerns, Mokpo officials filed a criminal suit against the mayor of Kwangju, whose city is the main upstream source of municipal and industrial waste in the river basin. They also filed suit against the head of the Cholla-namdo environmental office for allowing water drawn from the Yongsan basin to become contaminated.

The Ministry of Environment's weak explanation and the legal action brought by Mokpo gave leaders of the Democratic party's environmental study group a perfect opportunity to highlight their adherence to the cause of Korea's environment and public health and safety. They demanded and received a special hearing in the National Assembly, where they were joined by some majority DLP members in criticizing the ineffectiveness of government environmental policies and programs. Together the assembly members lashed out at the government's slow pace in responding to the environmental emergency. The assembly's Health and Social Welfare Committee grilled the minister of environment, Park Yun-Huen, and charged him and the Kim administration with wholesale negligence. Representative Lee Hae-Chan mocked the official explanation by suggesting that the "natural cause" of the problem in Mokpo was "the natural consequences of the long contamination of the Yongsan River." "How can the government officials discount the incident as being the natural result of a single fall of rain?" he asked. "Can precipitation of a mere 23 millimeters cause this kind of environmental disaster?"[28]

At the hearing the DP unveiled its own study of the problem. In it they contradicted the government's official version of the Mokpo incident that downplayed its long-term seriousness. The DP survey team found that the level of ammonia nitrogen was 13.74 milligrams per liter where the dead fish were found. This value was more than twenty times higher than the government's own river water-quality standard. The Yongsan "is a sewer not a river," Representative Kim Sang-Hyun asserted. "We tested the river water at the Mongtan Pumping Station and the result was shocking," he said. "We found 6.84 milligrams of ammonia nitrogen, 13 times the permissible levels." The fish kill was the result of worsening pollution levels in the Yongsan River, he concluded, and "the authorities have mocked the general public by not admitting the critical state of the pollution. . . ."[29]

The leadership of the Democratic party and almost every other party and politician in Korea have begun to learn the potency of the environment as a political issue. This recognition is, of course, a predictable response to widespread public concern that politicians hope can be transformed into votes at the polls. They may well be right. When questioned, students at Hanyang University and Seoul National University say firmly that they will be more likely to vote for candidates who support a clean environment than those who do not seem to hold pro-environmental views. This response is fairly typical of most Koreans today, especially those living in the nation's urban centers.[30] Seoul is, of course, the battleground for these nontraditional voters. In the capital city, where there are 7.5 million eligible voters, more than 60 percent are less than forty years of age. This large voter block has little consistent party loyalty, but polls repeatedly show they have a deep concern for the state of the natural environment.[31] This has given rise to hope that the June 1995 local elections, in whose campaigns environmental quality was widely discussed, would be the first step on a political road that will make the issue of paramount public importance in the 1996 National Assembly elections and the presidential election scheduled for 1997.

However, all political calculations must be tempered with a recognition that cynicism and suspicion remain the deepest held political traits in Korea. Many Koreans, if not a majority, express frustration and even hopelessness at the government's inability to address environmental problems. Korean political leaders, they remind themselves, have often failed to move beyond their own rhetorical flourishes and petty intraparty gamesmanship. The public's suspicions are well founded and can be illustrated by the legislative actions of the National Assembly shortly before it rose in anger over the water quality in the Yongsan River. The same lawmakers who so effectively used the issue for gaining public attention had just a month before adopted Korea's new land-use planning program as submitted by the Ministry of Construction. As noted earlier, this modification will make rural development much easier, further fragmenting green zones, weakening natural resource protection around the country, and inevitably leading to greater contamination of the nation's already polluted water supplies.

This kind of inconsistency is endemic, and it has created a clear gap between rhetoric and policy. Seeing this at every level of the government, the average Korean has long viewed domestic politics and political leadership as an elaborate stage play. To most it is an exercise of power; specific issues of public policy, programs, or ideology are of no real importance, and few think that they can actually have any input or substantive influence within the political process. As a result, personal and geographic loyalty remain the primary determinants of voter opinion. In the final analysis, many if not most Koreans still see themselves as part of an audience who will be entertained by politics but ultimately powerless to change the script. Politicians are generally dismissed as corrupt, and political activity is defined as being a waste of precious time. In turn, there is little in the ceaseless personal conflict of politicians that gives hope for the emergence of parties and politicians of consistency, principle, and reasoned policy.[32]

Even those who say that they steadfastly support democratization reflect the deep historic political cynicism of Korean domestic politics. Park Chang-Seok, economic editor of the English-language *Korea Times*, is typical. In a May 1994 editorial about the state of national politics, he noted that over the next two years there would be a "host of major political elections . . . which will surely be a waste of time and energies." Park continued, "A new opportunity awaits us. Politicians! Workers! Lose no time. Roll up your sleeves. Put your shoulders to the new economic juggernaut again."[33] Such comments from the established media are a sign that old political customs will not easily give way to full-fledged public participation.

Yet, despite this cynicism, there has been a perceptible change in Korea's national political culture. The habits of democracy may not be fully in place, but progress can be measured. In 1975 the highly respected Professor Kwon Sook-Pyo of Yonsei University published a short scientific paper detailing the level of industrial air pollution in the port city of Pusan.[34] After publication, Professor Kwon was interrogated by the Korean Central Intelligence Agency about his "negative" research, which was seen as a threat to the continued development of the national economy. Dr. Kwon was not alone. Many others concerned about the environment found themselves in similar situations when they openly discussed their concerns about the declining quality of the Korean environment in the late 1970s and 1980s.

Today democratization, liberalization, and a growing acceptance of pluralism have largely eliminated the direct and implied threats to physical, economic, and social well-being of those who speak out on behalf of the environment. No issue is more widely discussed in the increasingly independent Korean media, within government and political circles and the public at large. No one, except the most paranoid, feels seriously threatened by political repression or personal reprisals because of environmental views. What this means is that the environment as a political issue in Korea today is more than a social, economic, or scientific question. The issue itself has become an important measure of the progress of liberalization and political modernization in Korean political thinking and activism.

Notes

1. Cited in Chung Chin-Seung, "Origin and Development of Environmental Problems and Awareness," unpublished manuscript, 1994.

2. Korean Ministry of Environment, *National Report to the Secretary General of the United Nations to Be Reviewed by the Commission on Sustainable Development*. Seoul: December 1993.

3. This avalanche of media interest in the environment has not been met with universal support by environmental activists, some of whom have reacted to the commercialism of the newspapers' interests. Some leaders, especially those who are competitors of KFEM, worry that their own organizations will lose initiative just when the public mood is turning in support of environmental cleanup. See *Baedal Update*, Fall 1994.

4. "Beer Industry Shakes Off Staleness," *Korea Herald*, May 12, 1994. Oriental, Korea's largest beer maker, entered the "clean market" in March 1994 with OB Ice. Soon Jinro, the maker of Korea's soju liquor, will take its shot at the market in a joint venture with the American beer maker Coors.

5. This reflects a deep-seated traditional view of the role of government in Confucian societies. Government is paternalistic, and it and its officials have a duty to educate and enlighten the people about public and social responsibilities as well as to warn them about dangers.

6. N. Patrick Peritore, "Korean Environmental Attitudes: The New Environmental Paradigm and Traditional Values," University of Missouri–Columbia, unpublished manuscript, November 1992.

7. The observation is far from unique. Evidence of this can be found in reading three very different and useful books about Korea. See Roger L. Janelli, *Making Capitalism: The Social and Cultural Construction of a South Korean Conglomerate* (Stanford, CA: Stanford University Press, 1993). Janelli's work looks at the social landscape of Korean industrial society through the lens of the modern salaryman and his corporations. Paul S. Crane, *Korean Patterns* (Seoul: Royal Asiatic Society, 1978), offers a different approach to understanding the mannerisms, customs, and habits and the important complex social networks that these rest upon. One of the most endearing and enduring books dealing with Korea and the nature of Korean life, it is also one of the first to appear in Western literature. Produced as an "undiplomatic" memoir by the American foreign service officer William Franklin Sands a century ago, this account of Korean court life illustrates many of the cultural and emotional attributes that still lie just below the noisy surface of modern Korean society. See William Franklin Sands, *At the Court of Korea* (London: Century Hutchinson, 1987, reprint).

8. Walden Bello and Stephanie Rosenfeld, *Dragons in Distress: Asia's Miracle Economies in Crisis*. San Francisco: Institute of Food & Politics, 1990.

9. Martin Hart-Landsberg, *The Rush to Development: Economic Change and Political Struggle in South Korea*. New York: Monthly Review Press, 1993.

10. Shim Jae-Hoon, "Flawed Politics," *Far Eastern Economic Review*, May 26, 1994.

11. "South Korean Leader Struggles to Free Up a Regulated Economy," *Wall Street Journal*, March 30, 1994.

12. Shim Jae-Hoon, "Trial and Error," *Far Eastern Economic Review*, March 23, 1995.

13. Shim Jae-Hoon, "All Change: Political Reforms Set to Shake Up Campaigning," *Far Eastern Economic Review*, March 17, 1994.

14. Shim Jae-Hoon, "Package Deal: President Bids to Revamp His Reformist Image," *Far Eastern Economic Review*, March 10, 1994.

15. The challenge of reforming the legal system is daunting. It is estimated that 30 percent of all statutory law is antidemocratic at its foundation, and the legal profession itself is unskilled in the arts of democratic law. Moreover, the courts have been a traditional dumping ground for cronyism. Shim Jae-Hoon, "Judging the Judges: Legal System Begins Slow Process of Reform," *Far Eastern Economic Review*, December 9, 1993.

16. "Ex-Kukje Owner Again Fails in Bid to Reclaim 'Forcibly' Sold Shares," *Korea Times*, May 5, 1994.

17. Kim Ong-Ae, "Sales of Natural Water to Be Legalized Soon," *Korea Herald*, March 10, 1994.

18. "Marketing Bottled Water," *Korea Herald*, March 10, 1994.

19. Byun Eun-Mi, "Right-Wing Bodies Escalate Attack on Cho's Novel 'Tae-Baek-San-Maek,'" *Korea Herald*, May 11, 1994.

20. "Kim D.J. Still Backstage Force in Politics," *Korea Herald*, May 10, 1994.

21. The elections, held to elect 5,700 local officials throughout the country, produced a stunning reversal for the ruling Kim Young-Sam government. Kim's Democratic Liberal Party won control of only 5 of 15 metropolitan and provincial governments. It further suffered defeats in elections to select heads of dozens of smaller administrative districts, winning only 67 of 230 seats. In Seoul, the opposition Democratic Party's candidate for mayor, Cho Soon, handily defeated the DLP and independent candidates. Adding to the government's embarrassment was the loss of constituencies throughout the middle of the country to the splinter United Liberal Democrats headed by Kim Jong-Pil, who bolted from the DLP in February 1995. The elections have left Korean domestic politics in chaos and it is widely anticipated that a new constellation of political parties will now form to prepare for the 1996 national assembly elections. The strong presence of unbroken regional loyalties, however, is a measure of how far Korean democracy still has to travel.

22. Kim Chang-Young, "Second Generation of Tycoons Tighten Grips in Management," *Korea Times*, May 8, 1994.

23. This generational change is widely seen as an important force in Korean society. The new generation is breathing life into stale bureaucracies, individual businesses, and industrial organizations as well as social activist groups. This maturing generation is sincere, but most important its members come to their still-middle-management positions with significant international experience, excellent training, and, at least for the moment, a desire to implement change.

24. Critics have pointed out that as the president was using the rhetoric of environmental concern, his government was eliminating the need to incorporate testing for Chemical Oxygen Demand (COD) in water-quality measures.

25. This reformist drive on the part of the Kim Young-Sam administration has been uneven, and in the spring of 1994 it began noticeably to slow down, cata-

lyzed by two events. The first was the revelation that the president himself may have been involved in a significant electoral scandal (unproved as of this writing) involving Rev. Suh Eui-Hyun, immediate past chief of the Chogye sect, Korea's largest Buddhist group. This so-called Sangmundae Affair involved the funneling of $9.1 in illegal campaign contributions from businesses through the sect's officers and on to the Democratic Liberal party. See "Kim Faces Most Critical Moment Since Inauguration," *Korea Times*, April 26, 1994. See also "Assembly Probe Facing Rupture," *Korea Times*, May 14, 1994. Hard on the heels of this, the president fired his highly respected and liberal-leaning prime minister, Lee Hoi-Chang, for publicly challenging his views. Lee was apparently a victim of the Constitutions' ambiguous provisions on the role and responsibilities of the prime minister. He complained that he was not being consulted on matters of importance and went public with his complaint, confirming his reputation for honesty and inflexibility. "DLP, DP Exchange Political Tirades on Assembly Approval of New Premier," *Korea Times*, April 26, 1994.

26. "58 DP Lawmakers Step Up Anti-pollution Campaign," *Korea Herald*, April 13, 1994.

27. "Lawmakers Assail Gov't for Yongsan River Contamination," *Korea Times*, April 21, 1994.

28. Ibid.

29. Ibid.

30. The survey among the students involved fifty students filling out detailed questionnaires. Their views are fully consistent with anecdotal evidence provided by numerous personal conversations.

31. "Seoul Mayoral Candidates Look to Young Voters," *Korea Herald*, May 21, 1995.

32. In January 1995 Koreans witnessed political jousting in both major parties as new leaders prepared for local elections by ridding themselves of political ghosts and uneasy alliances. The process once again demonstrated that Korean politics is largely about personal power and influence, lacking even a polite veneer of ideological struggle. See Chon Shi-Yong, "Korean Politics Enmeshed in Regionalism, Factionalism," *Korea Herald,* January 18, 1995.

33. Park Chang-Seok, "Political Strife Drag on Booming Economy," *Korea Times*, May 3, 1994.

34. Kwon Sook-Pyo, "Health Effects of Industrial Exhaust in Urban Areas," College of Medicine, Yonsei University, Seoul, Korea, 1975.

5

Nongovernment Organizations: Environmentalism and Civic Democracy

The environment has become an important focal point for democratic political activism in Korea. Organized political parties are learning how to use the issue, and so are the leaders of nongovernment organizations (NGOs). Many environmentalist members of these NGOs are rapidly transforming themselves from antigovernment dissidents into democratic organizers for a clean and healthy environment. The amount of specific support NGOs enjoy in society is uncertain, but through environmentalism, they are plowing the fields of the middle class and learning the skills of democracy. As a result they are maturing as influential, if still relatively powerless, players in Korea's efforts to come to terms with the environmental price of its modern industrial prosperity.

The Emergence of Popular Environmental Movements

The first signs of an environmental or green movement appeared in Korea in the early 1970s when a handful of university professors and conservationists began to worry openly about the declining quality of the natural environment. Dissent, though, was dangerous, and the early environmentalists restricted their activities to the publication of research, professional conferences, and small-scale publicity campaigns aimed at cleaning up trash in national parks. Predictably, this concern was seen by the government as counter to industrial development and as a potential vehicle for protest against the military dictators who occupied the Blue House. Curiously, during this early period, social protest movement leaders largely ignored the potential harm of industrial pollution and urbanization. To be sure, they saw health and safety problems in the newly created industrial zones near Masan and Ulsan, but these seemed small and distant when measured against the weakness of the economy and grinding poverty. For mainstream dissidents and social campaigners, questions such as political liberty, labor rights, and social and economic equity were far more important than smoke in the atmosphere and brown streams of water in Korean rivers.

By the early 1980s, environmental concerns began to take shape as the side effects of industrial pollution and urban development became more evident. In 1982, Korea's first important environmental group was formed by the Korean Anti-Pollution Research Institute, a group of scholars and progressive church-based social activists. Through the institute, they printed papers and released information to the public about potential health hazards for people living and working near the rapidly expanding industrial complexes of Ulsan and Onsan. Special attention was paid to chemical and heavy-metal poisoning, but with the press tightly controlled by the military government, concern about the environment and information on health hazards were not widely known or appreciated among the public.[1] In 1986, Korean Anti-Pollution Movement Association (KAPMA) activists initiated Korea's first large-scale public environmental public relations campaign to publicize the Onsan disease. This environmental disease was discovered in the booming southeastern industrial city of Onsan, where tons of chemical wastes were dumped annually into local waters, which in turn were producing birth defects and other illnesses.

A unique and early role in raising environmental consciousness in public was played by the YMCA and the Catholic church. Those institutions had long been known as traditional rallying points for "careful" social protest. Under the guise of education and Christian fellowship, the leadership of the YMCA and the church decided to assist in educating the Korean public about the environmental consequences of the government's single-minded development strategy. Both organizations used their standing—international and religious—to promote community-based activities such as recycling drives and neighborhood cleanup efforts and to avoid the ire of the authoritarian government.[2]

Among the first attempts to mobilize broad public sentiment was a 1987 nationwide campaign led by the YMCA to reduce the use of phosphorous detergents. The YMCA was joined in its efforts by many other nongovernment organizations, including housewives' organizations and groups who found in environmental issues an outlet for their social concerns. In undertaking this kind of action, though, they were walking the fine line between protest and public education. The leadership of the YMCA, the Catholic church, and others continually ran the risk of government displeasure in a time when arrests and jailing, even torture, were common treatment for opponents of the military regime.[3]

Many mainline social activists viewed the early stirrings of the environmental movement with suspicion and even disdain. For those working to resist the authoritarian government, environmentalism was a diversionary issue that looked too much like the government's own citizen participation programs that sponsored and funded politically "safe" NGOs.[4] Such sanctioned NGOs were registered with the government and engaged in activities ranging from cleaning up litter in parks and streets to promoting environmental coordination between industries and environmental experts. Today many of those groups are still supported by the government. There are currently fifty-eight government NGOs. Seventeen of these are pollution control committees in industrial zones, and twenty-nine are civic organizations with environmental programs such as neighborhood recycling or education. Twelve are general social activity clubs that engage in some level of environmental activism.[5]

To those educated and committed to the ways of street protest and class warfare, the early environmental citizens' groups were too mild mannered and too similar to the official government-sponsored social action groups to be taken seriously. They were generally dismissed as just another expression of middle-class and intellectual interests. The environment was important, they conceded, but in the end, it was a diversion from what more progressive and radical political elements understood as the deeper and far more critical social and political problems of Korean life. Focused on Korean events and isolated by the government from gaining broader experience in the world, the social activist community had no real chance to learn from the powerful political and social impact of contemporary environmentalism in Europe and the United States. Had they been more connected to the outside world, they would have quickly grasped the true potential for broad social protest in mobilization around green issues.

By the spring of 1987, thousands of Koreans were taking to the streets daily to protest the Chun Doo-Whan government's policies. The demonstrations were aimed at the perceived continuation of Chun's repressive policies by his hand-picked successor and military academy classmate, General Roh Tae-Woo. Although the street protests were led by student and social radical groups, these were soon joined by the middle class, who demanded increased political and economic liberalization and an end to rampant corruption. Faced with rising violence and street protest, General Roh, who demonstrated an unexpected degree of political courage and independence by breaking with Chun, announced that he would submit himself to the voters in a direct presidential election. This announcement quelled the protests and began Korea's five-year march toward greater democratization. In the election that followed, Roh received a plurality of 36.6 percent of the votes, while the opposition was divided between the largely indistinguishable political camps of Kim Dae-Young and Kim Young-Sam.[6]

Popular enthusiasm for environmental causes and aggressive environmental activism were unleashed by the events of 1987. In that year, the first movement-style, nongovernment-sponsored environmental organization was born: the Anti-Pollution Movement Association, led by former dissident Choi Yul. Choi's organization assisted individual communities in protesting against local pollution problems. At the same time, the Anti-Pollution Movement Association turned its attention to resisting Korea's headlong rush toward nuclear energy. In doing so, it built upon the tactics and strategies of other social campaigners. The movement began to use public protest and the newly liberalized media to highlight environmental problems and the potential consequences of embracing nuclear power without reservation.

Between 1988 and 1991 there were numerous environmental protests and actions in Korea, but they tended to be localized and focused on specific actions or plans of the government or industry. However, they did serve to rally support for environmental concern and highlighted its importance for all of Korea. One of the major flash points for public protest and NGO activity has been the surge in golf course development. Among the Korean professional middle class, playing golf became a status symbol in the late 1980s (accompanied by the desire to own a four-bedroom condominium and a Hyundai Sonata and to tour abroad). The result was the largely uninhibited gobbling up of agricultural land for conversion to golf courses, the creation of which can contaminate water resources due to the use of high-nitrogen fertilizers. Protests against golf course construction also provided a handy way of knocking the establishment, whose expensive leisure activities were portrayed as an affront to the dignity of hard-working poorer Koreans.

One of the first golf course protests was in Kyungbuk Province in the country's southeast.[7] In August 1988, more than 70 percent of the residents of one area there signed and submitted a petition to President Roh Tae-Woo requesting suspension of the planned golf course. Protest organizers also contacted all political parties, local authorities, and every national newspaper in an effort to attract national attention to their complaints. The appeal fell on deaf ears, so when construction began in spring 1990, residents organized protests on the site and refused to send their children to school. In November, tents were erected and over five hundred people participated in a four-month camp-in campaign. This resulted in several clashes between the camping protesters and so-called unidentified people that resulted in numerous injuries. By February, people from the rest of the province joined the protesters in a province-wide coalition to oppose further golf course development in the region. By 1992, similar protests were found at thirty other golf course construction sites around the nation.

The mobilization of public opinion against golf course construction provided important symbolic imagery for Korea's environmental activists. It was, however, only one aspect of rising public environmental protest. Like other countries with ambitious nuclear power generation programs, Korea has had difficulty in locating a long-term waste repository for spent fuel and other waste nuclear materials. In 1988 the national government proposed to build a long-term storage site on Korea's southeast coast. Three sites were selected for consideration: Uljin, Youngil, and Youngduk. When the sites were announced to the public, antinuclear opponents organized protests and blockaded major highways. After months of confrontational protests, the government was forced to abandon its efforts to identify and open a permanent nuclear storage site.

In 1990, antinuclear activists became aware that the government had secretly identified remote Anmyundo Island off Korea's west coast as a proposed site for a permanent nuclear waste disposal site. The islanders, assisted by a coalition of fifteen environmental groups, launched protests against the unannounced project. Parents refused to send children to school, and police and government buildings were violently

attacked. Several buildings were set afire, and many people were injured during the protests. The government never admitted that it had
chosen the island as the nuclear site, but the minister of science and
technology, Dr. Chung Kun-Mo, resigned as a result of the public's
negative reaction to the unannounced site.[8]

In May 1994 the cycle repeated itself once again when the Korean
government announced that it was considering a new long-term storage site near the town of Uljin in Kyongsannam-do. No public hearings had been held, and a week of public protests ensued. Over a
period of four days, ten thousand demonstrators blockaded roads,
burned tires, and threw fire bombs at the five thousand riot police who
were called in to disperse the crowds.[9] The Ministry of Science and
Technology was forced to abandon its plan, and again the process of
establishing a permanent disposal site for nuclear wastes in Korea
stalled in the face of public displeasure.[10]

In late 1994 the internationally respected Dr. Chung Kun-Mo was
again appointed minister of science and technology. Among Dr.
Chung's primary tasks was to identify and develop a long-term nuclear
waste storage facility, a mandate that had cost him his earlier appoint-
ment as minister. In December 1994 Chung announced that his ministry had found a new site for the nation's estimated 2,250 tons of
high-level nuclear wastes.[11] This time a small Kulop island about fifty
miles off the west coast, near the port city of Inchon, was selected. The
island has only ten residents, who all agreed to accept financial compensation from the government for the loss of their lands. Almost
immediately, environmentalists raised a series of objections and began
to organize the island's people and those of neighboring Dukjock Island.[12] They pointed out that the Kulop island does not currently have
electrical power, fresh water, or developed port facilities. Questions
have also been raised about the geologic suitability for the storage of
radioactive wastes, although the government has said that any problems can be overcome with adequate technology and safeguards. It is
unclear whether the government will be successful this time in quelling
the protests of antinuclear activists.[13] Like so many other things in
Korea, the ability to manage, shape, and lead democratizing public
opinion is as yet an unsophisticated public art among political leaders.
It is small consolation that, where nuclear energy is concerned,
Korea's politicians and technocrats are in the company of nearly every
other industrial power.

In another environmental dispute, there have been long and loud protests against the government's construction of a new international airport on Youngjong Island, fifty kilometers west of Seoul. The decision to build the airport was made in the late 1980s based on the government's hope to make Korea the primary gateway hub airport in Northeast Asia, in direct competition to Japanese plans. On recovered land near Inchon, the government started work on the 10 trillion won ($12.5 billion) investment in 1992. The first phase of construction includes runways and a new passenger terminal. It was originally scheduled to open in 1998, but by late 1994 government planners had slipped the opening to the last day of 1999.[14]

However, the new Youngjong airport has become an important focus for environmentalists as a symbol of everything they see wrong with development planning. It is, they argue, an unnecessary environmental intrusion marked by questionable need, flawed economic thinking, and widespread corruption. The comprehensive national economic plan of 1980 made no mention of either the need or any evaluation of the need for the project. The idea simply surfaced in 1989 and was rapidly approved within one year by the government after the minister of transportation noted the urgency for such a facility to President Roh Tae-Woo. This rapid decision was unusual for the Korean bureaucracy, which is usually painfully deliberate in every aspect of economic planning. The government pointed out that Korea had to act, or it would find itself bypassed by regional competitors.[15]

As the plans for the airport were made public, fifteen NGOs established the Joint Council of NGOs to Save Youngjong Island. The group has issued a twenty-four-point paper outlining its complaints against the project.[16] In it they charge that the airport is unnecessary, given the realities of modern air travel, and that a Korean hub is unlikely to be geographically attractive to long-distance passenger and cargo aircraft. They also claim that the planned size of the airport (twice the size of Chicago's O'Hare Field) is too large for any conceivable need. The reason for this size, the environmentalists insist, is that the project is a honey pot of corruption and sweetheart deals for politicians, land owners, and Korea's powerful construction industry, which needs larger and larger projects to maintain its economic balance. To underscore this, opponents have released names of well-connected land owners in the region who will gain from the inevitable escalation of land values. This, they argue, points to a disturbing pattern of insider real-estate speculation. They further note that sites other than Youngjong were never seriously considered for the airport even though there are several that appear to have lower development costs and are closer to existing transportation networks leading to Seoul.

Aside from the economic and procedural complaints, environmental worries about the new airport are widespread. Those opposing construction of the airport point out that Youngjong Island and its neighbors in the giant Inchon estuary are a central feature of east Asia's waterfowl north-south migration corridor. Some 200,000 migratory birds visit the island each spring. This makes the site of the airport both disruptive to the birds and potentially dangerous to the airplanes that will eventually use the facility. The environmental coalition against the airport also points out that by destroying several thousand acres of wetlands, the project will only add to the problems of the already troubled, semi-enclosed Yellow Sea (known commonly as the West Sea in Korea). Finally, environmentalists have argued that when completed, the facility will use massive quantities of fresh water, thus contributing to the continued urbanization and pollution of the Seoul-Inchon corridor.

The combined forces of the NGOs concerned with the Youngjong airport development have been largely ineffective in stopping or slowing the project. The site is accessible today only by ferry, and this has made it difficult to organize public protests. When the project was dedicated by President Kim Young-Sam in 1993, environmental protesters were met by police, who blocked access to the island's ferry, detained the protesters, and dropped them off, without harm, in the remote countryside. These and other complaints against the project have not caught the public's imagination, many of whom see it as another powerful symbol of Korea's growing global stature as a newly industrialized nation.

Youngjong airport is only one of many environmental causes that have been given public exposure since liberalization began in 1987. Many of these have focused on environmental projects themselves, such as the siting of solid-waste landfills and garbage incinerators. Others have sought to rally public opinion against land reclamation, dam building, and the establishment of new industrial zones. As a result, Korea is rapidly becoming paralyzed by the NIMBY syndrome. By 1993, thirty-two of thirty-four national industrial-waste disposal and landfill projects had been delayed by public protest and would not be completed by the 1995 timetable established by the government.[17]

The NIMBY syndrome has made government planners wary of launching new development projects, and while many support public involvement, few are comfortable with the frustration inherent in public participation. Public protest remains largely a locally based phenomenon. Whether confronting the building of a golf course, an international airport, or a new dam, Korean environmental activism has remained highly dependent on specific local conditions to generate environmental awareness, and often that does not extend beyond affected communities. This is a severe limitation, made worse by the pursuit of narrow financial interests by those who are most immediately affected. For many local people, the monetary compensation for lost land or environmental harm often impedes the pursuit of environmental preservation. As a result, activists have repeatedly found that their local base of support melts away once developers or government representatives open their wallets.

In the final evaluation, the most significant limitations on increased popular participation in public decisions are the structures and habits of contemporary Korean government. In early June 1994, a Seoul appellate court declared that the Ministry of Construction could proceed with the construction of a 57.1-kilometer highway in Kyunggi-do. A citizens' group had asked the court to reroute the path of the highway because it "threatened the natural environment" of the largely rural city of Uiwang, which lies between the existing main expressway and one of Seoul's new satellite cities, Ilsan. In its ruling the court wrote, "The project is designed to improve the social infrastructure of the nation and the residents have no right to demand changes for selfish purposes." The ruling went on to note that even if the residents of the town work through their city council to propose changes to the master road plan, their suggestions are a "matter of reference and do not represent guidelines that must be adopted."[18] The ruling was consistent with current Korean law, but it is hardly in keeping with the trend toward greater democratization, liberalization, and public involvement. Thus it stands as a stark reminder of the hierarchical nature of Korean civil society and its governing institutions, even as Koreans search for new social and political balance points. Until more orderly and responsive vehicles for public participation are found, government resistance and clumsiness will continue to produce higher levels of popular anxiety, cynicism, and protest over environmental decay.

The Naktong Crisis and the Nationalization of Protest

In March 1991, the largely local and regional focus of environmentalists was suddenly transformed into a more widespread national concern when the Doosan Chemical Company accidentally spilled phenol into the Kumee River, a principal tributary of the Naktong. The solvent spill came from a circuit board manufacturing facility that released thirty tons of phenol through pipes directly into the river. The leak occurred because the firm's pollution abatement facilities were out of order, and plant managers were storing waste phenol in the tanks. When Doosan discovered the spill, it failed to report the presence of the phenol in the river water, and soon the tap water in the city of Taegu was discovered to have a strange chemical-like taste. The city, lacking trained staff, simply added extra chlorine to the city's drinking water supply to address the mysterious problem. The result was an even stronger unpleasant chemical odor that permeated every home tied to the municipal water system.

Authorities immediately suspended the operation of all drinking water plants taking water from the Naktong. They did not act quickly enough, however; many residents became ill, and several pregnant women who feared chemical poisoning underwent abortions. A number of downstream food processors were affected and were forced to discard products that could have been contaminated by the phenol-chlorine mix. Eventually, Doosan was discovered to have caused the problem, and charges were made in the press (later proved wrong and retracted) that the spill had been intentional. Environmental groups around the country sprang into action and loud public protest. Doosan, which besides circuit boards makes the popular OB Beer and is the Korean licensee for Kodak film, Kentucky Fried Chicken, and Coca Cola, found its products the object of a national boycott. OB Beer, Korea's best-selling brand, was poured into the streets of Seoul in front of Doosan's corporate headquarters before a large audience of reporters and television cameras.

Environmental groups also focused their attention on the government. The Ministry of Environment was accused of not doing enough to prevent the phenol spill, and its officials were accused of taking bribes from Doosan. Largely in response to public opinion, the public prosecutor's office arrested three officials of the Taegu Regional Office of the Ministry of Environment. The minister of environment, appointed just a few months earlier, took tough administrative action against Doosan. The offending factory was ordered closed for thirty days, at that time the most substantial penalty for environmental neglect ever levied in Korea.

However, the closure order fell victim to the larger Korean priority: economic growth. With the Doosan plant shut down, companies such as Samsung and Goldstar found they were threatened with a shortage of essential Korean-produced circuit boards for their products. After a short examination of national needs and priorities, the Ministry of Trade and Industry "requested" an administrative review of MoE's actions against Doosan. A week later the MoE Administrative Review Committee lifted the order, and the company began operation once again. But the story did not end there.

Shortly after Doosan returned to production, phenol was once again spilled into the Kumee River. This time, the spill was quickly reported, and the water plants downstream were closed while the phenol was diluted to safe levels. The government was again faced with national environmental protests, and the minister of environment and his vice minister were fired for their handling of the situation, which was given front-page play in all Korean newspaper, TV, and radio news headlines. Doosan was eventually fined for negligence, and a handful of women in the affected region were awarded damages for miscarriages. The chairman of Doosan made repeated public apologies and suffered the not-inconsequential burdens of public social embarrassment.

With the phenol spills in the Naktong basin, environmental consciousness was propelled to a new level in Korea. Koreans could no longer afford the convenience of seeing the environment as an issue for rich countries. Something was terribly wrong with their nation's environment and the way it was being managed, and the consequences were widely seen as being dangerous to health and welfare. For political activists the contamination of the Naktong River provided ample opportunities to tweak the noses of the national government, its bureaucracy, and the corporate establishment. At the same time, the dissident community finally understood the power of the environment to become a catalyst for broader social and economic goals.

The NGO Movement and Its Progress

If the water quality of the Naktong River served as the first national environmental wake-up call, the United Nations Conference on Environment and Development made Koreans aware that environmental issues were no longer simply local issues. Before UNCED, most Korean policy makers, government officials, and, in all probability, the public viewed international environmental concern as a luxury for rich countries. In 1985, when the United Nations sponsored an international conference in Vienna on the state of the ozone layer, Korea did not send a delegation. In a sense, participation was a luxury that Korea could not afford. As the rest of the world was coming to the conclusion that CFCs should be banned, Korea was increasing both domestic production and consumption of the chemical coolant.

When the Montreal Conference adopted the Montreal Protocol banning CFCs in 1987, Korea was caught unprepared.[19] The government's initial response was to delay signing due to fears about the economic impact the Protocol would have on Korea. Just one day before international sanctions were to go into effect, Korea became a signatory to the document. This pattern has repeated itself several times over since Montreal, most recently in Korea's last minute endorsement of the treaty banning international trade in endangered species.[20] In practical terms, Korea's late decisions to enter into international environmental agreements have probably unnecessarily caused economic dislocation, because Korean firms have often been forced to comply with little warning.

Given the level of Korea's international experience in environmental matters, it is no surprise that the country and its leaders were not fully prepared for the worldwide and domestic impact of the 1992 UNCED meeting in Rio de Janeiro. The Korean government approached the Rio conference with caution. It was initially concerned about the impact of the two principal treaties that were to be acted upon at the conference, the conventions on global change and biodiversity. Both, but especially the first, were understood as having the potential to directly threaten continued economic expansion in Korea.[21]

Still, in Rio, the Korean public saw for the first time the enormous power of international concern about the environment, and national domestic environmental affairs have not been the same since. The Rio conference concerned Korea's economic planners, but at the same time it served to embolden its environmentalists, who discovered that they were not as isolated as they had once thought, and that a significant portion of world opinion could be mustered in support of their efforts.[22] Everywhere in Korea, activists adopted the slogans of environmentally sustainable development and breathed life into a young environmental movement.[23]

In 1987 independent environmental NGOs were all but unknown in Korea. Those that did exist were government-sponsored and financed citizens' groups that were completely subservient to the government and civil bureaucracy. In 1995 there are more than three hundred private NGO organizations espousing environmental messages around the country. These NGOs are pursuing goals ranging from the shutdown of the nuclear industry to the development of community gardening, food cooperatives, and recycling efforts.[24]

The most extensive work detailing the nature of NGOs has been done by Dr. Kim ·Jong-Soon of Hon Kuk University.[25] In a 1993 survey of the independent Korean NGO community Dr. Kim found that more than two-thirds of the NGOs are located in Seoul, and about 70 percent are organized solely for environmental purposes. The rest have added environmental goals to more long-standing purposes such as demands for greater political liberty, women's rights, and social and economic justice.

More than half of the independent NGOs have been created since 1989, with 57.6 percent established between 1989 and 1993. Forty-five percent claim that they give first priority to publicizing serious environmental problems and seek to induce public participation in protests against the causes of pollution. They do so largely through public lectures, displays, protests, educational publications, and exposure of government and industrial neglect. A handful of NGOs have programs to monitor environmental conditions such as water and air pollution and to develop alternative proposals to government or industrial programs or plans. The majority of Korean NGOs, 51.3 percent, have fewer than two hundred members, but recruitment appears to be increasingly easy for the more aggressive organizations.

Korean NGOs, like others around the world, are perpetually short of money. Most remain dependent on donations, dues paid by those committed to environmental improvement, and the sale of products such as canvas tote bags, shirts, lapel pins, and publications. However, almost half of the NGO members fail to pay dues at all, and according to Dr. Kim's survey only 32.8 percent count themselves as activists. Financial assistance from the government and private industry is rare. Reflecting these financial limitations is the lack of professional staff to support NGO activities. Although 53.5 percent of NGOs manage to employ 1–3 full-time staff members, another 26 percent have no staff at all. As a result, it is not surprising to find that, as in NGOs of other countries, the level of professionalism and activism can range from highly efficient to haphazard.

As the environmental NGO movement has grown since 1987, it has become largely dominated by middle-class activists and leaders. Many of these are former radicals, who attended Korea's most prestigious schools and have years of experience in social justice, antinuclear, and democracy movements. They are almost all in their thirties and forties and can be found in government ministries, business, universities, and the professions. They are well educated and eloquent in their understanding of the environmental complexities that face Korea. The environmental movement has also attracted an unusually large number of female activists, although the number of students is surprisingly small.

While it is hard to characterize the new NGOs, they do share some common attributes. Most attempt to transcend class boundaries and define themselves as speaking from and to the entire national audience, from working-class laborers to wealthy housewives in Seoul's posh hillside neighborhoods. While many of the NGO activists are nonsectarian and secular, others are tied to religious groups and include clergy and lay activists from the Catholic church and Protestant evangelical organizations. The NGOs generally advocate policies that are reformist in nature and supportive of wider and deeper democratic change. These, they argue, will lead to a Korean-style social democracy that will also sow the seeds of respect for the natural environment. Although a few suggest a cessation of industrialization, the vast majority are comfortable with the inherent tensions between capitalism and environmentalism, and they see their roles as peaceful activists for greater attention to the environmental consequences of modern industrialized life.[26]

A common approach of many NGOs is to play off the Hansallim movement, which has wide emotional support throughout Korean society. Hansallim, which translates loosely as a combination of "great life," "great enlivenment," and "living together," is actually less a movement than an emotional expression of a Korean sense of communal shared values. Its advocates often stress the importance of national cultural and historic social cohesion. They place emphasis on what they see as the universal value of human life and harmony with the natural environment, and the importance of establishing a personal relationship with nature and its products. One expression of this is the joint campaign by the National Federation of Agricultural Cooperatives and the YMCA, which seeks to persuade people to eat only locally grown grains, fruits, and vegetables. This kind of activity has strong roots in the Hansallim belief that the body and the environment cannot be separated. Therefore, food grown close to home and on native soil is thought to be inherently healthier than food raised provinces or continents away.

Another illustration of the power of the Hansallim tradition is the reemergence of protest art in Korea. *Minjung,* or people's art, has long been part of the dissident movement. It is romantic and aimed directly at the emotions. In recent years, the themes of minjung practitioners have often highlighted environmental destruction in the cities and especially in the once tranquil countryside.[27]

The kind of sentimentality expressed in the Hansallim movement is not unique to Korean environmentalists. Similar expressions can be found in grassroots environmentalism all over the world. But in Korea it is perhaps more deeply felt than elsewhere because Hansallim is in part a product of centuries of foreign domination and the deep-seated urge to express national pride and independence. It is the same emotion that moves Koreans to buy only Korean goods and services, thus angering outsiders who see such actions as expressions of protectionist policy rather than cultural solidarity. At the same time, Hansallim carries with it a good deal of anti-Western opinion, especially anti-Americanism, which provides a ready explanation for all of Korea's industrial and environmental problems.

Hansallim is important in shaping individual thinking, but it is not capable of sustaining a modern environmental movement in Korea. It lacks the kind of rationalism and consistent scientific rigor necessary to counter the power of advancing industrialization and the seductions of prosperity and modernization. Given this, NGOs that are dependent on this emotional ideology are unlikely to play a strong and sustained role in addressing complex environmental problems. Similarly, other external and internal forces are at work limiting the growth of Korean NGOs. Externally, order and central authority in Korean life play too large a role in motivating public opinion to be overcome in such a short time by coat-and-tie activists and their allies in the streets, no matter how earnestly they present their cases for improving the environment. Korea, despite its seeming prosperity, is still only a half-developed country. The urge to strengthen the economy at all costs is a powerful and primary force working against green advocates. At the same time, after nearly five decades of security laws and drumbeat anticommunism, there is deep public suspicion of anyone who seems to oppose government policy and of community activists, environmental or otherwise, who appear too politically ambitious.

The NGO community can do little in the short run to eliminate the residue of forty years of military dictatorship and five thousand years of political and cultural history. However, what success it does achieve will depend on its ability to contend with the sweeping currents of political and social modernization and continued democratization. The challenge for all activists is to determine what effective social activism means for them and their ambitions for Korean society in an age of rapid but uneven political liberalization and democratization.

In the past, conspiracy and street actions ruled the day, but in the future, electoral activity, voter education, and legislative maneuvering may be the most important tools in fostering change. Already, many NGOs have mastered the art of the press release and understand how to use the media to get their point across to the public and the government.[28] Others have begun to develop political strategies and alliances that they hope will yield dividends in elections to come. Still, since the Korean democratic system and its institutions are evolving, many do not yet have a full appreciation of the sophistication they will need to help shape public opinion, and maybe more important, to move citizens to vote and act "green."

There also remains a strong rejectionist sentiment among some elements of the Korean NGO community. These elements hold fast to the tradition of suspicion and estrangement from the institutions of government. They resist all suggestions that fundamental change has occurred. In many cases, this tempers the cooperative position of the NGOs, but given Korea's history of authoritarianism and military rule, such caution seems warranted to many. In the extreme, this body of opinion rejects all accommodation with the government, though such hard-line views are increasingly difficult to find in the NGO environmental movements. Nonetheless, issues of accommodation and cooperation with the establishment will plague and perhaps severely restrict the development of independent NGOs well into the future.

A recent example of this sensitive subject surfaced in April 1994. The progressive *Hangyore* newspaper's chief environmental correspondent, Shin Dong-Ho, published a story about leading environmental activist groups who accept monetary contributions from industry as well as money for advertisements in magazines and newsletters published for group members. Shin's article set off a firestorm of recriminations and finger pointing. All of this embarrassed the tainted NGO organizations and caused internal and external debate over the degree to which they and their leaders were selling out. NGO leaders defended their acceptance of limited financial support from industry by saying that their organizations were not influenced by the money. Furthermore, they offered the ideological purists a choice of continued activity or fiscal starvation in a country with no real history of charitable giving for social and political causes.

It is apparent that this kind of ideological discussion will continue to intermittently plague the highly politicized Korean NGO movement, which still has some distance to go before it comes to terms with its well-placed suspicion of those in authority. Equally, the internal conflicts within the NGO movement, which often produce backbiting and bickering among separate groups, remain a hallmark of these organizations and severely limit their effectiveness. Still, many Korean NGOs today do have the talent to transform themselves into more effective advocates for the environment. This does not mean that Korea will develop a green political party, although Korean environmental activists and political leaders are increasingly working together to achieve joint political goals.

In April 1994 more than forty NGOs joined to create the Korean Environmental Forum to facilitate greater political cooperation on national environmental issues and to overcome their own fragmentation. While this is not the first step toward a green political party, it is an indication that the NGOs are emerging as important players in domestic affairs. Their organizations may not be large, but they are the only counterweight to the institutions of government and industry in newly democratized Korean society. They do not have anything approaching political power, but they are gaining political influence. The final form of their influence has yet to be seen, but for the moment it seems likely that NGO participation will be characterized by a unique Korean mix of cooperation and independent opposition.

Signs of this are already emerging. Throughout the winter and spring of 1994, numerous NGO leaders were invited to the Blue House to discuss the state of the environment with President Kim Young-

Sam. The leaders of the major NGOs have also openly moved to support the Ministry of Environment in its efforts to improve environmental administration, control, and management. In response to this cooperation, the ministry has established a special advisory council of NGOs chaired by the chair of Korea's YMCA, Kang Moon-Kyu. It is composed of a broad cross section of environmental activists and has begun to provide insight and recommendations directly to the minister. Naturally, there is concern that this council is little more than an attempt to co-opt and seduce the NGO leaders. And this kind of cooperation does have the potential to divide NGO organizations in future. At the moment, though, the NGO leadership is entering the relationship with cautious hope that they can effect change through formal participation and the exercise of political influence.

Many in the Korean NGO movement understand that to achieve real influence they will have to gain more international experience. They rightly point out that their lack of exposure is not surprising given the severe censorship and external travel restrictions that most Koreans lived under until very recently. As a result, many within the NGO leadership and certainly most of the followers have little knowledge about the outside world or the activities of international environmental movements.

The relative isolation of Korea and its environmental advocacy groups has produced some interesting anomalies. An illustration of this can be found in the discussion of recent international trade issues in Korea. Some elements of the international green community have objected to free trade because of environmental concerns and have demanded various restrictions on third world "brown products" in order to force environmental responsibility. Others have seen the potential for forcing greater global environmental responsibility through economic agreement. In contrast, the vast majority of NGO activists in Korea (green and otherwise) have opposed new international trade rules (General Agreement on Tariffs and Trade, or GATT) for purely nationalist reasons. In Korea, activists have resisted what they see as imperialistic interference by the developed countries in the West.[29]

Like many representatives of developing countries, Korean NGOs base their objections on fears that strict trade rules will unfairly damage continued Korean industrial expansion and prosperity. This, they charge, is an unfair burden that will maintain the economic and political dominance of the northern industrialized nations over the poorer southern nations of the globe. Korean environmental groups in full agreement with this view joined in the protests over the GATT agreements in the winter and early spring of 1994.[30]

Many Korean environmental groups objected to the new world trading rules because in their view, nations have the right to protect their agricultural markets for ecological, social, cultural, and health reasons. Applying this logic, environmental activists argue that if Korean farmers are driven from the fields by the importation of cheap foreign food, Koreans will inevitably be forced to adopt a less healthy diet contaminated by high levels of foreign petrochemical-based fertilizers, pesticides, and fungicides. Beyond the complaints about a decline in the quality of food, Korean environmentalists have claimed that open agricultural markets will only accelerate Korea's environmental problems. One important leader argued that traditional rice paddy cultivation is, in effect, a giant historic civil engineering project. It protects Korean cities from flooding due to the large-scale diversion and storage of water, and cools the countryside during the hot summer months (without air conditioners, thus saving energy); the rice plants themselves absorb tons of carbon dioxide from Korean air annually.[31]

The emotional content of such arguments is undeniable, and it has had a tremendous impact on Koreans of all classes. Of course, the very subsidies that have protected Korean farmers have led to excessive use of chemicals, which now severely pollute water and soil and leave high chemical residues on Korean-grown fruits, vegetables, and grains. Moreover, the subsidization of the domestic beef industry, which Koreans widely believe produces the best beef in the world, has made runoff from cattle farms and other animal husbandry activities a leading source of pollution in every river in Korea. Finally, it is clear that Korean agriculture has long been in decline. Its real enemy is the rapid depopulation and unimpeded development of the rural countryside that has been going on for nearly thirty years.[32]

These and other environmental consequences and the Korean policy decisions that have led to them are widely discussed among Korean environmentalists. However, in the noisy trade protests of December 1993 and January 1994, they were never thoughtfully linked. The blame was placed on the outside world rather than domestic Korean actions. This represents an unworldly parochialism that betrays the lack of significant international connections or experience in the Korean environmental community.

However, Korean NGO leaders openly acknowledge the inexperi-
ence of their young movements and are working to address the problem. Recently, leaders from the NGO movement have opened
communications with their counterparts in the United States, Europe,
and Asia. They are increasingly traveling to international conferences
and inviting outsiders to come to Korea to share their insights. International organizations such as the Asia Foundation have been active in
assisting in that process.[33] The foundation has provided funds for international conferences in Korea and has worked to identify key NGO
leaders and give them opportunities to gain overseas experience. For
the Asia Foundation, this has been an investment in democracy. In
May 1994 a group of eighteen NGO activists and two representatives
from the Ministry of Environment toured Europe and the United States
to learn about their counterparts. For the Korean NGO leaders it was
an opportunity to learn how to manipulate the tools of democracy with
greater efficiency and more effect. It will also likely accelerate the
process of "professionalization." Through such contacts with the wider
world, Korean NGO leaders and their organizations will learn new
strategic concepts that will bring them more into line with the forces of
worldwide environmentalism.

There are hundreds of environmental NGOs today in Korea; however, only three have achieved any real size or prominence. These
generally cooperate with each other, but at times there has been friction as they struggle for members, public attention, and financial support. The three, Hwan-Kyung Un-dong Yeon-Hap (Korea Federation
of Environmental Movements, or KFEM), Baedal Noksaek Yeonhap,
(Green Korea), and Kyungje Jeongeu Silcheon Siminyeonhap (Citizens Coalition for Economic Justice, or CCEJ), represent the major
forces in Korean independent environmentalism. None is a static organization—all are in a constant state of ideological and organizational
ferment (to say nothing of financial emergency). However, they represent the primary strands of NGO environmental activity in Korea.

The Korea Federation of Environmental Movements

The Korea Federation of Environmental Movements (KFEM) is Korea's
oldest and largest environmental NGO. Its roots lie in the Anti-Pollution
Movement Association, Korea's first purely environmental activist
group. Its founder and secretary general, forty-four-year-old Choi Yul,

began his environmental activism in 1982 and is among the best-known environmental antigovernment dissidents. Today he oversees every aspect of KFEM and remains its most visible public figure. He was been awarded a Global 500 award at the UNCED Rio conference and in the spring of 1995, Choi was selected for a Goldman Prize for his long-standing environmental activism in Korea. This $50,000 award was an important recognition of the new international standing that has been achieved by Choi Yul and the Korean environmental community.

KFEM publishes a monthly magazine called *Environmental Movement*, which has a circulation of twenty thousand. Recent issues have included stories about KFEM activities and environmental problems throughout Korea, high-quality photography, coverage of international issues, essays, and poetry. The magazine also includes corporate advertising and fundraising appeals.

KFEM's 120-member governing board reflects its diverse membership. More than 350 separate organizations are part of KFEM, including Korea's YMCA and YWCA, whose environmental education activities have long been an important center of activism in Korean life. The federation presently claims over twenty thousand members and has seventeen regional offices around the country, with the Seoul office as national headquarters. As in many similar groups in Korea, the vast majority of KFEM's members are supportive of the organization's goals but are not very active and their pursuit of those goals is loosely coordinated. Because many groups have agreed to work together under KFEM's umbrella, and constituent groups drift in and out of activism, the resulting loose organization and sometimes competing interests have often made it difficult for KFEM to maintain the solidarity of its coalition.

In 1994 the organization had an annual budget of over 10.2 million won ($1.3 million). It has a full-time paid staff of sixty people, augmented by approximately two hundred unpaid activists. The funds for daily operations come from membership fees and the sale of products such as carrying bags, posters, buttons, and pins. About 20 percent of the budget is derived from the publication and sale of books and pamphlets. However, like almost all Korean activist NGO organizations, KFEM is severely limited by its lack of resources. In 1994 it faced a deficit of 160 million won ($200,000), which was eliminated by a large public fundraising dinner early in the year.

KFEM is an umbrella group for many small environmental activist organizations, although some of those were merged under KFEM direct management during 1994. As part of its role, it coordinates interorganizational study groups and provides a sense of national cohesion for its diverse membership. The federation is strongly opposed to the expansion of nuclear energy in Korea and stages protests around nuclear power and proposed fuel and waste storage sites. The group has also sought to stimulate public resistance to further golf course development, new industrial complexes, and intrusions on the national parks. KFEM leaders have been active in the opposition to the GATT free trade agreements in defense of continued protection of Korean agriculture. Recently, KFEM has also spoken out against military exercises, both as an environmental problem and as an unnecessary escalation of tensions between North and South Korea.

Like many environmental groups in Korea, KFEM has focused its attention on water-quality issues. Its slogan for 1994 was Water Is Life. It has launched a series of public protest campaigns in each of the nation's watersheds and has begun research projects staffed by volunteers, who work during school vacations to collect water samples for analysis. The volunteers are also tracking the development of management plans for each of Korea's river basins. A significant goal of this project is to identify the causes of their contamination and major polluters. Similar programs are underway in coastal areas to work with fishermen to identify the level and cause of marine pollution. KFEM intends to release the results to the public through the media.

In 1995 KFEM selected seven major projects. It continued its campaign for clean air and water in Korea and launched activities designed to highlight the conservation of the nation's forest and sea ecosystems and to reduce the generation of consumer wastes. The remaining programs for 1995 are intended to establish alternative energy systems, restore damaged ecosystems, expand youth education programs, and promote greater involvement with international organizations, with special emphasis on cooperation with NGO organizations in Northeast Asia. This effort to internationalize KFEM has been one of its most important undertakings. Beginning in 1993 it aggressively expanded its contacts with foreign environmental groups under the direction of Mr. Kwon Hyun-Yeol, of KFEM's International Department. By 1995 the organization had become Korea's first environmental group to develop, acquire, and use the international computer network, the Internet, and become a participant in Eco-Net.

KFEM has generally avoided formal political or partisan electoral activity. Its leadership remains highly suspicious of the political system even in the wake of democratization. However, Choi Yul, who is widely perceived as being the most political of the major NGO leaders, has joined other environmental leaders in advising the Ministry of Environment. In the most recent National Assembly elections, KFEM did support two candidates, both members of the opposition Democratic party. One lost and the other won. A third candidate was going to be backed by KFEM, but he was arrested for antinuclear activities before the election.

KFEM has all the hallmarks of a classic environmental protest group. Its programs have high emotional content. It focuses programs on specific issues and concentrates on mobilizing its constituency. It has an ongoing boycott of over thirty Korean companies that have been identified for their poor environmental records, and it has led the movement against the construction of solid-waste incinerators. It also has become involved in a wide variety of social and labor issues well beyond environmental problems, which has led to a diffusion of organizational energy. Despite that, KFEM's staff is adept at staging protests and releasing attention-getting information to the Korean media to highlight its point of view. However, the staff is far less well equipped to conduct independent environmental research and to muster the technical expertise to deal with complex scientific and technological problems. This is a product of the personal history and experience of KFEM's leadership as well as the inclinations of its membership. Also reflecting this experience is the prevailing view within KFEM that Korea's environmental problems are unique and demand Korean answers. With the exception of antinuclear activities, that attitude has impeded the development of greater cooperation with both domestic environmental organizations and the international environmental movement.

Choi Yul and the KFEM leadership have not been blind to their organization's limitations in the growing complexity of a democratizing and liberalizing Korea. KFEM has made the important and financially risky decision to begin to pay its key full-time organizers, as another aspect of its desire to modernize its operations. In another move, Choi made a decision to try to professionalize the organization's thinking and to implement longer-term planning. To achieve that, a young Ph.D., Dr. Kwak Il-Chyun, left the government-supported research institute, KETRI, to help shape a new research institute, the Civil Institute for Environmental Studies (CIES). The goal of CIES is to assist KFEM in developing consistent policy directions and improving the organization's ability to develop policy ideas for government. After several months of full-time activity, however, Dr. Kwak abandoned his efforts, at least in part because of KFEM's inability to secure a stable base of funding. CIES remains an important part of KFEM plans, but the problems faced by Dr. Kwak point to the extreme difficulty inherent in bringing financial stability as well as intellectual consistency to Korean activist organizations.

Green Korea

Green Korea, known prior to 1995 as the Baedal Eco-Society, is Korea's second-largest environmental organization, with approximately ten thousand members. It has fifteen chapters around the country including a Seoul office, but its headquarters are in Taejon, 150 kilometers south of the capital. The avowed purpose of Green Korea is to give a greater degree of scientific credibility and "substance" to the Korean environmental movement. The organization had, in 1994, five full-time staff members and an annual budget of 480 million won ($600,000). Most of that money was earned through the sale of reports, books, and green products. About 20 percent of the operating budget is raised through donations and membership fees, and another 20 percent comes from personal loans from key members and bank borrowings secured by Green Korea's leadership.

Green Korea was founded by Dr. Jang Won, who holds a Ph.D. in environmental science from Drexel University. Jang Won serves as the secretary general of Green Korea, and its president is the well-respected Dr. Rho Young-Hee, the retired founder of Seoul National University's Graduate School of Environmental Studies. The leadership of Green Korea seeks to provide what it calls a "professional resolution" to environmental problems, to find and promote environmentally sound and technically achievable solutions to Korea's environmental problems. Green Korea enlists the support of trained scientists from universities and industry in developing and conducting projects, then publishes and distributes the results of their research. In focusing only on environmental questions, Green Korea prides itself on being Korea's principal purely environmental nongovernmental organization. It is also one of the best at attracting the attention of the

Korean media, a strategy that often earns it criticism among the environmental activist community for a lack of depth.

The various organizations under the Green Korea banner include the Korean Institute for Sustainable Development, the Baedal Flora and Fauna Research Institute, the Research Institute of Environmental and Natural Philosophy, and the Baedal Academy. The Baedal Academy is perhaps the most active. It is a nationwide education program through which volunteer scientists present seminars and lectures to the public. In this way Green Korea activists play an influential role in the development of Korea's informal environmental education. The day-to-day activities of the organization are run by Nam Sang-Min, who began his environmental interests as an antigovernment and antinuclear activist in the mid-1980s.[34]

The driving force behind Green Korea is the thirty-eight-year-old Dr. Jang Won, and the organization is heavily dependent upon his personal prestige, insight, commitment, and standing with the Korean public and media.[35] The organization emerged from Dr. Jang's Baedal Environmental Institute, which he formed in June 1991. At the time of the Rio Earth Summit conference, Jang moved to create the Baedal Eco-Society and its substructure of programs. Most of those programs, though, have little functionality and only represent expressions of interest by individuals or often a handful of activists.

Dr. Jang's activities first broke upon the public scene during the 1991 Naktong River emergency. His so-called Green Warriors conducted an independent water sampling program during the crisis and informed the public of their findings. That set a pattern of activity for Green Korea, which now sees its role as provider of accurate environmental data to the activist community as well as the public. A network of monitors has sampled the NO_2 levels in major Korean cities and issued Korea's first independent environmental assessment statements about the impact of the Kimpo solid-waste landfill, golf course construction, and the Youngjong-do airport project. Members have also released a green plan for the city of Taejon and studies of water quality in Korea's river basins. Among the organization's publications are periodic reports on environmental conditions in the entire country and a plan for developing environmentally conscious public policies and lifestyles. These studies are put together by teams of expert volunteers, typically university professors, who have access to necessary equipment and tools of environmental analysis.

The leaders of Green Korea see themselves as a complementary alternative to the approaches taken by KFEM and other more populist-based organizations. Green Korea prides itself on its academic approach to environmental problems. Jang, Nam, and their colleagues generally eschew political involvement, although Dr. Jang has been invited to the Blue House with other environmental leaders and participates as an adviser to the Ministry of Environment. Despite this, Green Korea has mixed an avowed academic approach with very aggressive public activism.[36]

In January 1994, the Green Korea Green Warriors (who have evolved since 1991 into a small cadre of activists who mount public environmental protests) launched a protest about the quality of Han River water. During the winter civil action, they waded into the cold water with banners that demanded improved drinking-water quality. In another action, in March 1994, the Green Warriors chained themselves to the front gate of the U.S. Eighth Army Headquarters to protest "the leakage of hazardous wastes, particularly lead and other heavy metals into areas surrounding U.S. military bases throughout Korea." They have also assisted local neighborhood groups in resisting the siting of trash incinerators and have worked with many other activists to mobilize people against nuclear power. Finally, in addition to street protest, members of Green Korea have worked for the release of government-gathered environmental data to the media and used an international network of friends to secure information about Korean environmental conditions published abroad for release to the domestic media.[37]

In almost every way, Jang Won is Green Korea, and he is aware of the dangers of personally being perceived as too distant and academic. To modify this he has sought to mix visible personal commitment with his avowed scientific approach. During the past several years, while maintaining his academic post, he has moved his family to various sites of environmental controversy. He lived for a while near Daechong Lake, a freshwater lake on the outskirts of Taejon that is extremely polluted. His presence there underscored his and Green Korea's message of concern for all social classes. He later moved his family near the Kimpo landfill, where he sought to play a role in the public and scientific disputes over the siting of the solid-waste facility and to serve as a visible public reminder of the need to reduce waste in Korean society.

Green Korea has made some tentative steps toward becoming part of the international environmental community. It has begun to publish its quarterly newsletter in English and mail it internationally. In 1993 Green Korea joined the Global Anti-Golf Network as part of its efforts to reduce the pace of golf course construction in Korea. In February 1994 Green Korea participated with other Korean and Asian NGOs in a program partially funded by the Asia Foundation to outline the environmental problems of the international timber trade caused by Korea. At that meeting the Korean NGO leaders had a chance to host colleagues from abroad in Seoul and to highlight the destructive activities of Korean timber companies in the deforestation of Southeast Asia.[38]

In its most ambitious international activity, Green Korea joined with KFEM and other NGOs to invite Greenpeace to Korea for a month-long antinuclear protest in April 1994. Green Korea is preparing additional international environmental symposia and programs in Korea, ranging from the present problems of urban Asia to issues of sustainable development. Through its sponsorship of these programs, Green Korea hopes to educate itself and the Korean public about the larger global issues and their potential connection to Korean environmental problems.[39]

Although Green Korea has generally maintained its nonpolitical stance, the organization took part in some political activities during the local elections of June 1995. It joined with forty other civil groups, ranging from environmental groups to labor unions and women's rights organizations, to form the Hankuk Shimin Dangye Hyoboye (Korea Civil Movement Association). Reverend Suh Kyung-Suk, founder of Citizens' Coalition for Economic Justice (CCEJ), was named general secretary. Nam Sang-Min and environmentalists from CCEJ and KFEM organized a Green Autonomy Campaign under the banner of the new group. In part, the purpose of this was to take pro-active action against the fear that local autonomy might create more not less pressure on the environment by leading to additional development in green spaces, national parks, and as yet still underdeveloped rural areas. Thus, Nam and his colleagues in other NGOs worked together to establish a base of support for environmentalist candidates seeking office at the local level. However, NGO and other civic organizations, from labor unions to neighborhood organizations, are still prohibited from endorsing candidates for elective office. The constitutional limitation was restated by the Supreme Court, which on the eve of the June 1995 local election declared that the exclusion of full NGO participation was constitutional because the ban provided for civil peace.

Despite this injunction, in practice many NGO activists work for candidates who are sympathetic to their causes, but they have been reduced to quietly supporting candidates and preparing manifestos for release to the public. An example of this is a multipart policy paper drawn up to outline the principles of environmentally friendly local government and released to the public. Candidates were asked to make it part of their campaign platforms. Electoral activity of that kind will surely rise as Korean democracy develops, and Korea may not be far away from fuller NGO political activity, even if the constitutional ban on candidate endorsements continues to be a barrier.

Still, for Green Korea, greater political activity raises some important questions about its future as an organization. Will it continue to emphasize its founding ideals of scientific inquiry and environmental research, for example, or become more avowedly political in its approach to environmental activism?

Citizens' Coalition for Economic Justice

Unlike KFEM and Green Korea, Citizens' Coalition for Economic Justice is not a pure environmental group. In fact, it has come to environmental issues only recently through its involvement with social and political problems. CCEJ was established in 1989 by approximately five hundred people, primarily religious activists, progressive lawyers, university professors, and writers. In creating CCEJ, the founders hoped to address growing social and economic inequities they saw emerging in Korea during the late 1980s. These problems, they suggested, could be resolved only if citizens were engaged in public discussion and the establishment of alternative public policies, ranging from taxation to social welfare. Like Green Korea, CCEJ seeks to promote thoughtful, studious, and nonviolent approaches to social activism as an alternative to, but in support of, more vocal political protest. Unlike Green Korea, CCEJ does not itself sponsor street activism and symbolic street actions

CCEJ is managed by a board of directors. Founder Reverend Suh Kyung-Suk oversaw the organization's daily activities as its secretary general until his retirement in 1995. Born in 1948, Suh attended one of Seoul's most prestigious high schools and later Seoul National University, where he became active in radical politics. He was sentenced to twenty years in prison for his antigovernment, prodemocracy political activity in the 1970s and 1980s. He served a year of his sentence and upon his release became active in the Student Christian Church Federation and several other religious groups. During the next several years, he helped move various Christian groups from political docility to radicalism. In 1979, as a result of his role in a labor dispute known as the Y.H. Affair, he was again arrested.[40] He was fined and released, only to be arrested again in 1980 for his repeated and persistent outspoken opposition to the military government.

In 1984 Suh Kyung-Suk left Korea for the United States, where he was ordained as a Presbyterian minister. He returned to Korea in 1988 and worked for the Korean Christian Social Institute. Ironically, he was subsequently forced from his position because he was no longer thought radical enough. His radicalism had given way to a desire to promote evolutionary social and economic reform. It was in 1989, after this break with his radical past, that he and others founded CCEJ, which today still reflects the religious foundation of his activism and his personal determination to rationalize dissent.

A more recent addition to CCEJ's leadership council has been Dr. Yoo Jae-Hyun, who has emerged as an influential member of CCEJ and the social reform community in Korea. Dr. Yoo, forty-four years old, is trained as an urban planner and architect and received his Ph.D. from Columbia University, returning to Korea after he completed his doctoral studies in 1987. During the next four years he served as the director of the Hansaem Housing Research Institute, sponsored by the Hansaem Company, a manufacturer of home furnishings. During that time he became a member of CCEJ and worked as a volunteer on the interrelated issues of housing and land speculation. In 1992, he became the director of CCEJ's research institute, and since then he has become both the spokesperson for CCEJ and a national figure in his own right, although Reverend Suh remains the most visible and influential CCEJ leader. In February 1995, Yoo was formally appointed as CCEJ's general secretary when Reverend Suh gave up day-to-day responsibility for CCEJ operations. The different backgrounds of Suh and Yoo represent an important aspect of CCEJ activities and motivations: the coexistence of the Christian social-activist founders and the secular social reformers who have been attracted to the organization's rational approach to dissent.[41]

CCEJ's membership has grown to approximately ten thousand people; the organization has an operating budget of 530 million won ($662,500) and a full-time paid staff of one hundred. Although it is managed from Seoul, CCEJ has established nearly fifty regional committees to serve in every Korean city. The Citizens' Coalition attracts members largely from a middle-class and well-educated population. Approximately 63 percent of its members are college graduates, and about a third are under the age of thirty, but many of the most active members are long-time friends and schoolmates of Reverend Suh. As a result, most members are clergy, white-collar workers, university professors, and lawyers. It is not surprising that representatives from the business community are a relatively modest part of CCEJ's memberships rolls. CCEJ has also made few inroads into Korea's working classes.[42]

Many of the professional members attracted to CCEJ are participants in the department that undertakes policy studies for the organization. Within that framework, they are brought together into informal activist study groups to explore specific issues and develop policy alternatives to those offered by the government and its ministries. The results of these working groups are published and widely distributed to influential policy makers in the government and its research institutes. This policy-centered approach to Korea's social and economic problems has paid dividends for the organization and has set it apart from others in the NGO movement. It claims several recent successes, including the incorporation of CCEJ-generated ideas about tax reform into government reformist policies. As CCEJ has grown, the network of expert researchers has developed rapidly under a former social radical, Chung Tae-Yun, who manages the policy development aspects of CCEJ as chief of the policy department.

The Citizens' Coalition for Economic Justice is further organized around major program activities that seek to expand public participation in every aspect of Korean life and government. The coalition has established an Economic Injustice Complaint Center that documents economic abuses in Korean society and addresses them through publicity and mediation. CCEJ also operates a program called Parliament Watch that collects information about parliamentary activities and works to identify cases of public and political corruption in and around the National Assembly.

One of CCEJ's most recognized programs is Chung Nong

Consumers' Cooperatives. Through these, CCEJ activists have organized farmers to provide organically grown food to urban consumers' cooperatives established at the neighborhood level throughout Korea. Another high-profile program is a network of neighborhood-based consumer cooperatives called Addle Shops, in which volunteers buy and sell used clothing and other goods. In 1990 CCEJ also began to publish a bimonthly Korean-language newsletter called *Economic Justice* to promote its programs. More recently, in 1993, it began to publish a newspaper, the *Weekly Citizens' Times*. This newspaper was financed through the investments of one thousand stockholders who contributed 150 million won ($1.874 million) to create the weekly publication. By June 1994, the paper claimed thirty thousand subscribers and celebrated the appearance of its fiftieth edition.[43] In 1993, *Civil Society*, an English-language quarterly magazine, was begun by CCEJ to communicate its message to an international audience. Unlike other NGO publications, *Civil Society* is an expensive publication, using color and high-grade paper in a magazine format. This newest publishing venture is seen as an important step. It is a reflection of the recently perceived need to internationalize CCEJ, the entire Korean NGO community, and the public activism they seek to lead.

CCEJ has been hugely successful at gaining public recognition in the Korean press for its activities. In its first year of operation, CCEJ's compendium of news clips ran forty-five pages, and this pattern has accelerated as the organization has matured. This press coverage has caused some friction between CCEJ and other NGOs, which have seen its aggressive (and very intelligent) positioning in the public arena as a competitive threat—a predictable result in Korea, where jealous turf battles erupt even among those who are allegedly working toward the same end. A good example of this occurred in 1991, when CCEJ took advantage of the Naktong phenol spill to stake out an environmental position for itself. CCEJ, which had largely ignored environmental problems up to that point, captured the lion's share of the national media coverage of NGO activities, much to the dismay of the other activist groups with longer histories of environmental involvement and protest.

The 1991 phenol spill convinced the CCEJ leadership, and especially Yoo Jae-Hyun, that the environment was an important issue for the organization to take up as part of its core portfolio. As one of his first efforts after joining CCEJ, Yoo Jae-Hyun began to evaluate the importance of environmental questions and their connections to the larger issues of social justice in light of increasing public alarm over environmental pollution. This process was underscored by the attention in Korea given to the Rio global forum in 1992. Yoo was selected to serve on Korea's committee to prepare for UNCED, and as part of this he and others went to New York to assist in the planning. This experience awakened him to the international environmental activist community and to the power of their issues. After the Rio conference, Yoo and CCEJ organized a twenty-six-member delegation to Japan to discuss and learn about regional environmental problems. Following his return to Korea, Yoo established the Hwan-Kyung Gaebal Center, Center for Environmental Development (CED), as a functional part of CCEJ.

The CED operates within the ideological confines of CCEJ, which means it works to place Korean environmental issues into their social and economic context. In 1995 CED had a full-time paid staff of seven and an annual budget of 15 million won ($18,750). It is directed by Lee Jina, a Seoul National University graduate, who was hired by Dr. Yoo after she interviewed him for a community newspaper. Unlike almost every other NGO leader, Lee Jina does not have a personal history of social activism. Instead, after graduating from the university, she spent more than ten years raising her family, attending to the development of her university-professor husband's career, and engaging in personal study and writing. Nonetheless, Lee has emerged as an energetic and respected advocate for the environment.

CED has worked to identify areas where its research approach can help address environmental problems. One of its earliest activities was to study the problems of waste management and recycling. Like everyone else, CED researchers identified the many gaps in Korea's recycling systems and made suggestions about how to fill them. The CED research team also suggested legal reforms it thought would improve the national recycling rate. At the same time, the team pointed out that government policies on solid-waste disposal needed to be harnessed securely to improved waste-reduction programs, such as those designed to encourage the elimination of excess packaging for consumer goods. Following the CCEJ model, the Center for Environmental Development released its report to the media and organized meetings to train community activists so that they might act upon the conclusions of the CED study. Another area of deep concern for CED has been energy conservation. During the spring of 1994 it launched a major project to study Korea's energy use and to propose strategies for national energy conservation.

The Citizens' Coalition for Economic Justice and its Center for Environmental Development, like other independent NGOs, have wrestled with the issue of accepting financial support from corporate and government sponsors. Still, more than other groups, CCEJ has aggressively searched out that kind of support. After much discussion, CCEJ decided to accept corporate advertising in its publications, as have nearly all other Korean NGOs. However, CCEJ researchers, in a few instances, have also taken corporate money to perform studies that are in turn used by industrial sectors to promote their products or services. One example of this is a research study done for Korea's glass manufacturers that properly cited the well-known and widely accepted environmental benefits of using recyclable glass bottles instead of plastic containers. The report is now used by the glass industry to promote use of its product, complete with an implied Center for Environmental Development endorsement. The center, however, has resisted corporate pressures to directly advertise the environmental benefits of glass containers in its publications and has refused to provide commercial testimonials.

CCEJ leaders have tried to carefully define their relations with industrial supporters. In doing so, they generally adopt a policy of refusing corporate money offered as "donations." Samsung, which has an impressive record of environmental concern, was recently honored by CCEJ as its corporate citizen of the year and responded with an offer of a large contribution. The offer divided CCEJ's board, but in the end it voted to reject the badly needed financial support. As CCEJ and other NGOs gain public recognition—and at least the patina of political influence—to match their moral position, they will increasingly be faced with conflict-of-interest problems, and it is apparent that they will need to evolve clear fundraising guidelines. These must have the support of their core constituencies and guard against the taint of compromise. If CCEJ and other NGOs get careless in this regard, they will run the risk of being viewed as simply the most recent examples of corrupted and corruptible domestic political interests.

Notes

1. Jang Won, "The History of the Korean Environmental Movement," speech text 1994. Dr. Jang is the founder and executive director of Green Korea.

2. Citizens' Coalition for Economic Justice, *Civil Society*, Fall 1993.

3. Martin Hart-Landsberg, *The Rush to Development: Economic and Political Struggle in South Korea*. New York: Monthly Review Press, 1993.

4. Korean Ministry of Environment, *National Report to the Secretary General of the United Nations to Be Reviewed by the Commission on Sustainable Development*, 1993. As might be expected, there is constant tension between those NGOs supported by government money and those that rely on grassroots organizing for income. The "citizens' " NGO movement generally dismisses the role of the government NGOs and sees them as mere extensions of the government.

5. Ibid.

6. Martin Hart-Landsberg, *The Rush to Development: Economic and Political Struggle in South Korea*. New York: Monthly Review Press, 1993.

7. Kim Jung-Wk, Jeon Eui-Chan, and Chung Sang-Ok, "Promoting Public Participation and Environmental Education in the Republic of Korea." Presented to the Expert Group Seminar on Environmentally Sound Management of Industrial Development in Asian Countries, Kitkyushu, Japan, September 25–28, 1991.

8. Chung Kun-Mo is a man of international reputation and close contacts with the National Science Foundation and other primary scientific bodies in the United States and throughout the world. In recent years he has devoted his energies to developing the Institute of Applied Engineering, which is sponsored by Daewoo Corporation.

9. *Baedal Update*, Fall 1994. Following the suppression of the protests, three leaders of the antinuclear movement were arrested and given prison terms of up to eighteen months.

10. "On Nuclear Allergy," *Korea Herald*, June 3, 1994.

11. *Baedal Update*, Fall 1994.

12. "Kulop: Condemnation of an Island," *Green Korea Reports*, vol. 2, no. 1, Spring 1995.

13. There has been widespread suspicion in the Korean environmental activist community that the government's selection of this remote site may have implications other than waste storage. At the time of the announcement government officials also outlined a plan for the creation of a research institute to explore reprocessing technologies for stored nuclear wastes. Given the presence of nuclear weapons in North Korea, some activists have suggested that the energy program could be easily turned into a bomb-building enterprise that would be well hidden.

14. Kim Soo-Chan, "Future International Airport Taking Shape on Youngjong Island," *Korea Economic Weekly*, February 7, 1994.

15. *Baedal Eco-Society Update*, Fall 1993.

16. Ibid.

17. Chung Chin-Seung, "Origin and Development of Environmental Problems and Awareness in Korea," unpublished manuscript, 1994.

18. "Residents Have No Say in Nat'l Projects," *Korea Times*, June 4, 1994. In its commentary on the ruling, the paper noted that the court "defies the common notion that residents have a right to voice their objections to development projects affecting them." The *Times'* editorial staff then went on to note that the decision could be "expanded to include the location of nuclear waste disposal facilities" whose site selection had been repeatedly stopped by public protest as recently as a week before the June court ruling.

19. Korea was one of several countries forced to cut production of CFCs by half in a single year, thus losing the opportunity to phase out the chemical as had been done in other countries. See Sue Chang, "The O-Zone: Ban of CFC's Has Korean Companies Panicking," *Business Korea*, June 12, 1992.

20. World Wildlife Fund Position Statement, "The GATT Trade and Environment Work Programme," January 1994.

21. The biodiversity issue was taken up by the Korean government, which created a central repository for the nation's genetic material in Taedok Science Town within the mandate of the Korean Research Institute of Bioscience and Biotechnology.

22. The Rio conference had a galvanizing effect on NGOs worldwide, especially those in developing countries that prior to 1992 had been largely isolated. It produced an explosion of networking among those groups that has recently been accelerated by increased access to the American-based computer network, the Internet. See Shelley Preston, "Electronic Global Networking and the NGO Movement: The 1992 Rio Summit and Beyond," *Swords & Plowshares: A Chronicle of International Affairs*, vol. 3, no. 2, Spring 1994.

23. Roy F. Weston, "Sustainable Development: The Economic Model of the Future." Unpublished paper presented at the New Mexico Conference on the Environment, Albuquerque, New Mexico, April 25, 1994.

24. Lee Su-Hoon, "Transitional Politics of Korea, 1987–1992," *Pacific Affairs*, vol. 66, no. 3, Fall 1993. In his short analysis Dr. Lee suggests that the emergence of NGOs in Korean society is a product of what he calls the "activation of civil society."

25. Kim Jong-Soon, "Present State of NGOs in Korea," *Hon Kuk University Journal*, 1993.

26. Kang Moon-Kyu, "The Role of NGOs in the Building Process of an Environmentally Sustainable Society," unpublished manuscript, Seoul, 1993.

27. Mark Clifford, "Art for Politics' Sake: South Korean Protest Movement Seeks New Directions," *Far Eastern Economic Review*, August 26, 1993.

28. This is evident daily in the media. The press has been eager to publicize NGO activities, and the NGOs have responded by seeking close ties to reporters. Reporters commonly complain that the relationship is too close and too dependent.

29. *Baedal Eco-Society Update*, Spring 1994.

30. Choi Sung-Jin, "Jump on the GR Bandwagon Before It's Too Late," *Korea Herald*, April 21, 1994.

31. *Baedal Eco-Society Update*, Spring 1994.

32. U.S. State Department, "Report on Environmental Trends in Korea," unpublished discussion paper, 1992.

33. Asia Foundation, *Annual Report*, San Francisco, 1993.

34. *Baedal Eco-Society Update*, Fall 1993.

35. Nho Joon-Hun, "Self-Interest Hinders Ecology: Jang," *Korea Times*, May 24, 1994.

36. Ibid., Spring 1994.

37. Ibid.

38. The International Workshop for Forest and Green Round Strategy in Asia-Pacific Region, Seoul, February 17–22, 1994. Sponsored by Global Environment Fund (Japan), World Rainforest Movement, Asia Foundation, and Pulmuwon, Ltd.

39. "Greenpeace Calls for Withdrawal of Carl Vinson Fleet," *Korea Times*, April 19, 1994.

40. Martin Hart-Landsberg, *The Rush to Development: Economic and Political Struggle in South Korea*. New York: Monthly Review Press, 1993. The Y.H. Affair was one of the most important and widely publicized labor disputes in the late 1970s. It involved the Y.H. Trading Company, a maker of wigs and, in the early 1970s, the country's fifteenth-largest earner of precious foreign currency. As its overseas markets declined, the company's largely female work force organized a union to defend the employees' position. The company at first agreed to the union but later changed its mind and announced that the company would close. Workers appealed to student and dissident groups for help. When the firm closed its doors, the government forced the evacuation of resistant workers and also plundered the local office of the New Democratic party, which had not been involved in the dispute. Shortly afterwards, the Korean C.I.A. "engineered" the suspension and removal of Kim Young-Sam from the leadership of the party for making critical remarks to the *New York Times*. The situation exploded in October 1979 when thousands of students and workers took to the streets in Pusan and Masan even though martial law had been declared. The crisis came to an end with the assassination of President Park Chung-Hee in late October 1979. At his trial, the assassin (who was the head of the Korean C.I.A.) claimed that he had acted to prevent a massive military assault on the workers and students that had reportedly been approved by President Park.

41. In June 1994 Reverend Suh announced his intention to retire from the leadership of CCEJ and to have Dr. Yoo replace him. This led to complaints from the old-line social activist members that Yoo lacked the credentials as a social campaigner necessary to lead CCEJ.

42. Lee Su-Hoon, "Transitional Politics of Korea, 1987–1992," *Pacific Affairs,* vol. 66, no. 3, Fall 1993. See also Citizens' Coalition for Economic Justice, *Civil Society*, nos. 1–3, 1993–94.

43. *Civil Society*, no. 3, May-June 1994. This public investment strategy was first pioneered by the liberal-progressive *Hangyore* newspaper as a defense against government control. The broad base of investors makes it difficult for the government to intimidate a single owner by threatening personal financial reprisals.

Choi, Yul. Founder and leader of the Korea Federation of Environmental Movement. He is Korea's best-known environmental activist.

Marching against the use of rural land for golf course and resort development as part of a pan-Asian movement.

Trash incinerator under construction.

A new massive water treatment plant in southern Seoul nearing completion.

Environmental protest outside U.S. military installation in 1994.

Riot police on duty. Democratization has not eliminated street riots or the government's determination to maintain civil order through tight security.

Dr. Jang, Won, Founder of Green Korea (formerly Baedal Eco-Society), one of Korea's three largest environmental activist groups.

Hand-pulled collection carts and neatly stacked cardboard ready for the recycler are common sights throughout urban Korea.

Woman collecting fresh water from a natural spring on Namsan in the heart of Seoul.

High sulfur compressed coal briquettes for heating and cooking, while still common, are being replaced by natural gas, propane, and other cleaner fuels.

Kwon, Hyun-Yeol, head of the international division of KFEM.

Beer bottles ready for reuse.

Mr. Nam, Sang-Min of Green Korea environmental group.

Roadside rest area recycling bin.

Lee, Jina, Director of the Center for Environmental Development and principal organizer within CCEJ.

Children's Day environmental art program.

6

Internationalization and the Environment

The forces of internal public pressure and democratization have raised environmental awareness in Korea in recent years. Nonetheless, few Korean government leaders subscribe to environmental values from a foundation of personal commitment. Rather, they fear the possible establishment of a link between international trade and environmental quality and the loss of economic competitiveness among green-conscious consumers. These new threats have captured the attention of Korean public officials and corporate leaders in a way that earlier international environmental concerns—open-ocean drift-net over fishing and endangered species, for example—did not.[1]

The Korean "economic miracle" was built upon four primary factors: the development of heavy industrial capacity, high productivity rates, the suppression of consumer demand, and an unyielding focus on export markets. These were managed by a command-and-control methodology backed up by rigid authoritarian rule that promised targeted and rapid economic development. This approach has been discussed widely by economists and adopted at least in part by other Asian economies as the pathway toward industrialization. Koreans take pride in their economic accomplishments, but many are concerned about the increasingly complex challenges to their nation's economic growth that lie ahead.

After two years of relatively slow growth, the Korean economy began to grow again in 1994 at an enviable rate of 8.5 percent. Despite this, Korea's economic foundation looks surprisingly shaky to analysts.[2] Inflation is a persistent problem, and the government has found it difficult to control the growth in consumer demand for higher wages and imported goods. One reflection of this weakness is the nation's trade imbalance, which stood at nearly 2.4 trillion won ($3 billion) during the first quarter of 1994.[3] The nation's heavy industrial base is aging, and managers are fearful of being outdistanced by competition from their now-cheaper rivals in Southeast Asia and China. As a result, products that built the nation's economic foundation, from shoes to textiles, are a declining part of Korea's industrial output.

Korea has attempted to replace these industries with high-technology goods and finished products such as machine tools, automobiles, and electronics. Similarly, the systems of industrial management and government control that worked well during the early years of national economic expansion are proving to be highly inefficient. They are constrained by patronage, corruption, and bureaucratic inertia.[4] Many Koreans, including President Kim Young-Sam, have noted these problems, and policies have been fashioned to implement liberalization and change. Since 1992, these include greater liberty for the nation's banks, opening up investment markets, and making foreign investment easier.

Individual companies recognize similar problems. Some leaders, most notably industrialists such as Lee Kuen-Hee, chairman of the Samsung Group, have worked aggressively to modernize management practices. They have promoted standards of high-quality production and employee training and the introduction of innovative technology, which will be the essential ingredients to their firms' future growth. Unfortunately, moving Korean government and industrial management is not an easy task. Internal cultural and political resistance is strong, and many government reforms, although laudable, are foundering on the rocks of bureaucratic intransigence. Still, many in Korea recognize that today's accelerated processes of global change have left them with little time to implement meaningful reform.[5] This deeply concerns thoughtful Koreans and leaves them feeling threatened and vulnerable, at times bordering on paranoia.

Korean government and industry have worried about the new realities of world economics for nearly a decade. To address these, they have sought to move the nation rapidly up the technology ladder through large-scale investment in what has become known as the G-7 project.[6] Named for Korea's desire to enter the ranks of the industrialized G-7 countries, the effort has led to significant investment in science and technology development. The most visible manifestation has been the creation of the Taedok Science Town, adjacent to Taejon. In Taedok the Ministry of Science and Technology has established dozens of large research centers, which have targeted a wide range of technologies, from microelectronics and telecommunications to biotechnology and materials for development. The government has also expanded its funding of research in the nation's universities and helped to establish dozens of research programs and centers. Korean business has also participated in the G-7 project, and Taedok is now also the home of many corporate research facilities.[7]

In 1995 the Korean government proposed to spend 1.92 trillion won ($2.4 billion) on science and technology, an increase of 32.7 percent over the previous budget year. Furthermore, the government has announced that it expects its science and technology spending to reach 4 percent of the nation's gross national product by 1998, which will bring it more in line with the rest of the industrialized world. Although many research areas have been designated as critical to the national interest, special emphasis is being placed on establishing a foundation for Korean technological innovation in semiconductors, computer engineering, telecommunications, and information technology.[8]

To complement this spending, the government is also increasing funds for scientific and technical education. Special emphasis is being put on the further expansion of applied science and technology education programs at the Korea Advanced Institute of Science and Technology (KAIST), which is also located in Taejon. The goal is to improve the education and preparation of students for entry into private industry. The Korean government has also launched a national program designed to speed the development of data communications or an "information highway" in Korea. To facilitate this, it recently signed an agreement with Japan to create a regional system capable of meeting the needs of the two nations in the next century.

These efforts have not yet produced much in the way of tangible products or services. They have, however, created new bureaucracies, and there have been repeated worries that technological innovation will fall victim to the kind of bureaucratic strangulation that remains a perpetual problem in Korean government, universities, and other institutions. A recent poll of scientists at government-run research institutes reveals the depth of this problem. Conducted by KAIST, it discovered a significant morale problem and reported that a majority of scientists are hoping to leave their institutions due to low wages and high management inefficiencies.[9] Thus, even in the government's lavish efforts to jump-start high-technology research and development, the corrosive effects of bureaucratic control and inefficiency are limiting the innovation and inventiveness of those who have been asked to lay the foundation for the new Korean economy.

Until 1992, international competition for most Koreans meant a continuation and expansion of its export economy. Any problems could be fixed later through greater access to and development of a Korean technological base. To be sure, there were significant challenges: new low-wage rivals, resurgent American competitiveness, the Japanese, and the need to incorporate innovative technology and higher quality into Korean goods. All of that has led to an increasing drive to go global and acquire the necessary management capabilities to compete on the international stage. Nonetheless, few understood how quickly those issues would become confused and complicated by new, noneconomic environmental and human rights considerations.

Just as UNCED awakened the Korean NGO community to the forces of international environmentalism, it jolted Korea's institutions of government and business into paying attention to global environmental demands. Prior to the announcement of the Rio meeting, most in Korean policy and government circles dismissed environmentalism as an issue for the developed world and as only an occasional inconvenience for rapidly developing Korea.

Rio changed that forever. It caused the Korean government to begin to think more broadly about the links between its economic policies, world trade and opinion, and the environment. The first visible step in this direction was the establishment of a ministry-level committee on the global environment in 1991. Headed by the prime minister, this committee was important not only for its preparations for the Rio conference but because for the first time it brought the entire institutional power structure of the government's economic planning and development agencies together to study environmental questions. As a result, in the preparations to attend and at the Rio meeting itself, Koreans finally saw the political realities of international environmental concern and the power of calls for sustainable economic development.

The government went to Rio resolved to become a strong advocate of newly industrializing countries, and Korea made three highly visible efforts to secure its leadership position. First, it managed to have its representative selected as one of the nine Asian vice presidents. Second, in his speech to the UNCED delegation, Prime Minister Chung formally suggested that South and North Korea work together to jointly survey the ecosystem of the DMZ, which has been undisturbed for forty years. Finally, Korea put forward its own Ministry of Environment as the host of a regional body for environmental cooperation on transnational issues in Northeast Asia. Those efforts were given wide press play in Korea. Although no real action took place, they did serve to underscore—for the public at home—the role Korea hoped to play in global and regional environmental issues, and the Korean government's newfound attention to environmental issues added legitimacy to those in Korea who had sought public approval for their pro-environmental views.

Following the Rio conference, there was a flurry of activity as government ministries and private corporations began to come to terms with Korea's new interest in international environmental issues. Government institutes and corporate think tanks released studies on every imaginable topic. The nation's news media kept up a steady barrage of coverage about international environmental questions and Korea's role in addressing them. In the public mind, environmental issues quickly blended with a larger domestic discussion about the need for internationalization in Korean life. This became shorthand for the need for Korea to end its relative isolation and for its companies to compete at a world standard in every aspect of business and international politics.[10]

In late 1993 the Uruguay round of the General Agreement on Tariffs and Trade was concluded. The outcome left an indelible impression on a Korean economic and political establishment that sees in the agreements a loss of national independence and greater international competition. Few if any Koreans, outside of trade policy circles, had even heard of the GATT talks prior to 1993. They were aware of Western and especially American efforts to open their markets to free trade, but such efforts seemed to come and go over time. When the GATT agreement was signed, Koreans learned that the world was going to adopt new and more open trade policies. The result was widespread public outrage at what was perceived as the collapse of the government's defense of vulnerable Korean industries and agriculture. Over the course of the winter and spring months, the reaction against the Uruguay round of GATT led to the resignation of three senior officials and greatly embarrassed the Kim Young-Sam government.

The conclusion of the GATT negotiations left many Koreans feeling defenseless and even victimized by what they viewed as bullying by the United States and the world's other industrial powers. This concern was quickly compounded by the stepped-up pressure by the United States on Japan and then Korea to open agricultural and other markets to foreign goods in the winter of 1994. In the midst of that, the Korean news media began to write about the coming "green round" as the first agenda for the World Trade Organization, which had been established as the new forum for evolving world trade rules. The green round was billed as the follow-up to GATT that would formally link trade with environmental issues such as global warming, endangered species protection, and environmental control in industrial production. Moreover, Koreans widely expect that the green round will be followed by a blue round, tying trade and labor issues, and then a technology round and a competition round.[11] Each of these global economic discussions is anticipated to present serious dangers, whether real or imagined, to Korea's economic stability and well-being.[12]

Korean government officials began to openly worry about the imposition of strict environmental standards through the adoption of international trading rules. They pointed out that it would be unfair to force Korea and other developing countries to adhere to strict standards when the older developed countries had not done so during their own industrialization. That might curb growth patterns by reducing capital for investment in production and economic expansion. At the same time, many are concerned that environment-linked trade rules are just another way for the Western countries, and especially the United States, to curb newly developed low-cost competitors in Asia and elsewhere. This, they argued, was not so much a level playing field as much as it was a raised playing field where only the rich could effectively compete.[13]

Newspaper editorials, public speeches, and street demonstrations aside, most thoughtful Koreans recognize that the nation cannot withdraw from the emergent international trading system. Rather, Koreans are going to have to learn how to represent their perceived interests and to accept the international pressure to address domestic and regional problems, including environmental pollution. In an unexpected way, Korea's governing elite has been caught in a vortex of complex domestic democratic pressures and international forces. At the center of this vortex lie global concerns about the environment and the preservation and thoughtful use of the earth's natural resources.[14]

Reflecting this presumed new reality, Kim Chul-Su, Korea's minister of trade, industry, and energy, noted that the changing global order calls for Korea to discard the old norms and practices and adopt new ones befitting the new trade order.[15] And now the entire power structures of the Korean government's most influential agencies, from the Economic Planning Board (merged with the Finance Ministry in December 1994) to the government's strongest ministries, are turning their attention to environmental issues. In 1995, many are still probably giving only lip service to the problems of environmental pollution, but even that is a sea change for Korean government and society. For the first time, the environment, due to its unavoidable linkages with vital economic issues and growing domestic pressures, has been advanced to the front rank of national political discussions and government planning. Real and substantial change will take time, but no one should be so cynical as to fail to understand that political recognition is the first, albeit small, step toward more effective environmental measures in Korea.

Industry and the Environment

Korea's major industrial combines, or chaebol, are caught in the same international economic, political, and social web as the government.[16] They understand their own weaknesses and have worked since the early nineties to become competitive global producers. They understand that they can no longer be low-cost producers, so they are now striving to improve quality and productivity. To accomplish that, the majority of large Korean industrial combines are working to shake off the reputation of producing cheap imitations of Japanese products and to become respected manufacturers in critical industries such as automobile manufacturing, construction, semiconductors, and domestic and industrial electronics.[17]

Korean industries remain prisoners of a small domestic market, and are all ultimately dependent on growing export market shares for survival.[18] As a result, they are acutely cognizant of two essential and inescapable realities of global business. First, international public opinion is vital to their success. To be branded an uncaring corporate ecological villain is not only bad public relations, it is bad business. And second, for Korean business, trade restrictions based on environmental issues—or any considerations other than the marketplace—are of immediate and profit-threatening concern. Thus, many Korean firms are beginning to develop a keen interest in learning how to become good environmental citizens of the world. Korean Airlines, for example, recently announced the adoption of a new environmental motto: The Creation of Prosperous Life and New Values through the Harmonious Combination of Aviation and Environment.[19] It is not alone in searching to acquire the mantle of commitment to global environmental security.

During the past two years, nearly every major Korean company has launched aggressive globalization efforts. These often involve sending corporate managers abroad for formal training and more informal cultural experience. At home they have begun private education institutes and corporate-sponsored universities. Foreign-language training and other continuing education programs are widely available for managers and workers alike.[20] As part of those activities, many large firms have established their own in-house capabilities to track worldwide technology and environmental trends through the creation of institutes and teams of Ph.D.-level researchers. These study teams often have external advisory boards of noted international scholars. It has also become quite common for these research groups to report to the president or chairman of the sponsoring corporation. Recently, the senior managers of the large corporate research groups have even formed their own loosely knit organization to establish a foundation for collaboration and the sharing of noncompetitive environmental information and trends analysis.

The acknowledged leader in such activities among Korean corporations is the Samsung Group. Founded in 1938 as a small trading company, Samsung has grown into one of Korea's largest chaebol. In 1992 it ranked eighteenth among the World Fortune 500 companies. It has annual sales of 3.92 trillion won ($4.9 billion), 190,000 employees, and 322 sales and production sites worldwide. Like other large Korean conglomerates, Samsung has broad business interests, including electronics, chemicals, trading, heavy machinery, and insurance.[21]

In 1992, the chair of the Samsung Group, Lee Kuen-Hee, announced the establishment of the Samsung Environmental Charter, which commits the company to an integrated approach to manufacturing and environmental management. Samsung also made a commitment to be in full compliance with its own global environmental standards by 1997 (an approach similar to that taken by Dow Chemical after the Bhopal disaster), which are approximately twice as restrictive as the current Korean government's domestic environmental guidelines.

The central elements of the Samsung Environmental Charter are to eliminate the use of CFCs and other ozone-damaging substances by 1995, replace high-sulfur fuels with clean energy resources such as LNG and LPG gas, reduce waste generation at the source, complete on-site treatment of waste water to the Samsung standard, and establish the Samsung Global Environmental Commission. The commission has been established and consists of the most senior managers across the group's affiliated businesses. Its role is to develop corporate-wide environmental strategies and integrate them with all aspects of Samsung's business activities.

One of the first acts of the Samsung Global Commission was to launch the company's "Clean Tech, Clean Life" campaign. This internally aimed effort is designed to alter the "end-of-pipe" mentality within the group and instill a commitment to prevention, reuse, and recycling. To implement this, Samsung undertook a complete evaluation of all its production sites and office operations and began a process of incorporating environmental principles into every aspect of daily corporate operations. Actions include recycling scrap office paper, retrofitting for energy efficiency and conservation, and installing new control technologies at Samsung industrial complexes.

An important part of Samsung's environmental program is its commitment to eliminate or treat all of its wastes on site by the end of 1995. To accomplish this, the company has launched a 40 billion won ($50 million) construction program designed to ensure that all of its corporate manufacturing sites in Korea meet the standards and goals established by the company's environmental charter. As of 1995, the company is nearing completion of these waste-treatment and handling facilities. Samsung claims that once in operation, the company will meet and in some cases exceed its 1995 goals as set out in its corporate environmental charter. Densities of all emissions have been reduced to between 25 and 33 percent of the generous allowable government standards.

As further evidence of their determination, corporate officials have proudly pointed out that the group has already beaten its own timetable to eliminate the use of CFCs in all its manufacturing processes and product lines. By mid-1995 the group claimed that it had reduced its total CFC usage by over 60 percent; officials recognize that the remaining 40 percent needed to bring the company in compliance with the Montreal Protocol will be difficult and expensive to achieve. The pace of environmental improvement in Samsung's operations has surprised even its environmental managers, who have been pleased at how quickly the group's individual plants and employees have embraced the commitment to environmental management. This success has led Samsung officials to prepare a second round of even more explicit and aggressive environmental goals. It is expected that those will be announced to the public sometime in mid- to late 1995.

Samsung's aggressive corporate environmental policies have been complemented with a strong public relations campaign that highlights its corporate commitment to environmental issues. In 1990 Samsung began its "One Company, One Mountain" care program, under which every Samsung operating site selects a mountain for care. Samsung employees are organized and given time from work to clean up trash from adopted mountain trails. Annually over ten thousand Samsung Group employees participate in this program. In 1993 they collected three hundred tons of trash during their cleaning excursions to mountains throughout Korea. In recent years the effort has grown into a national phenomenon, with 450 other Korean companies joining in the effort.

Samsung has also worked to set an example for other corporations by adopting a stretch of the Taehwa River in Ulsan City, where Samsung Petrochemical has its principal production facility. The river is heavily polluted, and its banks have been a dumping ground for all kinds of industrial refuse and household trash. The company announced that it would maintain the river near its plant under a "One company, One stream" care program, and it urged other companies in the area to join in the project. Today, although the river still has severe water-quality problems, the industrial zone is no longer a garbage-covered wasteland. In a similar venture, Samsung's electronics subsidiary has joined with the YMCA of Korea to sponsor public activity around the Han River with a donation of 128 million won ($160,000).

At end of 1993, Samsung sought to highlight its commitment to international citizenship through the establishment of the Samsung Global Environment Research Center. The role of this corporate institute is to provide the chair and other senior company officials with information about environmental trends, engage in strategic planning that integrates environmental activities with business interests, and develop environmental training programs for the corporation's business managers. The group followed that step with announcement of another innovative step: In December 1993 it would join a KFEM-sponsored program that advocates the boycott of environmentally irresponsible Korean companies; the company pledged that it would not purchase raw materials from those firms. This was the first time that a Korean company had made such an announcement and certainly the first time that a Korean chaebol had agreed to work with domestic NGO activists toward a common goal.[22]

In January 1994 Samsung sent a study mission to the United States to learn about industrial environmental management techniques from large American firms with operations similar to Samsung's in Korea. The mission was composed of eight director-level managers and Dr. Han Sang-Wook, a former assistant minister of environment who is a primary adviser to Samsung on environmental policy matters. The group visited several large American corporations, including DuPont, IBM, 3M, Motorola, and Amoco, to study their approaches to environmental citizenship. They also attended a special seminar at Northwestern University, where faculty briefed them on topics ranging from corporate responsibilities for environmental protection to planning, management, and external communications and public relations. That and other similar "internationalizing" programs have led Samsung to integrate the principles of total quality environmental management (TQEM) into its operations worldwide. Those efforts are highlighted in *Green Samsung*, a monthly corporate magazine about the company's environmental initiatives.

The Samsung Group was the first large Korean business group to develop a consistent approach to addressing its environmental problems. Other firms are beginning to follow Samsung's model. The Lucky-Goldstar Group has instituted major environmental management programs. The group is a diversified company with three primary business organizations, Lucky, Goldstar, and Honam Oil. Unlike the Samsung Group, Lucky-Goldstar does not centrally manage its member companies. Thus, although the chair, Koo Ja-Kyung, has expanded the corporate planning office to include an environmental planning expert, the expert's role is limited to dissemination of information, coordination of group-wide environmental planning, and representing Lucky-Goldstar before the Ministry of Environment. As a result of this distributed approach, each of Lucky-Goldstar's three firms has adopted its own environmental management plan. The plans have many common elements with those of the Samsung Group.

Goldstar makes consumer electronics and communications equipment. It is an export-driven company that in recent years has made significant strides toward improving the quality of its products. Because of the export focus of the firm, it has come to understand the importance of green manufacturing and products. As a result, it has the most advanced environmental management plan within the Lucky-Goldstar Group. In early 1994, Goldstar announced a six-point plan for environmental quality that it called the Goldstar System. This system, Goldstar announced, would impose a basic policy of incorporating environmental conservation, management, and quality in all of its corporate activities. To ensure its success, the company has established an environmental committee made up of senior managers from across the firm and chaired by a vice president.

Under this environmental policy Goldstar has placed itself on a timetable to meet the CFC elimination requirements of the Montreal Protocol by the 1996 deadline. Beyond that, the Goldstar System includes the establishment of the company's own environmental standards, which will meet or exceed Korean government and international requirements. High-sulfur fuels will be reduced and replaced by LNG gas and other clean fuels as part of a general effort to increase fuel efficiency and cut greenhouse gas emissions. Furthermore, Goldstar has moved to significantly improve its monitoring and management of all types of gas and liquid emissions in the environment. The firm will pretreat all of its gas and liquid emissions on its production sites and reduce packaging materials, especially those made of plastics, by 30 percent before the close of 1996.

Goldstar has also identified as a high priority the reduction of noise in its consumer product lines and manufacturing plants. In preparation, the company has instituted a facility-wide environmental noise and vibration self-assessment program that will be made public upon completion in 1995. The company will also perform a total environmental impact audit of all of its products. By 1996, the data collection aspects of the Goldstar System of environmental management will be integrated with government computers to allow the rapid transfer of emission data to the Ministry of Environment for real-time evaluation and rapid response in cases of accidental emissions into the environment.

In recognition of the importance of good community relations, a cornerstone of Goldstar's corporate environmental policy is to assist communities where it has plants in their efforts to improve environmental education and evaluation. Not surprisingly, Goldstar sees this kind of public activity as an important part of avoiding environmental disputes with communities where it has operations. The company has also undertaken an effort to assist its suppliers in acquiring appropriate environmental technology and management skills through a corporate financial loan program. Finally, it has adopted the Samsung-initiated One Company, One Mountain program. Every manufacturing site will adopt both a mountain and a river for employees to maintain through voluntary activities.[23] The Goldstar Group's activities recently won recognition by the national government for environmental progress, and the activities of five Goldstar plants were noted as models for others to follow.

Goldstar's sister firm, Lucky, produces chemicals, petrochemicals, and home consumer products such as soaps and shampoos. Although some of those goods are exported, Lucky's primary market is Korea. As a result of this relative isolation from foreign markets, Lucky has just begun to develop the specifics of its environmental policies. The broad outline includes an emphasis on health and environmental safety and a commitment to increased expenditures on research and development to reduce the damage its products do to the natural environment. Increased recycling, conservation of materials, and energy efficiency are also stated priorities of Lucky's environmental goals. But these, like the other aspects, are not yet incorporated into an implementation plan with specific measures of success as in the case of Goldstar. Lucky-Goldstar's final company, Honam Oil, which is Korea's second-largest oil refinery, has not produced its own environmental plan, but it has recently consulted the American engineering firm CH^{2}M Hill and solicited its advice in Honam Oil's environmental planning efforts.

The Samsung Group is widely recognized by the public as the most advanced example of corporate environmental management, but Lucky-Goldstar, Hyundai, and Daewoo are pulling even in the scope and depth of their environmental programs. Perhaps no large business group, though, has recently moved as fast and as decisively as the Hanwha Group to develop environmental programs. Hanwha is ranked as Korea's eighth- or ninth-largest company. Like the other chaebol, it is composed of a number of business ventures, including construction, petrochemicals, electrical energy production, machinery manufacturing, travel services, resort and land development, and financial services. The group also owns Seoul's Seoul Plaza hotel and has plans to build a new luxury hotel in the city's Mapo district.

Hanwha's young chairman, Kim Seung-Youn, who succeeded his father a decade ago, is well known for his personal commitment to environmentally sound practices. Educated in the United States, he is an avid hiker and has instituted a group-wide mountain and river care program. Once a month, during working hours on Saturday morning, all employees, unless specifically excused, climb their company's adopted mountain or visit the river chosen for care in order to clean up trash and maintain trails. However, it should be noted that there is an irony in this corporate commitment. As Korea's most active destination resort and golf course developers, Hanwha's business activities contribute to increasing the very water pollution and rural-area traffic congestion that the chairman would like to see ended. It is the kind of irony that is true of most if not all Korean business activities. It is also at the core of much conflict with environmental NGO activists, who argue, with little effect, that some business activities are so destructive that no amount of environmental rhetoric, pollution abatement, or improved planning will overcome the problems associated with development.

In 1991 the Hanwha Group launched its Eco–2000 program, which established environmental working committees in each of its operations as well as at the corporate level. The committees began to set environmental goals for each company in the group, with the expressed purpose of becoming a national leader in environmental quality and total quality environmental management. Throughout the group, programs have been established to support reuse, reduction, reformulation, recycling, and reengineering in every aspect of business activity. By 1994 the group's strategy had evolved to include a proactive goal of implementing environmental quality practices that aimed to exceed all government regulations for air, water, and development of environmental management systems. The group has also been a leader in its attention to indoor air quality and was the first Korean company (followed by Samsung in January 1995) to recommend to its employees that they not smoke in the company's office buildings. Such a senior management suggestion is tantamount to an official ban on indoor smoking due to peer pressure.

In 1995, Hanwha's corporate environmental management programs began to yield significant results compared to other Korean firms. Beginning in March 1995, five of the group's member firms participated in a Ministry of Trade, Industry, and Energy pilot program aimed at demonstrating how Korean firms in various sectors could begin to develop improved environmental management systems and prepare for achieving ISO 14000 certification. Fifty-four firms participated and were evaluated on a checklist of 930 separate technical standards and environmental management functions. Thirteen of the participating firms were medium-sized companies, and forty-one were large firms. Of the total, five Hanwha companies participated. After the first six months, all of the Hanwha firms had reached 100 percent of the technical and environmental management goals established by the sponsoring ministry.

Although environmental programs are uneven across the rest of Korea's corporate community, the remaining chaebol are also engaged in efforts to improve their environmental activities. Their motivations are, of course, largely driven by a strong sense of changing "green demands" in the domestic and international marketplaces. Groups like Samsung, Lucky-Goldstar, Hyundai, Daewoo, Hanwha, and others recognize that the world has changed and that associating corporate identity with the green cause is an important marketing asset.[24] Thus, at least in part, Korean companies have become green not because of conviction or belief but as part of their overall marketing strategies, and they have not been shy about highlighting every environmental measure taken, no matter how small. While not a primary motivator yet, business leaders already can see how green rhetoric in the media and among NGOs, elected officials, and government bureaucrats has entered the political discourse of the newly democratizing nation. They fully expect to see this result in a greater degree of improvement in the mechanisms of environmental regulation and enforcement and are determined to be ready for it when it comes.

For many of Korea's large chaebol, environmental activity is also clearly understood as a business opportunity. They have not been blind to the growing worldwide demand for environmental technology. In the case of Samsung, the company has consciously used its forward-looking environmental programs as a foundation for technology development. In this way it is hoping to turn what has been seen as principally a financial drain into exportable commodities and higher corporate sales in the future. This is certainly one of the reasons Samsung and Lucky-Goldstar are assisting some of their suppliers by training them in environmental management.

These smaller and at least partially dependent firms will form a ready market for new products across the spectrum of environmental control and management. Another chaebol, Hyundai Heavy Industries, has also defined environmental technology as a significant future market opportunity. In 1994 it launched its build, operate, and transfer (BOT) strategy, which is aimed at securing new markets for Hyundai water purification, waste-water treatment, and incineration products and technologies. Under this strategy the company is seeking to develop turnkey operations for customers in Southeast Asia and in the domestic Korean economy. Hyundai Electric Company has also set an ambitious goal of reaching the ISO 14000 standard for all its products by 1996.[25]

Many of the firms engaged in new environmental activities actively promote their activities in press releases, speeches, and informational brochures, and their efforts have not gone unnoticed by the public. Although the efforts are bringing important changes, they remain quite immature by international standards. Key environmental managers in Korean companies are often very inexperienced. They and their staffs are sincere but young. In general, they are technicians without sufficient training or resources to move their large companies toward strong and sophisticated environmental management systems that make use of the latest methodologies of statistical process control, employee participation, environmental cost accounting, and wholesale waste reduction through reuse and replacement of primary materials. At the same time, many companies, although seemingly committed to an environmentally sound course, still see the environment as an issue separate from their primary businesses. It clearly has an impact on operations, but with only a few exceptions it is not an integrated part of normal business activity.

A good example of the way Korean business groups approach environmental issues lies in their efforts to move toward adoption of the new ISO 14000 standard that establishes and defines appropriate environmental management systems. Although the ISO standard calls for continuous improvements through environmental target setting, employee participation, and systemic approaches, many company managers seem confused by notions of environmental management systems and are content to simply compile manuals for emergency response and document goals, programs, and objectives without integrating these into fundamental daily plant or business operations. Once mobilized, however, at least Korea's large companies will be able to climb this learning curve, if they are indeed sincere in their desire to curb their own environmental excesses.

No element of Korean society has been left untouched by its awakening to the environmental cost of rapid industrialization. Popular environmental movements have been created and energized, politicians have discovered new vehicles to reach voters, and corporations have found in environmental concern both threats and commercial opportunities. The coalescence of interests, ambitions, and motivations around Korea's domestic environmental crisis and the larger global concerns has been rapid. Still, it remains unclear whether the coincidence of interests will actually produce the large-scale change in thought and action that will be necessary for Koreans to fully enjoy the fruits of their hard-won prosperity. Without a doubt, Koreans should look to Europe, Japan, and America for positive and negative examples of environmental management. But, as with many things, Korea is different even if the scientific and technological nature of the environmental problems are well known and present in every industrial and industrializing country. Its history, its unique cultural isolation, and the character of its people may well demand that it forge its own answers to chronic and severe environmental decay. This leaves the question, can Korea reverse its environmental tragedy, or will its industrious and intelligent people be condemned by their own limitations to a poisoned prosperity?

Notes

1. "Government Needs New Strategy for WTO Era," *Korea Herald*, Special Supplement, April 29, 1994.

2. Lee Chang-Sup, "Korea Sees 8.5 Percent Economic Growth in 1st Quarter: Bok," *Korea Times*, May 1, 1994.

3. Ibid.

4. David Terrence Cassell, "Stifling Bureaucracy," *Korea Herald,* April 28, 1994.

5. Lori Valigra, "National Project Aimed at Making It the Leading Tiger," *Science*, vol. 262, October 1993.

6. Nho Joon-Hun, "GR Greater Challenge to Securing High Tech," *Korea Times*, Supplement, April 22, 1994. "Business Prepares for Environmental Green Round," *Korea Economic Weekly*, February 28, 1994.

7. Nho Joon-Hun, "GR Greater Challenge to Securing High Tech," *Korea Times*, Supplement, April 22, 1994.

8. Yoo Cheong-Mo, "Low Morale Plagues Institutes," *Korea Herald*, April 22, 1994.

9. "Korea to Face Strong US Demand for 'Barrier' Lowering in Trade Talks," *Korea Times*, April 3, 1994.

10. Jeong Jin-Ho, "Under New International Order: Korea Needs a New Growth Paradigm," *Korea Times*, April 19, 1994.

11. Mary Tiemann and Susan R. Fletcher, "Trade and Environment: Treatment in Recent Agreements—GATT and NAFTA," *Congressional Research Service*, February 24, 1994.

12. Choi Sung-Jin, "ISO Green Standard to Revolutionize Business," *Korea Herald*, June 9, 1994

13. Han Taek-Whan, "The New World Trade System and Trade-Environment Issues: A Korean Perspective," Trade-Environmental Issues and Korea's Alternatives, Conference sponsored by Institute for International Economic Policy and Korea Environmental Technology Institute, Seoul, Korea, April 22, 1994.

14. "Government Needs New Strategy for WTO Era," *Korea Times*, April 29, 1994.

15. Kim announced his candidacy and campaigned aggressively for the position of WTO secretary general. He was, however, forced to withdraw in 1995 when it became apparent that he did not have enough support to gain the post.

16. There are approximately thirty chaebol in the Korean economy, each of which is a large integrated trading and manufacturing group. They vary in size but individually and collectively hold great power over the Korean economy, and in the past they have not hesitated to play a significant political role as well. Two views of the chaebol as uniquely Korean institutions are provided in Richard M. Steers, *The Chaebol: Korea's New Industrial Might* (New York: Harper & Row, 1993), and Walden Bello and Stephanie Rosenfeld, *Dragons in Distress: Asia's Miracle Economies in Crisis* (San Francisco: Institute for Food & Politics, 1990).

17. Robert Keatley, "South Korea Loses Ground in Asia's Race," *Wall Street Journal*, February 25, 1994.

18. Kim Chang-Young, "Leading Conglomerates Face Losing Top 10 Status," *Korea Times*, May 14, 1994.

19. "Korea Air Adopts New Environmental Motto," *Korea Times*, May 20, 1994.

20. Yu Kun-Ha, "Reform Drive Brings Management Award to Goldstar," *Korea Herald*, May 12, 1994.

21. Chung Hae-Jae and Han Sang-Wook, "Forward to Environmental Excellence," Asia Pacific Environment & Management Institute, unpublished report, Seoul, 1994.

22. Ibid.

23. Goldstar spokespeople claim that this program is voluntary and employees are not "forced" to participate but do so of their own free will.

24. Lucky-Goldstar, for example, recently announced its own environmental charter and plans to more aggressively incorporate environmentalism into its already mature emphasis on "quality" in all aspects of its operation. "Goldstar Holds Seminar on Environment, Trade," *Korea Herald*, April 28, 1994. See also

Chae Hee-Mook, "Corporate Globalization: Overseas Training Expands," *Korea Times,* May 1, 1994; Choi Nam-Hyun, "Hyundai Eyes Greater Localization: Pushing Joint Ventures Abroad, Increasing R&D Investment," *Korea Times,* April 28, 1994.

25. ISO 14000 (International Standards Organization) is a new (1995) international standard for environmental management systems. Under it, companies can apply for certification by meeting the requirements of a checklist that involves the establishment of top management commitments for implementing and continuously improving management systems for recycling, waste reduction, and reuse. The ISO program also requires the development and maintenance of documents and manuals outlining company environmental programs, regular internal and external environmental audits, employee participation in every aspect of environmental management, environmental cost accounting, and enhanced worker training.

Although the ISO 14000 standard will not be mandatory, there will be significant government and peer pressure to conform. The ISO standard will push complying firms to use only those suppliers who are also certified, and failure to comply may create significant government or competitive marketplace barriers in the future. Many Korean industry leaders assume that certification under the ISO 14000 standards will be not a luxury but a necessity for their export-driven companies.

7

Environmental Stability and the Prospects for Progress

It would be a gross mistake to conclude from Korea's current situation that the country is irrevocably on the road toward environmental improvement. Despite the power of democratization, popular green enthusiasm, and international pressures, the forces working against improvement are strong and at times seemingly immovable. Many, if not most, Koreans have not thought deeply or seriously about the consequences of their own environmental demands. They have yet to discover the inconveniences of having to readjust their economic thinking and alter their social and business behavior to accommodate their desire for cleaner water and air and safer food.

Even more limiting are the Korean legal, regulatory, and bureaucratic systems. Although Korean environmental law is quite sound and at times far reaching, it cannot be supported by the current legal system, which lacks most of the checks and balances that are essential for measured environmental progress. Compensatory damages and the rights of redress by citizens are severely restricted both in law and by the Confucian system that stresses cooperation and civic harmony. Similarly, regulation and compliance with environmental laws remain weak. The government officials responsible for enforcement often lack the experienced staff needed to carry out their duties, and although public administration is less corrupt today, abuses, both formal and informal, remain a daily fact of Korean life. This is compounded by a uniquely Korean civic attitude that sees laws and government regulations as less than absolute mandates for obedience. Rather, from traffic rules to bans on extravagant hotel wedding receptions to environmental standards, laws are often idealized goals to strive for but not always to achieve.[1]

For thirty years the sole and unimpeded role of government administration has been economic expansion. Success has been measured in the growth of the annual gross national product and the number of factories, roads, and apartment blocks built. Anything perceived as a barrier to that growth was ignored or at times brutally suppressed. One result was that the permanent Korean bureaucracy, until very recently, had not taken notice of environmental problems. Many senior government officials are finding that they do not have the necessary base of experience to respond adequately to the public and political pressure being placed on them. Many are scrambling to find those resources, but greater understanding will take a degree of time and commitment that few fully appreciate today. Environmental management is an administrative challenge involving subtle management of natural ecosystems that do not always respond as expected to the latest engineering feat. Environmental protection is not constructed just once; it is a process of constant reevaluation of the interaction between human activities and natural processes.

Moreover, concerns about environmental quality do not stand alone. They exist as part of the broader sweep of Korean industrial society, where attitudes toward the environment have often been mirrored in the acceptance of lackluster quality and a disregard for worker and public safety. The costs of this are just now becoming apparent. Shoddy construction and careless maintenance were blamed for the collapse of the Song-su bridge in October 1994. Three days later, thirty people were left dead when a fire swept through a crowded and unfit sightseeing ship on a lake south of Seoul. Other recent disasters have included a plane crash on Cheju Island that killed sixty-six people and a train derailment that left seventy-eight dead. More than three hundred people were killed when an overloaded ferry sank in heavy seas while sailing between Japan and Korea. And on April 28, 1995, a huge early-morning gas explosion in Taegu left more than one hundred dead, at least forty-two of them middle-school children. This recent accident was caused by a careless worker who punched holes in liquefied propane gas tanks and sewer lines while working at the site of a shopping center. The gases subsequently collected at a nearby underground subway construction site, where they were ignited by a welder's torch.

The Taegu explosion produced a national outcry against corrupt inspectors and local officials, low-quality workmanship, and the widespread lack of concern for public safety. One member of the opposition party spoke for many Koreans when he bitterly suggested that the nation was rapidly becoming known around the world as the Republic of Disaster.[2] President Kim Young-Sam, hoping to allay public fears and avoid political embarrassment in the face of the June 1995 local elections, ordered safety checks at major construction sites throughout the country. He further hinted that unless immediate improvements were made, his government would consider requiring builders to make use of foreign safety inspectors on all construction job sites.[3] These changes, though, did not avert electoral defeat for the president, nor did they bring an end to the string of embarrassing and deadly civic catastrophes.

Just two days after the largely corruption-free June 27, 1995, local elections, the most sensational and tragic civil disaster yet occurred in Seoul. The upscale Sampoong department store, in the city's Kangnam district, collapsed during the busy early evening shopping hours on June 29. Five hundred and one people were killed, 937 injured, and 6 declared missing in an accident caused by the now all too common trinity: poor construction practices, nonexistent maintenance, and a management that refused to take action. Like Americans during the Oklahoma City explosion in the United States two months before, Koreans found themselves glued to their television sets, watching in horror as bodies were pulled from the rubble and exhausted rescue workers dug by hand to reach survivors. Unlike the case of the federal building in Oklahoma City, the collapse of the Sampoong department store could not be blamed on a lunatic fringe. The managers of the department store knew of the problem but ignored the crumbling walls and falling debris that preceded the collapse by at least two days. Even so, they failed to close the store for fear of losing the roughly $500,000 in daily revenues that were generated by the affluent clientele. Following the collapse, the owners and managers were quickly arrested, but the Korean public was left in a somber and introspective mood. Like earlier tragedies, the department store itself stood as a symbol of hard-won affluence and the prestige that it has brought. In its collapse, many Koreans saw a stunning metaphor for a country whose rush to development may have been accomplished with too little reinforcing steel and too much sand in its concrete.[4]

Despite the limitations and barriers within Korean government, business, and industry that have been highlighted in this discussion, it is a mistake to conclude that Korea has not turned an important corner in her short history as a developing industrial power. The forces of democratization, international competitive pressure, and growing global and domestic concern about the environment are driving Korea to a rough kind of environmental equalization. Things may not be getting much better, but they also may not get much worse.

The government's existing commitment to build new waste-treatment and purification plants, although late and still inadequate, will go a long way to alleviate the nation's drinking-water problems by the end of the present decade if implemented. Emission controls on cars and an expansion of mass transit and road systems in the major cities will at least hold air quality levels stable at today's poor levels. Moreover, if the government can manage to control the number of cars on the nation's roads and reduce the automobile's contribution to air pollution, there may well be some additional marginal improvements. A reduction in automobile miles traveled, though, is highly unlikely. Already nearly one-fourth of the national tax base is tied to cars and their use, and the auto manufacturers have announced that they are seeking to double their domestic sales over the next two years. People will complain loudly about noise and air pollution and traffic congestion, but as with Americans, it will be nearly impossible to pry Koreans out of their cars.[5] Even if Korean bureaucrats do manage to place tighter controls on auto use and other pollution sources, the country faces the prospect of having its already despoiled environment made worse by the consequences of large-scale Chinese industrialization.[6]

To some extent, industrial pollution may decline as low-wage, heavy manufacturing industries are forced by international competition to transform themselves into value-added manufacturers of goods and services. As government standards of enforcement and the costs of waste disposal are raised, industry will accelerate its investments in environmental conservation, control, and waste-reduction technologies and in the training of employees. Still, the Korean economy is not just the rich chaebol, which are quite capable of investing in environmental controls and management. Much of the domestic economy is made up of small to medium-sized industries, and these contribute a disproportionate share to environmental damage. Unlike the chaebol, these thousands of firms usually lack the resources, the experience, and often the desire to make their business practices more environmentally sound. Improving the environmental awareness and responsibility of this industrial sector is probably Korea's greatest challenge. Success in that will demand not just new environmental programs and vigilance but in all probability a new development policy. Finally, even if everything goes as planned, public demand for ever-higher living standards (more cars and air conditioners) will make it difficult for Korea to do much more than stabilize its current environmental conditions at the present-day intolerable levels.

A Korean Model for Change?

Any study of the social and political forces shaping the Korean response to environmental problems is bound to be a frustrating experience. Environmental administration and public attitudes are evolving and in a constant state of flux as the government lunges from one environmental crisis to the next. To non-Korean eyes it is not a very heartening sight. Crisis management and end-of-pipe strategies simply are not capable of addressing environmental needs, especially when the basic ingredients for effective management, regulation, and enforcement are either wholly or partially absent.

Yet something is happening that may defy all the rules of Western management experience. Korea is beginning to make some small but perceptible strides in coming to terms with its modern environmental neglect. Powerful forces are driving this progress, and they will only increase in intensity. To be sure, the forward movement is slow and uneven. It is also without a consistent strategic core of public policy and is usually motivated by panic and fear. Still, the coalescence of opinion and the desire to act can be seen and felt in the country. Thus, the real challenge is not to focus on what is not working but rather to look toward what might bring environmental improvements given the political, social, and economic realities in Korea today.

It is apparent that government-driven and regulatory-centered environmental management may not be an effective methodology for environmental improvement in Korea. There are simply too many institutional, cultural, and political obstacles to surmount. Instead, Koreans might look in another direction toward a mixed environmental management system that uses the power of government and the vertical organization of the nation's economic base to bring not only environmental stability (at the current unacceptable level) but longer-term environmental improvement.

Many of the pieces for a new environmental management system are already in place and need only to be organized and repositioned by government policy and corporate cooperation.[7] A clue to what this might look like lies in existing government programs that are already committed to building infrastructure, public participation, and a stronger environmental enforcement by the end of this century. A massive program to increase the nation's capacity to reduce its production of wastes and clean up its water and air is already being implemented, albeit unevenly. This will be an expensive and complicated social undertaking—one that the Korean public and its government officials will have to recognize and accept as the price for the next stage of modernization. Still, it will take time to complete the construction of waste-water-treatment and water-purification plants, hazardous-waste disposal facilities, and an effective regulatory system. The Korean public and the international community can do little but be patient and watchful as these vital elements of environmental management are put into place.

The forces driving Korea toward environmentalism will continue to be fueled by an expansion of democracy and liberalization. In turn, the environment as a political and social issue is itself becoming a potent driver of social and industrial modernization and democratization. This symbiotic relationship alone provides a foundation for cautious optimism regarding future change and improved environmental management and protection. In Korea the environment has become what American political professionals call a wedge issue. It has attached itself to or otherwise stands in the way of other critical problems. Because of this, environmental-quality issues have the potential to shift and divide constituencies in novel ways.

For Koreans, the environment is no longer a simple question of quality of life, public health, or aesthetics. It now has to be understood as an essential component of trade and economic policy and as a political weapon in the hands of democratized domestic political and social leaders. In effect, it has begun to intrude on every aspect of public and private decision making and is forcing Koreans at all levels of society to reevaluate long-standing practices and views. The question for Korea and its natural environment, given both the problems and realities of life—culture, politics, and economic development—is where to turn to find an environmental policy and management strategy capable of meeting the environmental demands of the public and the expectations of the world community.

Toward a "Natural Policy" of Environmental Control, Regulation, and Progress

In looking at the trends of Korean environmental problems, administration strategies, and public attitudes, it is clear that more than just specific tools of management are missing. Korea lacks an easily understood, integrated, and comprehensive policy to effectively disseminate environmental attitudes and regulatory measures throughout the economy. Clearly, what is needed is such a policy: one that is both enforceable and whose implementation will not drive hundreds of thousands of small and medium-sized firms throughout the country into bankruptcy. At the same time, greater environmental control must not be allowed to lead to further consolidation of economic power in the hands of either the government or big business. Either outcome would be counter to the progressive drive for liberalization in all facets of Korean life. What then can be suggested as a plausible foundation for an effective Korean national environmental policy?

Since 1994 the Korean government has sought to implement a mixed internal economic strategy that combines reform and anticorruption efforts with looser government control and market incentives. The government of Kim Young-Sam has worked to broaden economic power in the country and to curtail the historic and widespread culture of corruption that can be found at every level of Korean society. Real-name banking and real estate ownership are just the most recognized aspects of those reforms. Nonetheless, the government is also concerned that its financial capacity for new social overhead capital (SOC) in infrastructure is severely limited and falling behind that of international competitors. As a result, the government devised a policy of privatizing infrastructure developments that relies heavily on private capital and inevitably on the chaebol as a replacement for wholly public sponsorship.

With this policy of privatization, the government is seeking to spur social investment by encouraging private firms to build public infrastructure in exchange for concessions and tax abatements. Already modern roads are being built by private developers. Companies with massive financial assets such as Hyundai are planning to build and operate waste-water plants and other facilities that in most nations are thought to be purely public responsibilities. At the Nanji-do landfill near central Seoul, giant engineering and development companies are scrambling to gain access to the largest undeveloped parcel in the capital city. Lured by government financial incentives to clean up and stabilize the closed landfill, companies are standing in line to invest millions in private funds to transform Nanji-do into the proposed San-gram International Information Center within ten years. In 1995, the national government allocated some 800 billion won ($10 billion) for this and other privatized social overhead investments. More money and resources are being added by local governments. At Nanji-do, for example, the city government is offering to provide 64 million won ($8 million) to the redevelopment project and billions more to its four other planned SOC efforts (Youngjong Airport, Yongsan Advanced Information Center, Yoido Park, and Tooksum Riverside Leisure Town).[8]

It is precisely here, where public meets private, that the efforts of the SOC programs and of large chaebol such as Samsung, Lucky-Goldstar, and Hyundai might be instructive in formulating a larger, national, uniquely Korean approach to the nation's environmental problems. Instead of trying to mandate environmental standards that can't or won't be enforced, the central government might try to manip-ulate the levers of economic power that already exist in the country to bring environmental change. In doing so, Korea would be establishing a "natural policy" that follows the established boundaries of Korean economic, political, and administrative traditions. It would not impose wholly new concepts, yet it would meet the important test of being able to fully accommodate expansions of democratization and eco-nomic liberalization.

For example, Samsung, Lucky-Goldstar, Hyundai, Daewoo, and the other large trading groups might be asked (or volunteer in the name of national need) to insist that their suppliers subscribe to the same global environmental standards by the end of the century that they themselves are adopting. In doing so they could provide technical assistance while building markets for their new environmental control and management products. Small and medium-sized companies who chose to participate would be greatly improved in management skill and technical profi-ciency well beyond the initial environmental concerns. Firms that do not participate in "environmental modernization" would eventually find declining domestic markets for their "brown" products. Moreover, these nonparticipants will eventually run afoul of improving government capabilities to enforce environmental regulations. In this manner, effective environmental management will be pushed downward throughout the Korean economy.

The national government has a crucial role to play as the essential ingredient in this or any successful environmental strategy. It will have to improve and refine its own regulatory systems and its enforcement of environmental standards at all levels of society and throughout industrial sectors. Given the traditions of autonomy and independence within Korean government, achieving the necessary interagency coordination and cooperation will be a daunting task. Still, improved central administration will be only part of the challenge. Special attention will have to be paid to local and provincial governments, who are themselves major polluters due to their inability to pay for the effective treatment of municipal sewage and solid wastes. The national government will have to work overtime to give local agencies the skills and resources to bring transgressors into full compliance with the tougher national environmental quality standards.

Overcoming the barriers to effective, reasoned, and corruption-free environmental management at all levels of government will mean new investments in training, higher salaries, and increased rates of inspection and enforcement, to say nothing of infrastructure development. Those investments will be difficult to make. The Korean national government is impoverished, and funds for services beyond those devoted to national defense are relatively modest by modern international standards. Local governments suffer from similar fiscal constraints. However, improved environmental management, when coupled to an economically based cleanup strategy, can form the foundation for the establishment of achievable and enforceable environmental targets.

One way to begin this is by example. The national government can lead the way by immediately insisting that its own projects and facilities be brought into full and verifiable compliance with the nation's environmental regulations and goals. The national government might also use its control of twenty-three government-invested enterprises to set an example for the private sector in environmental management. These government-controlled firms include the Korea Electric Power Corporation, the Petroleum Development Corporation, the Korean Housing Corporation, and the Korea Tobacco and Ginseng Corporation, among others. These and others employ approximately 1.2 percent of all Korean workers and are responsible for nearly 10 percent of the GNP. Their managers have also enjoyed exemptions from environmental laws and regulations, and only recently have these state businesses been asked to come into compliance with the national standards.

Most government-controlled corporations are energy-, land-, and resource-intensive enterprises, and when combined with other government activities, their operations have a tremendous impact on environmental quality in Korea. As a result, the real incorporation of environmental quality into management plans is both a necessity and an opportunity for the government to demonstrate leadership and commitment to action. The same is true of those government-controlled firms that are scheduled for privatization. To be sure, they have to be economically attractive to investors, but the government has the ability to set reasonable, even attractive terms for their eventual public sale.[9] Through negotiation with the eventual buyers, that power could be used to promote a high standard of environmental compliance for those entering the private sector under new, independent management—what better place to showcase the nation's commitment to long-term environmental management than those companies?[10]

To make such a system work, the government must play an aggressive, consistent, and balancing role as the focal point for national policy and regulation and enforcement activity. The large industrial combines already have strong incentives to address their environmental problems. However, the use of pollution abatement tax credits or other free-market incentives, which have been widely discussed in Korea and used effectively elsewhere, are perfectly compatible with the proposed policy. The government will also need to focus its energies and resources on assisting companies and municipalities in need of direction and technical assistance to smooth their way toward full compliance with environmental standards.

The centerpiece of the government's commitment must be long-term, inexpensive capital available to the smaller firms that choose to become part of the national environmental improvement effort. A similar strategy will have to be put in place for local government, which in addition to being a fairly recent innovation in Korean political life, is also generally impoverished. Financial assistance can take many forms. It could be provided either directly or through incentives (government guarantees) to private lenders. Or Korea might seek assistance from entities such as the World Bank, which is turning its attention to the environmental results of its own historic efforts to spur industrialization.

This kind of mixed approach—private-sector incentives and public-sector financing—will reduce the potential for economic blackmail and be consistent with the government's efforts to reduce chaebol domestic economic power. It will also allow for the combination of financial assistance with mandatory technical standards and expanded training and education of environmental managers. Under this approach, energy efficiency and emission standards for new construction, to cite just two examples, could be moved to higher regulatory levels, while phased retrofitting of existing plants and facilities could be given more time to meet improved standards.

In embarking on this path, Korea can put in place a new approach to environmental improvement that does not demand difficult and unlikely administrative and legal reforms. This strategy will be compatible with the historical patterns of Korea's industrialization and consistent with the now irreversible trends of democratization, economic liberalization, and globalization. Perhaps most important, such a policy is politically attractive. It would allow the government to point to a consistent, flexible, and simple plan for addressing domestic environmental problems. Such a policy would be both reformist and respectful of the realities of Korean economic conditions. Moreover, for the first time, there would be the kind of measurable goals toward improvement that are increasingly being asked for by developed countries and international environmental pressure groups. What better defense can the Korean government mount against its internal and external critics than a plan with goals that are realistic, founded on unique Korean conditions, and reflective of a commitment to reach them along a clearly defined timeline?

Implied in the above policy is a recognition of Korea's special and maybe unique diplomatic position as a newly developed and maturing industrial nation. Its economy remains fragile, but with more than three decades of sustained growth rates of 7–12 percent, Korea can no longer credibly claim that it is in the same class as Bangladesh, the Philippines, or Indonesia, though many Koreans honestly believe that their country is poor, backward, and deserving of special international treatment. Korea will find it increasingly difficult to obtain special treatment as the world works to resolve transnational environmental problems. Nonetheless, Korea has an opportunity to turn its position as a newly developed country to its advantage in regional and international environmental negotiations.

International trade and concern for the global environment are becoming firmly linked in global economic discussions. At the same time, regional environmental issues in Northeast Asia are visible and pressing. These range from rising levels of pollution in the Yellow Sea and acid rain caused by emissions in China to nuclear dumping by Russia and the potential of large-scale environmental pollution resulting from the Tumen River basin development project. Korea's adoption of novel domestic environmental policy, if linked securely to its dramatic struggle to implement democracy and economic and social liberalization, can give the country a rare and valuable moral authority in regional affairs. If it chooses to use this authority, Korea can become a unique mediator in both regional and international affairs. It can come to occupy the space between the growing international environmental demands and the needs for economic expansion and a reduction of poverty in the developing world. If this role is successfully embraced, Korea will achieve something its leaders and people have long sought: The nation can move decisively from its colonial and Cold War isolation to a global role of influence and authority.

The above is suggestive of a possible environmental policy and strategy for Korea based on this examination of the issues swirling around its contemporary environmental dilemmas. It is impossible to know if Korean environmental policy will actually evolve in the direction sketched above. It is quite possible that Koreans will continue to thrash about from emergency to emergency without any apparent sense of direction. However, it is clear from trends since 1987 that the new political tools and technical and administrative capabilities are taking shape. To be sure, the process is and will be painfully slow and uneven. Even the most optimistic observers understand that meaningful and measurable change will take several more rounds of elections, further democratic maturation, and political modernization to overcome the historic cultural and social habits inherent in Korean systems of governance.[11] At the same time, democracy, Korean style, will have to consciously choose to avoid the systemic boxed canyon now evident in the aimless wanderings of Japanese democratic politicians and their parties and institutions.[12]

Yet the changes already evident throughout Korean life contain the seeds of effective environmental management. At the highest level, there are fundamental interactions and relationships taking shape that may push Korea toward a higher valuation of environmental quality: democratization, pluralism, modernization, globalization, and inevitable generational change. Integral to these are the Korean people themselves, who have consistently demonstrated the ability to bring energy and intelligence to their problems. Repairing the nation's natural environment will surely test Korea's human and institutional resources. The key to measuring their impact is to watch the gaps and calculate the narrowing between political and administrative rhetoric and goals and observable quantitative evaluations of the condition of Korea's environment.

It is for Koreans themselves to choose to improve the quality of their natural surroundings in accordance with their nation's perceived self-interest. There are many native and foreign cynics who have strong doubts that Korea will be able to sustain a commitment to environmental improvement. The problems are immense, and although Korea has embraced many of the outward forms of modernization, its people and institutions have been highly resistant to substantive structural change. Nonetheless, the political and social forces at work inside Korean society and institutions, especially those related to chronic environmental problems, are persistent and durable. Even the most jaded observers do not think that they are likely to disappear, and most concede that they will only grow stronger and more pervasive. This is giving shape to a community of interest for environmental reform and improvement. In this sense, rising Korean environmental concern should be seen as a sign of the modernization of Korean politics and society and an impetus for change well into the next century.

Politicians, industrialists, NGOs and social activists, and a large section of the newly enfranchised public have concluded that the environmental conditions in the country are unacceptable. For the foreseeable future, the demands of environmental management and an awakening public green consciousness will challenge Koreans and their leaders to think much more expansively in the search for solutions to their pressing problems. Their motivations will not always or even often be altruistic. Instead, motivations for action will be founded on a uniquely Korean blend of selfishness, ideology, aesthetics, and even morality and spirituality. This produces frustration, diversity, and inconsistency, but it also is producing the first signs of hope and progress for the environment. Environmental problems are tough under any circumstances, but they are even tougher in a newly industrialized nation like Korea. Nonetheless, public and private motivations are pushing Koreans toward a surprisingly broad consensus that environmental pollution must be addressed seriously and with commitment. This consensus will only grow stronger under the influence of internal and external political, social, and economic pressures.

The question is how this new recognition of environmental responsibility will be aligned and incorporated into Korean social and economic planning and organization. Most critically, how will it alter future behavior to make Korean society more environmentally sound and sustainable while addressing the problems of past neglect? The implications go well beyond the environment. No one can yet imagine the full details of Korea's approach to its massive environmental problems. Still, in understanding Korea's evolving responses to industrialization's environmental legacy, we can observe the gears of democratization, plurality, and a greater integration with the world at work. That alone makes Korea worth watching, understanding, and helping.

Industrialization in the United States took more than a century. In Korea it has been accomplished in less than thirty years. The United States began to come to terms with its environmental problems in the 1960s and has yet to solve them. Although Korea drafted its first environmental laws twenty years ago, it has just begun to seriously look for solutions to environmental pollution. To be sure, there are enormous barriers to progress in environmental improvement, and no one should expect immediate action. However, recent Korean history can be instructive not only to the West but to the other developing nations of East and Southeast Asia.

In its unceasing drive to build an industrial base, Korea has poisoned and despoiled much of its natural environment and resources. As we have seen, many of its traditional principles of government administration and social organization are unable to contend with the complex demands of environmental management. Of course, Korea is not alone in being overwhelmed by the environmental consequences of industrial processes. From Seoul to Bangkok and from Taipei to Beijing, pollution is going hand in hand with rising rates of productivity and profits. The whole East Asia region is being overwhelmed by pollution on a scale and at a speed unprecedented in human history.

The international community has taken notice of the environmental problems of the developing industrializing world. First in Rio in 1992 at the Earth Summit, and now in international trade talks, green attitudes are being infused into world concerns under the banner of the sustainable-development movement.[13] But for many developing countries, environmentalism is perceived as a threat to further industrialization. They will resist the pressure of the United States and Europe on the grounds that their fragile economies cannot support the burdens of reducing pollution and preserving resources. This is not to say that people in the developing world don't recognize the damage they are doing to their own land and water or the global environment; they do, but they still fear grinding poverty far more than bad air and foul water.

That is why Korea is such an interesting case study. In a sense, the Korean countryside and urban landscape have suffered for the Korean people's relative political and social isolation under a military dictatorship and the lack of an early environmental shock. In contrast to Korea, the Japanese were forced by the public scandals and embarrassment surrounding outbreaks of the Minamata and Itaitai diseases to come to terms with environmental problems at a relatively early stage of their modern industrial development.[14] Until the first Naktong River crisis in 1991, Koreans barely understood the environmental problems their own industrialization was producing. As a result, Korea's environmental conditions continued (and are continuing) to deteriorate well past the point of easy remedy.

There are massive barriers, and Korea's environmental needs are overwhelming. Almost every problem one can imagine, from capital to technology, from technical training to legal reform, from a tradition of corruption to budget shortfalls, stands in the way of cleaning up the nation's environmental mess. Many of them rest on the very cultural attitudes that have made Korean government and society a model for modern industrial development and efficiency, but they are ill suited for the country's next stage of economic and social development. As a result, problems of all kinds in Korea will be overcome only slowly and with consistency of purpose. This is a quality that at times has eluded Korean leaders. Democratization will surely help, as will the rising level of domestic demand for environmental change.[15] Those forces will be powerfully augmented by growing international pressure for environmental safeguards.

The outlook for successful environmental cleanup and security is complicated by the many internal contradictions in contemporary Korean society. The political reforms since 1987 are not yet deeply rooted. Evidence of the weakness of Korean democracy can be found almost everywhere in Korean society. It is seen in the constant division and subdivision of the political parties, in which members still place blind personal loyalty to individual leaders above principle, ideology, and historic mission.[16] Institutional weakness has been evident in the aborted actions of President Kim Young-Sam, when he failed in his attempt, in the name of harmony (and his own political unpopularity), to eliminate organized political parties from the first and long-anticipated June 1995 local elections.[17] Most of all, the shallowness of democracy's roots are found in the timidity of the Korean public in embracing pluralism and demanding openness and honesty at every level of Korean society.

Are the reforms of recent years a bold, if incomplete, departure from cronyism and secrecy or simply the seedbed for a new variation of the ancient Korean patterns of political, social, and financial micromanagement? Will the anticorruption campaigns of recent years really reduce the endemic culture of payoffs and underground deals in Korea? And, most important, can democratic reforms, the culture of tenacity, and environmental awareness overcome the historic and at times pathological ethos of conformity, aversion to social and personal risk, and deeply held suspicion of individualism?

Given these difficult questions, it is arguable that Korea will fail in its environmental control and cleanup efforts and that her people will have to learn to live in an unhealthy post-modern haze reminiscent of the dark setting of the movie *Blade Runner*. If this happens, Koreans will not be the only ones to suffer. The global community will find its environment a lot dirtier and the problems blocking cleanup even more intractable as other countries, still behind Korea on the development curve, choose rapid and nonsustainable development models over environmental security, and short-term economic improvements over long-term adverse health and quality-of-life consequences.

Korea and other developing nations cannot be allowed to become resigned to the inevitability of permanent environmental decay. To prevent this, the industrialized West will have to decide how best to help, through encouragement, aid, and at times scolding. Neither blind relativism that accepts national cultural differences as excuses for inaction nor absolutism about what needs to be done to prevent environmental disaster will work. To be sure, striking a balance will not be an easy task. Western motives will be suspected as either post-colonial bullying or efforts to check future economic competition. Still, if the world's citizens want a cleaner global environment, the industrialized West is going to have to invest a lot more time in a thoughtful foreign and trade policy that listens as much as it talks, that gives as much as it takes, and that practices patience even in the face of frustration. In the final evaluation, international environmental policies must have at their foundation a goal tempered by practical experience and a clarity of purpose that seeks to minimize environmental damage while allowing for steady economic expansion that reaches the most impoverished corners of the globe.

It will be a hard balance to strike, and there are no reliable models yet to follow. But Korea is especially useful in both a negative and a positive sense. Its heavy industrial development model, rigid and inflexible administrative systems, and authoritarian political history provide evidence for environmental failure. Nonetheless, events since 1987 point to the possibility of improvement through the creation of linkages between democracy, domestic liberalization, and globalization. Without a doubt, the emergence of these powerful trends offers the prospect of improved environmental protection to Koreans and encouragement to countries seeking to follow Korea's progress toward first world economic status. This is not to say that the process will be easy or fully effective at any given point in time. Equally, the announcement of environmental goals and speeches about the necessity of cleanup are the simple and cheap parts of environmental consciousness. Long-range planning, coordination, consistency, enforcement, and a willingness to change three decades of environmental abuse will be the hard part.

Speaking before an audience in Seoul in April 1994, U.S. Ambassador Dr. James T. Laney said that "Korea is one of the most improbable places on earth."[18] In 1960 no one would have dared suggest that by the early 1990s the Korean economy would be the thirteenth in the world. Fewer still, in the late 1980s, would have predicted that Korea's ruling military elite would peacefully transfer power to a civilian government led by a former radical popularly elected in a relatively corruption-free election. And only the most optimistic observer could have foreseen President Kim Young-Sam's anticorruption campaign of

1993 and his insistence on electoral reform and economic liberalization in 1994. Korea has often been underestimated, and the ambassador's commentary is a seasoned reminder that all things in Korea seem improbable until they happen. The cleanup of Korea's natural environment may be the next improbable case in point.

Notes

1. Kim Byong-Kuk, "Realistic, Equitable Law Enforcement," *Korea Times*, February 2, 1994.

2. "All Things Considered," National Public Radio Report, April 28, 1995.

3. Sang-Hun Choe, "Fatal Blast in South Korea Stirs Rage at Government," *Portland Oregonian*, April 30, 1995.

4. "Rescuers Quicken Their Pace to Save Korea Mall Survivors," *New York Times*, July 2, 1995.

5. Although the government is expanding mass transit quickly, its policies designed to support the domestic automobile industry work to place more cars on the streets. The government's transportation and environment plans call for the encouragement of car pooling every "ten days," but this is an all-but-useless step toward reducing the interrelated problems of traffic congestion and noise and air pollution. Korean Ministry of Environment, *National Report to the Secretary General of the United Nations to Be Reviewed by the Commission on Sustainable Development*. Seoul: 1993.

6. Nho Joon-Hun, "Self Interest Hinders Ecology: Jang," *Korea Times*, May 24, 1994.

7. Chung Chin-Seung and Chung Hoi-Seong, "Environmental Policy at the Age of Decentralization in Korea," Korea Development Institute, unpublished manuscript, Seoul, 1993.

8. In 1995, investment in public infrastructure under the Social Overhead Capital program stood at 3.1 percent of total gross national product. Of this, 2 percent comes from central government resources, 1 percent is drawn from state-invested industries, and currently 0.1 percent is contributed by private investment. Emphasis is placed on railways, subways, and an expansion of cargo distribution facilities. The forecasted increase in these programs amounts to 25 percent per year and is planned to reach 5.5 percent of GNP by 1999. As in the Nanji-do project, the government is hoping to secure greater private-sector participation in the SOC program, rising to 0.8 percent of the total at the end of the decade. "Gov't Expects SOC Investment to Total 5.5 percent of GNP by 1999," *Korea Economic Weekly*, May 29, 1995.

9. The stated challenge to the Kim Young-Sam government in accomplishing this sale of assets is to prevent the companies from falling into the hands of the chaebol, thus increasing their share of the nation's economy. Unfortunately, only the chaebol have the resources necessary to purchase the assets. As a result, privatization of the state-owned industries is also tied to the reform and liberalization of financial markets, banking and other financial foundations of the Korean economy. "Preparation Set for Futures Trading," *Korea Times*, May 12, 1994.

10. Chung Chin-Seung and Chung Hoi-Seong, "Environmental Policy at the Age of Decentralization in Korea," Korea Development Institute, unpublished manuscript, Seoul, 1993. The idea of asking these entities to be judged in part by their environmental performance has been suggested a number of times by researchers at the Korea Development Institute. KDI has suggested the implementation of a graded-performance cash bonus system for workers and managers alike.

11. Park Kwon-Sang, "Six Tasks for Realizing Democracy," *Shin Dong-A Monthly*, December 1994.

12. Since the start of their industrialization, Koreans have closely hewed to their interpretation of the Japanese economic model. This strategy has been shaped by a mix of historical hatred and modern envy for the emergence of the postwar Japanese industrial state and has led to a difficult-to-admit admiration for the efficient organization of Japanese society and the social and political systems it rests upon. This has been further blended with a palpable suspicion of Western forms. With the collapse of the "bubble economy" and the exposure of deep-seated political and social corruption, some thoughtful Koreans are beginning to ask if Koreans can afford to follow Japanese democracy into an apparent dead end. See "Oriental Renaissance: A Survey of Japan," *The Economist*, July 9–15, 1994.

13. Richard Estes, "Toward Sustainable Development: From Theory to Praxis," *Social Development Issues*, vol. 15, no. 3, 1993.

14. These diseases were caused by poisonings due to the industrial pollution in Japan in the 1960s and provided stark examples of the consequences for human health of environmental neglect.

15. Cho Jin-Sang, "Local Autonomy and Environmental Protection in South Korea," *Green Korea Reports*, vol. 2 no. 1, Spring 1995.

16. "Renewal for the Ruling Party," *Dong-A Ilbo*, February 8, 1995. In February 1995, Kim Jong-Pil, an old political war horse who had served as the chairman of the Democratic Liberal party since the end of the Roh Tae-Woo government, split with Kim Young-Sam to form his own minority conservative faction. At the same time, President Kim edged closer to the leadership of the Democratic party, which itself had begun to display deep internal divisions between the followers of the current leadership and those who defined them as part of the Kim Dae-Jung faction of the party. These fissures in the ruling elite reflect the continuing importance of personality and historic personal ties over democratic sensibilities that, although surely not immune from personality cults, tend to stress ideas about institutional or constitutional governance and political policy.

17. "South Korea: Home Takeover," *Far Eastern Economic Review*, March 16, 1995. Partly in response to rising political confusion and the increasing volume of criticism, President Kim attempted to strangle party pluralism. He used his National Assembly majority to decree that the parties would not be allowed to participate formally in the long-anticipated June 27, 1995, local elections. This caused a tremendous outcry. Although he reversed himself, the maneuver left many thinking that Kim's personal commitment to democracy had reached its limits.

18. Ambassador James T. Laney, speech before the Fulbright Forum, Seoul, April 1994.

Bibliography

"Advanced Environmental Technologies Swarm into Korea," *Kyonghyang Sinmun*, June 7, 1993.

"Aerators' Vital Role in Olympic Clean-up of Korea's Suyong River," *Waste Water Treatment*, 1988.

Ahn, K. H., "A National Program for Environmental Control in Korea: Water Supply, Waste Water Management, Pollution Control," Ph.D. Dissertation, Cornell University, 1983.

"Air Pollution Regulations to Tighten to Standards in U.S., Japan by 1999," *Korea Times*, May 12, 1994.

"Air Pollution Worsens Due to Heating," *Korea Times*, November 29, 1993.

"Alert on Water Quality," *Korea Times*, June 8, 1993.

"All That Remains: A Survey of Waste and the Environment," *The Economist*, May 29, 1993.

Anderson, Kym, "Trade, Environmental Issues and Asian Economic Growth," Conference on Trade-Environmental Issues and Korea's Alternatives," Conference sponsored by Institute for International Economic Policy and Korea Environmental Technology, Seoul, April 22, 1994.

Asia Development Bank, *Economic Policies for Sustainable Development: Ministerial Brief*. Manila, Philippines: 1991.

Asia Foundation, *Annual Report*. San Francisco: 1993.

"Assembly Probe Facing Rupture," *Korea Times*, May 14, 1994.

Bardal Update, 1993–1994. See *Green Korea Reports*.

Bedeski, Robert E., *The Transformation of South Korea: Reform and Reconstruction in the Sixth Republic under Roh Tae Woo, 1987–1992*. London: Routledge, 1994.

Bello, Walden, and Rosenfeld, Stephanie, *Dragons in Distress: Asia's Miracle Economies in Crisis*. San Francisco: Institute for Food and Politics, 1990.

"Benzene Found in Naktong River," *Korea Herald*, January 14, 1994.

Berniker, Mark D., "South Korea Lifts Import Curbs," *Journal of Commerce*, March 6, 1989.

Biers, Dan, "Pollution in China Reaches Dangerous Levels," *Korea Herald*, May 16, 1994.

Blatner, K. A.; Schreuder, G. F.; Govett, R. L.; and Youn, Y., "The Market for

Solid-Wood Products in Korea: Past and Future Opportunities," *Forest Products Trade: Market Trends and Technical Developments*. Seattle: University of Washington Press, 1988.

Bohlin, F., "Planning of Forestry for Rural Development," *Sveriges Lantbruksuniversitet*, 1984.

Booth, Jason, "Bad Karma: Monks Fight for Control of Buddhist Order," *Far Eastern Economic Review*, April 28, 1994.

Breskin, Ira, "Korea Toxics Law Imperils Exports of US Chemicals," *Journal of Commerce and Commercial*, July 27, 1992.

Brooks, D. J., "Forest Resource Conditions in Japan, Taiwan, Korea, and the Southern Pacific Rim in Pacific Rim Forestry," *Bridging the World: Proceedings of the Society of American Foresters National Convention*, San Francisco, August 1991.

"Business Plan, United States–Asia Environmental Partnership," unpublished report, Seoul: 1994.

"Business Prepares for Environmental Green Round," *Korea Economic Weekly*, February 28, 1994.

Byun Eun-Mi, "Right-Wing Bodies Escalate Attack on Cho's Novel 'Tae-Baek-San-Maek,'" *Korea Herald*, May 11, 1994.

"Cabbies Earn Extra W260,000 Monthly from Joint Rides, Tips," *Korea Times*, May 15, 1994.

"Cancer-Causing Chemicals Foul Water Supply in South Korea," *Chicago Tribune*, March 22, 1991.

Cassell, David Terrence, "Stifling Bureaucracy," *Korea Herald*, April 28, 1994.

Chae Hee-Mook, "Corporate Globalization: Overseas Training Expands," *Korea Times*, May 1, 1994.

Chang, Sue, "The O-Zone: Ban of CFCs Has Korean Companies Panicking," *Business Korea*, June 12, 1992.

Chipello, Christopher J.; Darlin, Damon; and Mark, Jeremy, "Seoul Set to Join Tokyo in Banning Drift-Net Fishing," *Asian Wall Street Journal*, December 2, 1991.

Cho Jae-Hyon, "Average Household Savings Hit W11 Mil.," *Korea Times*, May 26, 1994.

Cho Jin-Sang, "Local Autonomy and Environmental Protection in South Korea," *Green Korea Reports*, vol. 2, no. 1, Spring 1995.

Cho Lee-Jay and Kim Yoon-Hyung, eds., *Economic Development in the Republic of Korea: A Policy Perspective*, Honolulu, HI: East–West Center University of Hawaii Press, 1991.

Choe Sang-Hun, "Fatal Blast in South Korea Stirs Rage at Government," *Portland Oregonian*, April 30, 1995.

Choi I. H., "Developmental Process of Planning and Management System of National Forest in Korea," *Bulletin of the College Experimental Forests* (Hokkaido University), Hokkaido, 1991.

Choi Nam-Hyun, "Hyundai Eyes Greater Localization: Pushing Joint Ventures Abroad, Increasing R&D Investment," *Korea Times*, April 28, 1994.

Choi Suk-Jin, "Curriculum of Environmental Subjects in Korean Middle School," *Journal of the Korean Society for Environmental Education*, no. 4, 1992.

Choi Suk-Jin and Yoo Jae-Taik, eds., "National Seminar on Developing Strategies and Action Plans for Development of Environmental Education in Korea in Seoul," Korea Educational Development Institute, Seoul: 1990.

Choi Sung-Jin, "ISO Green Standard to Revolutionize Business," *Korea Herald*, June 9, 1994.

———, "Jump on the GR Bandwagon Before It's Too Late," *Korea Herald*, April 21, 1994.

———, "Korean Firms Play Catch-up in Race for Green Market," *Korea Herald*, May 19, 1994.

Choi Yearn-Hong, "Water Crisis," *Korea Herald*, February 15, 1994.

Chon Shi-Yong, "Korean Politics Enmeshed in Regionalism, Factionalism," *Korea Herald,* January 18, 1995.

Chuan Wen-Hu and Wolfe, George, "Nuclear Power Development in Asia," *IAEA Bulletin*, April 1993.

Chung Chin-Seung, "Directions and Tasks of Social Education for Environmental Preservation in Korea," *Journal of the Korea Society for Environmental Education*, April 1993.

———, "Origin and Development of Environmental Problems and Awareness in Korea," unpublished manuscript, 1994.

Chung Chin-Seung and Chung Hoi-Seong, "Environmental Policy at the Age of Decentralization in Korea," Korea Development Institute, unpublished manuscript, Seoul, 1993.

Chung Hae-Jae and Han Sang-Wook, "Forward to Environmental Excellence," Asia Pacific Environment and Management Institute, unpublished report, 1994.

Chung Hae-Jae, Paik Jae-Bong, and Han Sang-Wook, "Forward to Environmental Excellence Management," unpublished report, Asia-Pacific Environment and Management Institute, Seoul, 1994.

Chung Yong, "All-Out War Proposed for Preserving the Environment," *Koreanana*, January 1991.

———, "Environmental Expert Training in the Republic of Korea," *Environmental Education*, January 1990.

Citizens' Coalition for Economic Justice, *Civil Society*, nos. 1–5, 1993–94.

"Civic Groups Push Water Bill Boycott, Move to Start Water Quality Watchdog," *Korea Times*, January 16, 1994.

Clifford, Mark, "Art for Politics' Sake: South Korean Protest Movement Seeks New Directions," *Far Eastern Economic Review*, August 26, 1993.

———, *Troubled Tiger: Businessmen, Bureaucrats, and Generals in South Korea.* Armonk, NY: M.E. Sharpe, 1994.

———, "The Ups and Downs of a Korean Politician," *Far Eastern Economic Review*, June 24, 1993.

———, "Wealth Can Damage Health," *Far Eastern Economic Review*, September 19, 1991.

"Controlling Growth for Stability in '95 Goal," *Korea Herald*, January 10, 1995.

Crane, Paul S., *Korean Patterns.* Seoul: Royal Asiatic Society, 1978.

Darlin, Damon, "Doosan Chairman Quits, Takes Blame for Toxic Scandal," *Asian Wall Street Journal*, April 29, 1991.

———, "Foreign Makers of Chemicals Pan New Import laws," *Asian Wall Street Journal,* July 27, 1992.

——, "South Korean Law on Imports Worries Chemical Companies," *Wall Street Journal*, July 29, 1992.

"Decontrolled Military Protection Areas to Come under Ecological Preservation," *Korea Times*, May 25, 1994.

Deuchler, Martina, *The Confucian Transformation of Korea: A Study of Society and Ideology*. Cambridge, MA: Harvard University Press, 1992.

"DLP, DP Exchange Political Tirades on Assembly Approval of New Premier," *Korea Times*, April 26, 1994.

"DP Leader Lee Demands Drastic Hike in Investment in Environmental Field," *Korea Times*, November 29, 1993.

"DuPont Wins S. Korean Approval to Build Controversial Plant," Reuter's, December 30, 1989.

"The Dying Yellow Sea, "*Kyunghyang Shinmun*, January 7, 1995.

"Entretien avec Sang Wook Han, Président de l'APEMI," *Corée Affaires*, March 1993.

"Envelope Recycling Begins," *Korea Times*, April 10, 1994.

"The Environment in Asia," *Far Eastern Economic Review Focus*, November 17, 1994.

"Environment, Construction Ministries Clash over Tap Water Safety Program," *Korea Times*, November 25, 1993.

"Environment Min. Whang, KFEM Clash over EIA Filing Libel Suit," *Korea Times*, November 12, 1993.

"Environmental Education Needed at Pre-School Age," *Korea Times*, June 5, 1993.

"Environmental Equipment Demand Increases," *Korea Economic Weekly*, August 30, 1993.

"Environmental Facilities, Tech Will Be Promoted as Export-Oriented Ind.," *Korea Times*, December 28, 1993.

"Environmental Levy Imposed on Cigarettes from July '94," *Korea Times*, June 2, 1993.

Environmental Management Corporation, *Annual Report*, Seoul: 1994.

Environmental Officers Training Institute, *Program Guide*, unpublished internal document, Seoul: 1994.

Estes, Richard, "Toward Sustainable Development: From Theory to Praxis," *Social Development Issues*, vol. 15, no. 3 (1993), 1–9.

"Ex-Kukje Owner Again Fails in Bid to Reclaim 'Forcibly' Sold Shares," *Korea Times*, May 5, 1994.

"Expansion of No-Smoking Areas," *Korea Times*, January 11, 1995.

"58 DP Lawmakers Step Up Anti-pollution Campaign," *Korea Herald*, April 13, 1994.

"Foreign Ministry Mulls Installing Nuclear, Environmental Bureaus," *Korea Times*, December 30, 1993.

"Foul Odor Detected Again in Tap Water in E. Seoul," *Korea Times*, March 25, 1994.

"Garbage Charges by Volume Due in Apr.," *Korea Times*, November 26, 1993.

"Garbage, Old Furniture Dumped in Back Streets," *Korea Herald*, January 5, 1995.

Glain, Steve, "Shackled Tiger: South Korean Leader Struggles to Free Up a Regulated Economy," *Wall Street Journal*, March 30, 1994.

Goda, T., "Circulation and Pollution Dispersion in Masan-Jinhae Bay of Korea," *Marine Pollution Bulletin*, 1991.

———, "Mariculture and Eutrophication in Jinhae Bay," *Marine Pollution Bulletin*, 1991.

"Goldstar Holds Seminar on Environment, Trade," *Korea Herald*, April 28, 1994.

"Government Needs New Strategy for WTO Era," *Korea Herald*, special supplement, April 29, 1994.

"Gov't. Expects SOC Investment to Total 5.5 percent of GNP by 1999," *Korea Economic Weekly*, May 29, 1995.

Green Korea Reports, formerly *Baedal Update*, 1994–95.

"Green Round Committee Operation Due," *Korea Times*, December 30, 1993.

"Greenpeace Calls for Withdrawal of Carl Vinson Fleet," *Korea Times*, April 19, 1994.

"Ground Water Contamination Found at Dangerous Levels," *Korea Times*, November 12, 1993.

Haas, Peter M.; Levy, Marc A.; and Parson, Edward A., "Appraising the Earth Summit: How Should We Judge UNCED's Success," *Environment*, vol. 34, no. 8, October 1992.

Hahn Pyong-Chon, *Korean Jurisprudence: Politics and Culture*. Seoul: Yonsei University Press, 1986.

Halvorsen, David E., "Confucianism Defies the Computer: The Conflict within the Korean Press," *Special Report*, East-West Center, 1992.

Han Do-Hyun, "Environmental Movements against Golf Course Development," *Korea Focus*, June 1994.

Han Sang-Wook, "Environmental Issues and Projects in Korea," unpublished report, Asia-Pacific Environment & Management Institute, Seoul, 1994.

Han Taek-Whan, "The New World Trade System and Trade-Environment Issues: A Korean Perspective," Trade-Environmental Issues and Korea's Alternatives, conference sponsored by Institute for International Economic Policy and Korea Environmental Technology Institute, Seoul, April 22, 1994.

"Hankook Develops Viable CFC Substitute for Use by '95," *Korea Economic Weekly*, September 5, 1993.

Hart-Landsberg, Martin, *The Rush to Development: Economic Change and Political Struggle in South Korea*. New York: Monthly Review Press, 1993.

"Health Ministry Prohibits Smoking in Its Work Areas," *Korea Herald*, May 31, 1994.

Henderson, Gregory, *Korea: The Politics of the Vortex*. Cambridge, MA: Harvard University Press, 1968.

Ho Nam-Hyun, *Report of the Asia Pacific Environmental Management Institute to the Ministry of Environment on Environmental Assessment Process*, December 1993.

Holman, Richard, "Seoul to Allow Bottled Water," *Wall Street Journal*, August 12, 1991.

Hong Joon-Hyun, "Abandoned Environment, Unkept Promise," *Law and Society*, vol. 9, September 1994.

———, *Environmental Law*. Seoul: Hanwool Press, 1994.

Hyman, L. L., and Faulkner, G., "U.S. South Increases Hardwood Chip Exports to Meet Far East Demand," *Pulp and Paper*, vol. 63, no. 7, July 1, 1989.

"Inaugural MPs Environment Confab to Open Here Monday," *Korea Times*, June 5, 1993.

Janah, Monua, "Korea's Environment Plan," *Wall Street Journal*, May 26, 1992.

Janelli, Roger L., *Making Capitalism: The Social and Cultural Construction of a South Korean Conglomerate*. Stanford, CA: Stanford University Press, 1993.

Jang Won, "The History of the Korean Environmental Movement," speech text, 1994.

Jang Y. C. and Youn H. C., "An Economic Analysis of Oak Stand Management in Korea," *Research Bulletin of the Seoul National University Forests*, 1990.

"Japan, South Korea Conclude Environmental Accord," Kyodo News Service International, Inc., March 21, 1988.

Jeong Chin-Seung and Chung Hoi-Seong, "Environmental Policy at the Age of Decentralization in Korea," *Environmental Policy toward the Year 2000*, Korea Development Institute, Seoul, unpublished proceedings, June 2–3, 1993.

Jeong Jin-Ho, "Under New International Order: Korea Needs a New Growth Paradigm," *Korea Times*, April 19, 1994.

"Joint Efforts Needed for Environment Issue," *Korea Herald*, Special Supplement, April 13, 1994.

Jones, Clayton, "Water Shocks Rouse South Korea," *Christian Science Monitor*, May 29, 1991.

Jun S. K., "Greenways for the Provision of Recreation and Open Space: A Literature Review and Application of the Greenway Concept to Korea, Plan B Paper," University of Minnesota, College of Natural Resources, 1990.

Kang Moon-Kyu, "The Role of NGOs in the Building Process of an Environmentally Sustainable Economy," *Environmental Policy toward the Year 2000*, Korea Development Institute, Seoul, unpublished proceedings, June 2–3, 1993.

Kang Yeoun-Sun, "Beer Industry Shakes Off Staleness," *Korea Herald*, May 12, 1994.

———, "Environment Day Points to Future of Earth," *Korea Times*, August 19, 1993.

Keatley, Robert, "South Korea Loses Ground in Asia's Race," *Wall Street Journal*, February 25, 1994.

Korea Electric Power Company (KEPCO), *Annual Report*, Seoul, 1993.

"KIEP Stresses Need for Economic Dynamism," *Korea Herald*, May 12, 1994.

Kim B. I. and Yoo C. S., "A Study of the Forest Workers of the Private Forest in Korea," *Research Reports of the Forestry Research Institute*, Seoul, 1990.

Kim B. I. and Yoo E. G., "The Status and Proposals for Forestry Tax System," *Research Reports of the Forestry Research Institute*, Seoul, 1987.

Kim Byong-Kuk, "Realistic, Equitable Law Enforcement," *Korea Times*, February 2, 1994.

Kim Chang-Young, "Leading Conglomerates Face Losing Top 10 Status," *Korea Times*, May 14, 1994.

———, "Second Generation of Tycoons Tighten Grips in Management," *Korea Times*, May 8, 1994.

"Kim D.J. Still Backstage Force in Politics," *Korea Herald*, May 10, 1994.

"Kim D.J.'s Remarks Have Politicians Guessing," *Korea Herald*, May 11, 1994.

"Kim Faces Most Critical Moment Since Inauguration," *Korea Times*, April 26, 1994.

Kim Ilpyong J. and Kihl Young Whan, eds., *Political Change in South Korea.* Seoul: Paragon House, 1988.

Kim J. C., "End-Use Markets for Tongass Forest Products in Japan, South Korea, and Taiwan," *The Future of the Timber Industry in Southeast Alaska.* Ketchikan: University of Alaska Southeast, 1989.

Kim Jong-Soon, "Present State of NGOs in Korea," *Hon Kuk University Journal,* 1993.

Kim Jong-Won, "An Ecological Strategy for Conservation and Rehabilitation of Korean Biodiversity," *Journal of Environmental Science* (Kyungsook National University), vol. 7, July 1993.

Kim Jung-Wk, "Current Environmental Problems and Policies in the Republic of Korea," unpublished paper, November 1994.

————, "Environmental Aspects of Transnational Corporation Activities in Ulsan/Onsan Industrial Complexes, Republic of Korea," Japan Environmental Congress, Osaka, Japan, January 14–15, 1991.

————, "Environmental Cooperation in North-East Asia," *Proceedings of the Conference on Political Economy of Development and Cooperation in North-East Asian Rim,* sponsored by UNDP and UN ESCAP, Changchim, China, June 30–July 2, 1993.

Kim Jung-Wk and Jeon Eui-Chan, "Policy Responses towards Improving Solid Waste Management in Seoul City," *Journal of Environmental Studies* (Seoul National University), vol. 25, 1989.

————, "Strategies for Developing Responsive Solid Waste Management in Seoul City: Institutional Arrangement," *Journal of Environmental Studies* (Seoul National University), vol. 28, 1991.

Kim Jung-Wk, Jeon Eui-Chan, and Chung Sang-Ok, "Promoting Public Participation and Environmental Education in the Republic of Korea," *Expert Group on Sound Environmentally Management of Industrial Development in Asian Countries: Focus on Developing Local and Regional Capabilities,* United Nations Centre for Regional Development Conference in Kitkyushu City Government, Japan, September 25–28, 1991.

Kim K. C., "Water Pollution of the Naktong River—(II)," *Korea Times,* January 30, 1994.

Kim K. C. and Sung C. S., "Studies on the Formation of Forest Products Price in Korea," *Research Reports of the Forestry Research Institute,* Seoul, 1991.

Kim Kwang-Woong, "Government Restructuring Has Only Begun," *Shin Dong-A Monthly,* January 1995.

Kim Kyu-Eung, "Environmental Policy and Environmental Education in the Republic of Korea," *Environmental Education,* Korea Educational Development Institute, Seoul, 1990.

Kim Ong-Ae, "Sales of Natural Water to Be Legalized Soon," *Korea Herald,* March 10, 1994.

Kim S. B., Youn Y. C., Park M. K., and Lee Y. D., "A Study on Productivity Analysis of Plywood Industries and Lumber Industries in Korea," *Forest Research Institute Research Reports,* Seoul, 1985.

Kim Seong-Hwan, "A Case Study on Environmental Education and Teacher Training in Korea," *Seminar Sponsored by Korean Educational Development Institute and British Counsel,* Seoul, 1991.

Kim Soo-Chan, "Future International Airport Taking Shape on Youngjong Island," *Korea Economic Times*, February 7, 1994.

Kim Soo-Shan, "Business Prepares for Environmental Round," *Korea Economic Weekly*, February 28, 1994.

Kim Sung-Bok, "Kim Faces Most Critical Moment Since Inauguration," *Korea Times*, April 26, 1994.

Kim Yong-Man, Environmental Education in Elementary Schools in Korea, *Environmental Education*, Korea Educational Development Institute, Seoul, 1990.

"Korea Air Adopts Environmental Motto," *Korea Times*, May 20, 1994.

"Korea, China Agree on Atmospheric Program," *Korea Times*, June 6, 1993.

Korea Educational Development Institute, *Environmental Education in Korea, Final Report to UNESCO*, Seoul, April, 1990.

Korea Environmental Technology Research Institute, *Environmental Measures in Korea: Answers to the Questionnaire of UNCTAD/TCMIS*, Seoul, March, 1993.

"Korea to Face Strong US Demand for 'Barrier' Lowering in Trade Talks," *Korea Times*, April 3, 1994.

"Korea, Japan Sign Accord on Cooperation in Water Treatment," *Korea Times*, June 4, 1993.

"Korea Ranks 13th in Terms of GNP in 1992," *Korea Times*, March 17, 1994.

"Korea Set to Ratify Montreal Protocol," *South Magazine*, November 1990.

"Korea Shoe Industry and Its Competitors," *Korea Economic Weekly*, May 16, 1994.

"Korea Tap Water," *Wall Street Journal*, September 20, 1990.

"Korean Firms Begin Producing Non-Polluting Detergent," *Korea Economic Daily*, April 27, 1991.

Korean Ministry of Construction, *Third Comprehensive National Development Plan: 1992–2001*. Seoul: 1992.

Korean Ministry of Education, *The School Curriculum of the Republic of Korea, 6th Curriculum Revision*. Seoul: 1994.

Korean Ministry of Environment, *Environmental Acts of the Republic of Korea*. Seoul: 1993.

———, *Environmental Protection in Korea*. Seoul: 1993.

———, *Environmental White Paper*. Seoul: 1990.

———, *Korea Report to the World Bank*, unpublished manuscript, 1993.

———, *National Report of the Republic of Korea to UNCED*. Seoul: 1992.

———, *National Report to the Secretary General of the United Nations to Be Reviewed by the Commission on Sustainable Development*, unpublished report, Seoul: 1993.

———, *1993 Report on Environmental Status of Korea*. Seoul: 1993.

"Kulop: Condemnation of an Island," *Green Korea Reports*, vol. 2, no. 1, Spring 1995.

Kwak Il-Chyun, "Nuclear Power, Public Acceptability and Democratic Change in South Korea," Ph.D. dissertation, University of East Anglia (UK), 1989.

———, "Reconciling Free Trade and the Protection of Global Commons: The Tasks for Korean Environmental Policy Makers," Trade-Environmental Issues and Korea's Alternatives, Conference sponsored by Institute for International Economic Policy and Korea Environmental Technology Institute, Seoul, April 22, 1994.

Kwon Sook-Pyo, "Health Effects of Industrial Exhaust in Urban Areas," College of Medicine, Yonsei University, Seoul, 1975.

————, "Rapid Economic Development Calls for More Social Investment," U.S. Environmental Protection Agency Document Report, undated, unpublished briefing paper.

————, "Study on the Standards of Ground Water Quality and Setting of Evaluation Standard of Ground Water Pollution," Interim Report submitted to Korean Research Council on Environmental Sciences, Seoul, August 1993.

"Lawmakers Assail Gov't for Yongsan River Contamination," *Korea Times*, April 21, 1994.

"Leaded Gasoline Banned," *Oil Daily*, December 23, 1992.

Lee B. I. and Yoo S. Y., "The Case Study of Private Forest Management Activities in Korea," *Research Reports of the Forestry Research Institute*, Seoul, 1989.

————, "A Study of the Forest Insurance System in Korea," *Research Reports of the Forestry Research Institute*, Seoul, 1990.

Lee Chang-Sup, "Government Asked to Revive Investment in the Environment," *Korea Times*, August 19, 1993.

————, "Korea Sees 8.5% Economic Growth in 1st Quarter: BOK," *Korea Times*, May 1, 1994.

Lee Jina, "The NGO's Role in Environmental Protection in Korea," *Civil Society*, 1993.

Lee Man-Woo, *The Odyssey of Korean Democracy, 1987–1990*. New York: Praeger, 1990.

Lee Su-Hoon, "Transitional Politics of Korea, 1987–1992," *Pacific Affairs*, vol. 66, no. 3, Fall 1993.

Lee Sun-Yong, "Economic Incentives to Control Pollution: A Case Study of Korea's Non-Compliance Charge System," Indiana University dissertation, 1992.

Lee W. Y., Joo J. S., Kim Sa-I, and Kim Seong-I, "A Study on the Evaluation of Potential Recreation Forests," *Research Reports of the Forestry Research Institute*, Seoul, 1991.

"Level of Benzene in Naktong River 1.8 Times Higher Than WHO Standard," *Korea Herald*, January 15, 1994.

Levin, Mike, "Beware the Green Tide," *Asian Business*, April 27, 1991.

Lewis, B., "The Markets for Softwood Lumber in Europe, Korea, and Taiwan," *Marketing of Chips, Lumber, and Other Manufactured Forest Products of the Pacific Rim*. Seattle: Jay Gruenfeld Associates, 1991.

Lorbach, J., "Road Construction and Harvesting in the Republic of Korea," in *Role of Forest Research in Solving Socio-Economic Problems in the Himalayan Region*, M. I. Sheikh, ed. Peshawar: Pakistan Forest Institute, 1987.

MacDonald, S., *Koreans: Contemporary Politics and Society*. Boulder, CO: Westview Press, 1989.

"Marketing Bottled Water," *Korea Herald*, March 10, 1994.

Merson, John, "Korea Wakes Up to the Environment," *New Scientist*, June 8, 1991.

"Ministry Considers Creation of Water Management Body," *Korea Times*, January 14, 1994.

Moon C. H., "Seasonal Variations of Heavy Metal Contamination of Topsoils in the Taejun-Industrial Complex," *Environmental Technology*, May 1991.

Moreinis, Josh, "Zoning Policy and Neighborhood Transformation in Seoul: The Case of Shillim-Dong," *Interplan*, no. 49, December 1994.

Morris, P., and Maxwell, J., "Export Potential of Pulp and Paper to South Korea," *Proceedings of the Forestry and Forest Products Industries Economists Conference*, Brisbane, Australia, 1985.

Nahm, Andrew C., *Korea: Tradition & Transformation—A History of the Korean People*. Seoul: Hollym, 1988.

"Naktong River Contamination Identified in Oct.," *Korea Times*, January 20, 1994.

"Naktong River Pollution Source Not Identified," *Korea Times*, January 18, 1994.

"Naktong River Scandal: Citizens Refuse to Pay Tap Water Bills," *Korea Herald*, January 24, 1994.

Nam Il-Chong, "Using Price Mechanism in Waste Management," *Toward Environmental Policy in the Year 2000*, Korea Development Institute, Seoul, unpublished proceedings, June 2–3, 1993.

Nam Yong-Mahn and Kim Sang-Joon, "Environmental Education in Primary and Secondary Schools in Korea: The Present and the Future," *Journal of the Korea Society for Environmental Education*, December 1994.

National Forest Products Association, *Market Development Opportunities for the U.S. Wood Products Industry in the Republic of Korea*. Washington, D.C.: National Forest Products Association, 1989.

"New Garbage Disposal System: Everything You Want to Know about It," *Korea Times*, January 7, 1994.

Nho Joon-Hun, "Environment Policies Make No Progress," *Korea Times*, June 6, 1994.

———, "GR Greater Challenge to Securing High Tech," *Korea Times*, Supplement, April 22, 1994.

———, "Koreans Must Be Patient about More Improvement in Quality of Tap Water," *Korea Times*, March 26, 1994.

———, "Nation to Take on More Environmental Obligation," *Korea Times*, 1994.

———, "Plastic Recycling Plants Due by June," *Korea Times*, January 11, 1995.

———, "Self Interest Hinders Ecology: Jang," *Korea Times*, May 24, 1994.

"1994: A Year to Forget," *Maeil Kyungje Shinmun*, December 31, 1994.

"The O-Zone: Ban of CFC's Has Korean Companies Panicking," *Business Korea*, vol. 9, no. 12, June 1992.

OECD, *OECD Environmental Data Compendium*, 1993.

Oh H. S., "Economic Development and Changing Forest Problems and Policies: The Case of Korea," in *Community Forestry: Lessons from Case Studies in Asia and the Pacific Region*, Y. S. Rao, ed. East–West Center, Environment and Policy Institute, Honolulu, 1988.

"On Nuclear Allergy," *Korea Herald*, June 3, 1994.

"1 in 5 Seoulites Buys Bottled Water, 0.6 Pct Drink Tap," *Korea Times*, March 17, 1994.

"Oriental Renaissance: A Survey of Japan," *The Economist*, July 9–15, 1994.

Pacific Consultants Corporation, Republic of Korea: Market Studies on Softwood and Hardwood and Other Information. Washington, DC: National Forest Products Association, 1986.

Paik Wan-Ki, *Korean Administrative Culture*. Seoul: Korea University Press, 1991.

Paisley, Ed, "Sleek or Sluggish," *Far Eastern Economic Review*, March 24, 1994.

Palais, James B., *Politics and Policy in Traditional Korea*. Cambridge, MA: Harvard University Press, 1975.

Park Chang-Seok, "Political Strife Drag on Booming Economy," *Korea Times*, May 3, 1994.

———, "Re-engineering of Workers," *Korea Times*, April 26, 1994.

Park Hyun-Ok, *Resource Mobilization Theory in the Authoritarian State: A Study of the Korean Environmental Movements*, University of Hawaii, Honolulu, 1986.

Park Kwon-Sang, "Six Tasks for Realizing Democracy," *Shin Dong-A Monthly*, December 1994.

Park Sang-Yeol, "Environmental Law in Korea," *Journal of Environmental Law and Practice*, vol. 1, no. 3, November 1993.

Park Tai-Shik, "Forest Planning and Management Policy in Korea—With Emphasis of Forest Management Plan and Management Operation by Proxy System," *Research Bulletin of the Seoul National University College of Forestry*, vol. 21, Seoul, 1985.

Park Yun-Heun, *National Report to Secretary General of the United Nations, Commission on Sustainable Development*, Ministry of Environment. Seoul: 1994.

Peritore, N. Patrick, "Korean Environmental Attitudes: The New Environmental Paradigm and Traditional Values," University of Missouri–Columbia, unpublished manuscript, November 1992.

Platt, Anne E., "Dying Seas," *World Watch Magazine*, vol. 6, no. 1, January/February 1995.

"Pollution in China Reaches Dangerous Levels," *Korea Herald*, May 16, 1994.

"Pollution Measure Results Found Conflicting," *Korea Times*, November 26, 1993.

"Preparation Set for Futures Trading," *Korea Times*, May 12, 1994.

Preston, Shelley, "Electronic Global Networking and the NGO Movement: The 1992 Rio Conference and Beyond," *Swords & Plowshares: A Chronicle of International Affairs*, vol. 3, no. 2, Spring 1994.

"Private Sector to Take Over Water Purifying Business Biz," *Korea Times*, January 19, 1994.

"Proper Hiking Culture," *Korea Herald*, January 15, 1995.

"Rain in May Found Most Acid," *Korea Times*, May 20, 1994.

"Regional Overview," *Business Journal*, vol. 1, no. 1, March/April 1995.

"Renewal for the Ruling Party," *Dong-A Ilbo*, February 8, 1995.

Republic of Korea, *Third Comprehensive National Development Plan*, 1992.

"Residents Have No Say in Nat'l Projects," *Korea Times*, June 4, 1994.

Rhee Deok-Gil, "Environmental Challenges in the 1990s: A Korean Context," *Energy & Environment*, vol. 2, no. 4, 1991.

Ro Chung-Hyun, *Public Administration & the Koreans' Transformation*. Seoul: Kumarian Press, 1993.

"ROK Suffers Trade Deficit for 4 Consecutive Months," *Korea Times*, May 3, 1994.

"S. Korean Officials Arrested in Water Pollution Case," Reuter's, March 24, 1991.

"S. Korean President Backs Minister over Pollution Scandal," Reuter's, April 25, 1991.

Sands, William Franklin, *At the Court of Korea*. London: Century Hutchinson, reprint, 1987.

Sanger, David E., "Chemical Leak Brings Forth a New Era," *New York Times*, April 16, 1991.

Schreuder, G. F.; Vlosky, R. P.; and Youn Y. C., "Forest Products Sector Profile of South Korea," *CINTRAFOR Working Paper*, University of Washington, College of Forest Resources, 1987.

"The Scourge of Water Contamination," *People's Korea*, March 30, 1991.

"Scourge of Water Contamination: 7 Officials Arrested for Forging Document," *People's Korea,* April, 1991.

"Seoul Mayoral Candidates Look to Young Voters," *Korea Herald*, May 21, 1995.

"Seoul Sluggish in Improving Foreign Investment Climate," *Korea Times*, April 26, 1994.

"Separate Disposal Reduces Garbage," *Korea Times*, September 6, 1993.

Shendon, Philip, "Asia's Having One Huge Nicotine Fit," *New York Times*, May 15, 1994.

Shim Jae-Hoon, "All Change: Political Reforms Set to Shake Up Campaigning," *Far Eastern Economic Review,* March 17, 1994.

————, "Flawed Politics," *Far Eastern Economic Review*, May 26, 1994.

————, "Judging the Judges: Legal System Begins Slow Process of Reform," *Far Eastern Economic Review*, December 9, 1993.

————, "Package Deal: President Bids to Revamp His Reformist Image," *Far Eastern Economic Review,* March 10, 1994.

————, "Trial and Error," *Far Eastern Economic Review*, March 23, 1995.

Shin Dong-Ho, "Economic Growth and Environmental Problems in South Korea: The Role of Government," in *Asia's Environmental Crisis*, Michael C. Howard, ed. Boulder, CO: Westview Press, 1993.

"Small Firms Must Hone Competitiveness to Cope with WTO System: Seminar," *Korea Herald*, June 9, 1994.

Smith, David A., and Lee Su-Hoon, "Anti-Systemic Movements in South Korea: The Rise of Environmental Activism," 15th PEWS Conference, University of Hawaii, unpublished paper, 1991.

Soh Chung-Hee, *The Chosen Women in Korean Politics: An Anthropological Study*. New York: Praeger, 1991.

Song B. I. and Yoo Y. G., "A Study on Basic Policy for Private Forestry in Korea," *Research Reports of the Forestry Research Institute*, Seoul, 1991.

Soussan, J. G., "Fuelwood Strategies and Action Programs in Asia: Comparative Experience in Bangladesh, Indonesia, Nepal, Republic of Korea, Sri Lanka, and Thailand," *Report of a Workshop Jointly Organized by the Commission of the European Communities and the Asian Institute of Technology in Thailand*, Asian Institute of Technology, Renewable Energy Resources Information Center, Bangkok, 1984.

"South Korea to Discuss Environmental Topics," *Japan Economic Newswire*, February 6, 1990.

"South Korea: Home Takeover," *Far Eastern Economic Review*, March 16, 1995.

"South Korea Reacts to Water Pollution Incidents," *Haznews*, June 1991.

"South Korea: Trade and Investment," *Far Eastern Economic Review*, May 26, 1994.

"South Korean Government Awards L.A. Based Dasibi Environmental Contracts for Nine Air Pollution Stations," *PR Newswire*, October 30, 1989.

"South Korean Leader Struggles to Free Up a Regulated Economy," *Wall Street Journal*, March 30, 1994.

"South Koreans Plan to Halt Drift Net Fishing," *New York Times*, December 7, 1992.

"Southeast Asia: Facing Development Challenges," *Environmental Science and Technology*, Special Issue, vol. 27, no. 12, 1993.

"Special Edition for Environmental Education," *Kookmin Ilbo*, September 25, 1990.

Stammer, Larry B., "S. Korea Pressed to Ban Drift Nets," *Los Angeles Times*, November 27, 1992.

Steers, Richard M., *The Chaebol: Korea's New Industrial Might*. New York: Harper & Row, 1993.

Stewart, Peter, "Korea Refiners Wait on Plant Upgrades," *Platt's Oilgram News*, December 7, 1992.

"Strikers Demand Japan, South Korean Funding for Forest," *Japan Economic Newswire*, October 3, 1989.

Sung K. C., "A Study on the Improvements of Private Forest Management Planning," *Research Reports of the Forest Research Institute*, Seoul, 1988.

————, "Survey on the Wood Consumption and the Forecasting of Its Future Demand of South Korea," *Research Reports of the Forestry Research Institute*, Seoul, 1987.

"Taiwan and Korea May Be Penalized for Drift-Net Use," *Asian Wall Street Journal*, August 19, 1991.

"Tangled in Drift-Nets," *Los Angeles Times*, April 1, 1989.

"3 Chemical Waste Facilities to Be Constructed in Inchon, Kyunggi-do," *Korea Times*, January 11, 1994.

Tiemann, Mary, and Fletcher, Susan R., "Trade and Environment: Treatment in Recent Agreements—GATT and NAFTA," *Congressional Research Service Report*, February 24, 1994.

"W3.5 Trillion Water Quality Plan Seen Failed," *Korea Times*, September 19, 1993.

"Toothpicks to Disappear at Restaurants Next Mo.," *Korea Times*, January 18, 1995.

"Two Ministries in Korea Clash on Diesel Use," *Automotive News,* June 10, 1990.

United States State Department, "Report on Environmental Trends in Korea," unpublished discussion paper, 1992.

"Users to Bear More Cost for Clean Water," *Korea Times*, January 17, 1995.

Valigra, Lori, "National Project Aimed at Making It the Leading Tiger," *Science*, vol. 262, October 1993.

"Waste Water to Be Funneled into Sea," *Korea Times*, April 3, 1994.

"Water Rationing Continues in Mokpo," *Korea Times*, April 18, 1994.

Wells, Kenneth M., *New God, New Nation: Protestants and Self-Reconstruction*

Nationalism in Korea, 1896–1937. Honolulu: University of Hawaii Press, 1990.

Weston, Roy F., "Sustainable Development: The Economic Model of the Future," presented at the New Mexico Conference on the Environment, Albuquerque, New Mexico, April 25, 1994. Unpublished paper.

White, Gilbert F., et al., "Taking Stock of UNCED," *Environment*, vol. 34, no. 8, October 1992.

"Woes of Noise Pollution," *Korea Herald*, January 15, 1995.

Woo H. T., "An Assessment of Tourism Development in the National Parks of South Korea," in *Resident Peoples and National Parks: Social Dilemmas and Strategies for International Conservation*, P. C. West and S. R. Brechin, eds. Tucson: University of Arizona Press, 1991.

———, "The Social Impacts of Land Use Zoning in the National Parks of South Korea," *Resident Peoples and National Parks: Social Dilemmas and Strategies in International Conservation*, P. C. West and S. R. Brechin, eds. Tucson: University of Arizona Press, 1991.

Woo Jung-En, *Race to the Swift: State and Finance in Korean Industrialization*. New York: Columbia University Press, 1991.

Woo, T. M., "Status of Management of the Protected Areas in the Republic of Korea," *Tigerpaper*, 1991.

———, "A Study on the Change in Forest Ownership Structure," *Research Reports of the Forestry Research Institute*, Seoul, 1990.

World Wildlife Fund Position Statement, "The GATT Trade and Environment Work Programme," World Wildlife Fund, Washington, DC, January 1994.

Wu Pei-Tse, "DuPont to Build Plant in S. Korea: Titanium Dioxide Facility," *Journal of Commerce and Commercial*, January 22, 1990.

"Yersinia Germs Found in Spring Water," *Korea Times*, January 20, 1994.

Yim Seong-Hi, *The Impacts on Korean Society*. Seoul: Nutinamo, 1990.

Yoo Byoung-Il, "The Case Study of Private Forest Management Activities in Korea," *Bulletin of the Forestry Research Institute* (Seoul), no. 39, 1989.

Yoo Cheong-Mo, "Low Morale Plagues Institutes," *Korea Herald*, April 22, 1994.

Yoon Chan-Won and Lee Byung-Min, "Pollution in Masan Bay, A Matter of Concern in South Korea," *Marine Pollution Bulletin*, vol. 21, no. 5, May 1, 1990.

Yu Kun-Ha, "Government Needs New Strategy for WTO Era," *Korea Herald*, April 29, 1994.

———, "Reform Drive Brings Management Award to Goldstar," *Korea Herald*, May 12, 1994.

"Yukong Ltd. Dedicates Environmental Facilities," *Korea Economic Weekly*, December 6, 1993.

Index

Norman Eder is vice president of public affairs and associate professor of environmental science and engineering at Oregon Graduate Institute of Science and Technology in Portland. He also serves as an assistant professor at Pacific Northwest College of Art, also in Portland. He holds a Ph.D. in history from the University of Illinois at Chicago. During the past decade he has been a frequent contributor to science and technology policy discussions. He was a Senior Fulbright Scholar at Korea's Hanyang University in 1994.

363.7　　Eder, Norman R.
Ede
　　　　Poisoned prosperity.

DATE			